The GOVERNANCE of CURRICULUM

1994 Yearbook of the Association for Supervision and Curriculum Development

RICHARD F. ELMORE AND SUSAN H. FUHRMAN
EDITORS

Alexandria, Virginia

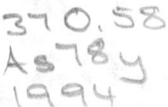

Association for Supervision
and Curriculum Development
1250 N. Pitt Street
Alexandria, VA 22314-1453
Telephone (703) 549-9110
FAX (703) 549-3891

The mission of ASCD, a diverse international community of educators, is to forge covenants in teaching and learning for the success of all learners.

Acknowledgments: Chapters 1, 3, 4, 6, 9, and 10 of this book draw directly on work undertaken by the Policy Center of the Consortium for Policy Research in Education (CPRE), Grant No. R11G10007, from the Office of Educational Research and Improvement, U.S. Department of Education. The opinions expressed are those of the authors and are not necessarily shared by the funding agencies or the institutional members of CPRE.

Copyright © 1994 (except the preceding chapters) by the Association for Supervision and Curriculum Development. Permission to reproduce or transmit in any form or by any means must be sought in writing from ASCD.

ASCD publications present a variety of viewpoints. The views expressed or implied in this book should not be interpreted as official positions of the Association.

Printed in the United States of America.

Ronald S. Brandt, *Executive Editor*
Nancy Modrak, *Managing Editor, Books*
Carolyn R. Pool, *Associate Editor*
Jennifer Beun, *Assistant Editor*
Gary Bloom, *Manager, Design and Production Services*
Karen Monaco, *Senior Designer*
Stephanie Kenworthy, *Print Production Coordinator*
Valerie Sprague, *Desktop Publisher*

Price: $19.95
ASCD Stock No.: 1-94000
ISSN: 1042-9018

The Governance of Curriculum

Foreword v
Barbara Talbert Jackson

1. **Governing Curriculum: Changing Patterns in Policy, Politics, and Practice** 1
Richard F. Elmore and Susan H. Fuhrman

I. Policy Development at the National and State Levels

2. **National Curriculum Standards: Are They Desirable and Feasible?** 12
Marshall S. Smith, Susan H. Fuhrman, and Jennifer O'Day

3. **Legislatures and Education Policy** 30
Susan H. Fuhrman

4. **Governors and Education Policy in the 1990s** 56
Susan H. Fuhrman and Richard F. Elmore

5. **Commentary on National and State Education Policy Developments: A State Legislator's Perspective** 75
Ken Nelson

II. State Curriculum Reform Development and Management

6. **Achieving Consensus: Setting the Agenda for State Curriculum Reform** 84
Diane Massell

7. **Systemic School Reform: The Challenges Faced by State Departments of Education** 109
Susan Follett Lusi

8. **Will This Be on the Test? Reflections on State Curriculum Leadership** 131
Richard P. Mills

III. District and School Roles in Curriculum Reform

9. **Standard Setting as a Strategy for Upgrading High School Mathematics and Science** 138
   Andrew C. Porter, John Smithson, and Eric Osthoff

10. **How Districts Mediate Between State Policy and Teachers' Practice** 167
    James P. Spillane

11. **Coordinating Top-Down and Bottom-Up Strategies for Education Reform** 186
    Michael G. Fullan

12. **Commentary on the District and School Roles in Curriculum Reform: A Superintendent's Perspective** 203
    Thomas W. Payzant

13. **Education Professionals and Curriculum Governance** 210
    Richard F. Elmore and Susan H. Fuhrman

About the Authors 216

ASCD 1993–94 Board of Directors 218

    Executive Council 218

    Review Council 218

    Members-at-Large 218

    Affiliate Presidents 219

ASCD Headquarters Staff 222

ASCD Networks and Facilitators, 1993–94 223

Foreword

Traditionally, in American public education, curriculum matters have been the prerogative of the local school district. State and local governments have played only marginal governance roles in deciding the content of the curriculum. But more and more, as student performance overall continues to be lackluster, and as employers and the news media continue to make comparisons with students in other developed nations, there is a growing advocacy for a national voice in the curriculum to provide coherence and a standard of accountability. In *The Governance of Curriculum*, Richard F. Elmore and Susan H. Fuhrman lay out the function that the federal government is poised to assume in setting standards for curriculum policy and student performance.

With the groundswell of demands coming from the states, the call continues to intensify for demonstrable evidence that students are being prepared to function successfully in the work world and to hold their own when compared with their counterparts in other nations. The demand is couched in the context of the national interest and economic needs. As a result, performance-based curriculum initiatives have gained widespread support nationally.

This yearbook brings together the collective thinking and expertise of a diverse group of contributors, each with a unique perspective on the subject of education reform as it relates to national standards and governance. The key question is, Who will decide what students will be taught in schools?

Today, the majority of educators see national standards as a profound shift in the governance of education. Yet, as the authors point out, national involvement has always been a part of education in the United States; total local control has never been the reality. And they suggest that the schools already face strong national influences in some areas, for example, textbook selection. But they note that curriculum oversight in the broad "monolithic sense" is not a possibility.

The education professionals for whom this book is intended will be interested in its major thematic emphases: national influence and local control, the political character of curriculum decisions, the need to work across institutional boundaries, and the importance of the capacity of individuals and institutions to help shape curriculum policy. Indeed, this yearbook can be viewed as a handbook on policy and procedures relating to curriculum governance in public education.

The authors of this yearbook address many questions related to national curriculum standards: What will be the effect of such standards on the increasing movement toward local school and district autonomy? What about state and regional differences in the assessment of student performance? What are the roles of state legislatures, governors, and education agencies in providing "ambitious content" for all students?

As the nation moves toward standard curriculum requirements and an emphasis on performance-based student outcomes, educators must become aware of the policy decisions that will be involved and be prepared to play an active role in shaping those policies. We educators who have oversight of curriculum matters must be cognizant of impending change and prepare to act with knowledge and insight. This book points us in that direction.

BARBARA TALBERT JACKSON
ASCD President, 1993-94

1

Governing Curriculum: Changing Patterns in Policy, Politics, and Practice

Richard F. Elmore and Susan H. Fuhrman

U.S. educators, policymakers, and community members currently face some fundamental choices about who will determine what is taught to students in schools. These choices have potentially large consequences for education professionals whose central responsibilities involve the development and oversight of curriculum in schools. Since the stakes of these choices are potentially quite high for professionals, for students, and for the public, everyone must understand the full scope of these choices. Hence, we have assembled writers who reexamine the entire structure of curriculum policymaking and implementation, from the political and administrative systems that surround curriculum policy to the district-, school-, and classroom-level systems that directly influence what students are taught. We have also tried to connect current empirical research on the nature of curriculum policy and governance decisions with the practical observations of those who make and implement those decisions.

The United States is perceptibly moving toward a more national, performance-based view of curriculum policy. That is, curriculum is increasingly a topic for national policy debate; and the debate increasingly focuses on curriculum as one mechanism for improving student performance, measured against national goals and international standards of achievement. One should not confuse national policy debate, however, with federal policy. To say that curriculum is increasingly a subject for national policy debate is *not* equivalent to saying that the federal government will get into the business of making curriculum policy any more than it has in the past. Indeed, most of the forces operating to nationalize curriculum policy are state and local in origin. Governors, chief state school officers, local superintendents, teachers' unions, and discipline-based professional organizations are playing a major role in raising curriculum issues to a national level. These groups are not only working together across state and local boundaries through their professional networks to improve the quality of teaching, but they are also influencing state and local policy decisions using the results of their national discussions. The federal government will play a modest role in nationalizing curriculum policy issues, largely by exerting pressure on states and localities through national standards. But the chief agents of nationalization are, and will continue to be, state and locally based constituencies.

Curriculum policy is becoming more performance focused because the broader policy debate about U.S. education is becoming more performance focused. For better or worse, public officials and corporate leaders are concerned about the gap between the current academic performance of students and what they perceive to be the future economic, political, and social needs of the country. This concern occurs at a time when educators are reconsidering the role that traditional tools of educational measurement play in assessing student performance. Educators are increasingly concerned that traditional measures of school performance give an inadequate picture of what students know and can do. Consequently, both lay leaders and professional educators are arguing for measures of performance that are more clearly based on what students are expected to learn, rather than on more general, more difficult-to-interpret standardized measures of student performance. Hence, assessment techniques will probably become more explicitly curriculum based. That is, students' performance will increasingly be measured against what they have actually been taught, rather than what some general population of students might have learned by a certain age. As performance assessment and curriculum are drawn more tightly together, curriculum will increasingly become a subject for public policy debate.

This yearbook attempts to lay out the terms of the present national debate on educational reform, educational standards, and governance in a way that is relevant to educational professionals whose primary responsibility lies within schools and districts. We believe that the consequences of this broader debate depend heavily on whether and how education professionals choose to play a part. In a sense, this book is a short course in the politics of curriculum reform and governance, designed to provide the wherewithal for educational professionals to play a more prominent and effective role in the current policy debates. In this chapter, we provide a broad framework, sketching out the major changes that we see taking place in the governance of curriculum on the national, state, and local levels and providing a context for the specific chapters that follow. In the final chapter, we try to distill some practical lessons for educational professionals who may be interested in playing a larger, more systematic role in the changes that we see occurring around the governance of curriculum.

Cutting across the chapters in this book are a number of major themes. These themes are not new; they run deeply in the history of politics around curriculum issues in the United States. But they take a slightly different form in the context of the present debate.

National Influence and Local Control

As we have noted, curriculum policy debates have increasingly taken on a more national focus. State and local policymakers are beginning to see their role as focusing on the improvement of teaching and learning in schools by influencing what is taught to students, within the context of broad national and state goals that are designed to hold schools to higher standards of performance for a broader cross-section of students. The locus of policymaking around curriculum issues has increasingly become the states. The chapters by Diane Massell and Susan Lusi illustrate how states are using their leverage to introduce significant changes in the way curriculum decisions are made and implemented. What distinguishes these latest state initiatives from earlier ones, however, is that they are connected to broad national themes about the improvement of schooling; and the key actors at the state and local levels are increasingly taking their guidance from national networks of like-minded people in other settings. Hence, while the locus of policymaking is indisputably at the state level, the key ideas that shape that policy are coming through national networks.

For many, these developments will seem like a threat to the hallowed tradition of local control in American schools. Indeed, local control has been, and continues to be, the most durable myth, or operating principle, of educational governance in the United States. Before we try to understand the impact that recent changes in curriculum policymaking will have on local control, we should be clear about what local control actually means in the present context. In fact, from its very inception, public education in the United States has been a composite of national, state, and local influences. David Tyack and Elisabeth Hansot (1982) demonstrate in their influential history of education administration, *Managers of Virtue*, that public schools in the 19th and early 20th centuries were heavily influenced by national networks of professional educators using a model explicitly drawn from the evangelical religious tradition. To be sure, funding and governance were decidedly local in the early years of U.S. public education, but many of the ideas that shaped curriculum and school organization were purveyed through national networks of educators. As states became more

THE GOVERNANCE OF CURRICULUM

and more powerful educational actors in the mid-20th century, these national professional networks were forced to compete with other influences. States became more assertive in establishing minimum standards for the provision of education and in assuring adequate minimum financing. From its inception, then, the U.S. education system has never been characterized by total local control; educational practice has always been a product of the interplay of local, state, and national forces. Hence, the emergence of strong national networks around core issues of education, such as curriculum, is not necessarily new. It is simply a new form of a long-standing phenomenon.

It is also legitimate to ask whether attention to curriculum issues at the national level, of the sort discussed by Smith, Fuhrman, and O'Day in their chapter, will lead to a national curriculum. Critics often invoke the term *national curriculum* to raise the specter of a single inflexible structure that would govern all local decisions about what is taught, regardless of variations in local preferences. In fact, a national curriculum in this monolithic sense is not remotely possible in the United States and won't result from national attention to curriculum issues. As the chapters by Smith, Fuhrman, and O'Day, and by Fuhrman and Elmore show, the politics of state and national decisions about curriculum are highly complex and allow for the interplay of many local, state, and national influences.

There are other reasons, as well, to be skeptical about the specter of a "national curriculum" undermining local control. Curriculum decisions have, for a long time, been subject to strong national influences. Textbook adoption, for example, is primarily a local decision, often made literally by groups of teachers and school district curriculum specialists sitting together evaluating competing texts for adoption in specific schools. In this sense, curriculum is determined locally. In another sense, though, the choices that teachers and curriculum specialists face are largely determined by textbook publishers' prior judgments about what content will sell in a national market—a market that is, incidentally, dominated by a few key states, like Texas and California, with statewide textbook adoption policies. In an important sense, then, local school people already face strong nationalizing forces in curriculum, because the criteria that determine the content of textbooks are national in character and largely beyond the influence of any single school or district.

Textbooks are not the only nationalizing force in curriculum determination. Policy is another. For example, since at least the mid-1960s, federal, state, and local governments have made a concerted effort to focus on the educational needs of poor, educationally disadvantaged students, through a variety of mechanisms, including categorical programs designed to focus more resources on special populations of students. These efforts have percolated through the structure of U.S. education, resulting in many practices that are quite common from one local setting to another. For example, children across the country are routinely removed from their regular classrooms for remedial instruction. Remediation often takes the form of so-called "basic skills" instruction—that is, focusing on the most elementary components of the content in which students are having difficulty. These approaches to teaching disadvantaged children are widespread, even though they are currently under attack from some quarters. For our purposes, the point is not whether the practices are good or bad, but that policies focused on the educational needs of disadvantaged children over time created strong nationalizing pressures on teaching and learning in local schools. One can argue whether the results are exactly what one might wish they had been, but the effect of such policies has been to create widespread national consensus on how and what to teach a specific group of students.

By presenting a broad perspective on how curriculum is determined, we are taking a particular point of view about the relationship between national influences and local control. We think that, in some fundamental sense, curriculum is always simultaneously "national," "state," and "local" in focus. The issue is not whether increased national discussion and policymaking on curriculum will result in a "national curriculum," but how that national discussion will influence the balance among key interests that currently shape debate on curriculum. New parties will enter the debate. Old parties will either fade or adapt to the new realities and play a different role. In this yearbook, we are trying to present a picture of the interdependent relationships among key actors at various levels of the system that surrounds curriculum decisions so that education professionals may identify and use opportunities to exert influence.

Politics and Professional Judgment

Another theme that cuts through the chapters in this book is the essentially political character of curriculum decisions, from the national level to the school level. For many education professionals, saying that curriculum is inherently political is a deeply disturbing observation. People who have invested their professional lives in developing an expertise in how academic content should be taught are typically queasy when they hear that their expert judgment is heavily influenced by political forces. This book presents a different view. Understanding one's political environment, we argue, is an important precondition to being able to operate effectively as a professional. We take as a given that curriculum will be heavily influenced by politics, because curriculum deals with a fundamental and deeply meaningful political reality—what professionals are entitled to teach other peoples' children. If such an issue were not the subject of political debate and conflict, one would wonder why. To say that curriculum will be heavily influenced by politics, however, is not to say anything in particular about whether the professional concerns of educators will be represented in curriculum or whether the curriculum will be "good" by professional standards. The quality of curriculum is determined by how well professional concerns are made to operate in tandem with the political realities of curriculum.

The political nature of curriculum is deeply knit into the history of education in the United States. In the early years of the Republic, whole classes of people—women and slaves, for example—were excluded from certain types of learning, and leading educators developed elaborate explanations for who was suited and who wasn't to certain types of knowledge. What was taught, to whom, in other words, was, in the deepest sense, a subject for determining who was allowed to participate in the political processes of society. More recently, debates over whether to teach the German language in public schools during the First and Second World Wars, over whether to teach human reproduction as part of high school biology, or over whether to provide elementary school children with knowledge of cultures in which euthanasia is practiced—all of these debates have been part of the history of curriculum decisions in the late 20th-century United States. Moreover, not all political debates around curriculum issues take the form of disputes between the public and professionals over curriculum content. Professionals themselves often engage in intramural political debates over curriculum content, as represented, for example, in the current disputes between reading specialists who espouse phonics and those favoring whole-language approaches to reading.

If we can't keep politics out of curriculum, then perhaps we should think about how to harness basic political processes to the improvement of curriculum. By giving a broad picture of how various political institutions work on issues of curriculum and educational reform, we hope to provide the raw material for a professional discussion about how to harness politics to curriculum improvement. Knowing, for example, how legislatures are organized to operate on education reform, as Susan Fuhrman's chapter suggests, allows us to understand how to engage legislators in productive discussions about what should be taught to whom. Knowing about the increasing importance of state governors in the reform debates of the 1980s and 1990s, and about their increasingly national focus through the National Governors' Association on issues of standards and curriculum, as the Fuhrman and Elmore chapter suggests, allows us to understand how to tailor curriculum issues to draw governors into a more productive discussion. Knowing how states organize themselves for large-scale curriculum reform, as Diane Massell's chapter suggests, allows us to develop more sophisticated ways of influencing those structures. In other words, harnessing politics to curriculum improvement requires an understanding of how basic political institutions operate and what opportunities they present for influence.

Education professionals are also concerned about another kind of politics—the politics of highly mobilized and focused community interests, such as groups on the political right and left with specific objections to curriculum and teaching practice. Again, this form of political mobilization is not new to American education and will undoubtedly be a recurring theme in the future. One of the reasons why extreme political groups are often successful in influencing public decisions about curriculum is that they know how to organize politically and they understand enough about the way political institutions work to make their views heard. To the degree that education professionals are concerned about the influence of extreme political groups on curriculum, it seems incumbent on professionals to develop at least the same level of sophistication in their knowledge of how political institutions work as those with whom they disagree.

We have assembled yearbook chapters that are designed to draw education professionals into a more detailed and constructive view of how politics and curriculum relate to one another. Increased political sophistication on the part of education professionals is an important precondition to harnessing the political system to curriculum improvement.

Spanning Institutional Boundaries

A third theme that cuts across the chapters in this yearbook is the necessity for working across institutional boundaries in the education system. For most education professionals, policy is something that is "done to" rather than "done with" them—particularly in policy issues related to curriculum. Teachers' worlds are often bounded by the classroom; and in that context, curriculum means what teachers teach on a day-to-day basis and what the outside world tells them they are expected to "cover" in a given year. The world of the district curriculum specialist is often bounded by a specific content area, a specific set of materials that the district would like to see schools use in their classrooms, and a specific group of teachers with whom the specialist interacts around teaching and curricular issues. The principal's world is often bounded by the special problems of her school and the relationships with community, parents, and higher level administrators that she must orchestrate to make a school run effectively. We could similarly characterize the "boundedness" of other influential actors in the process of determining what is taught to whom—local superintendents, school board members, state legislators, and governors, for example. In each case, the world of these actors is bounded by certain important, if somewhat parochial, concerns. But we also know that when people who play different roles in the education system don't work effectively with each other across their respective institutional boundaries, we often fail to provide real benefits to students. When teachers and principals operate at cross-purposes, students often suffer. When district administrators and principals don't have effective working relationships, schools often don't operate effectively, and so forth. By taking a broader view of the institutions that operate on curriculum in the United States, and by providing specific examples of how they do and do not work in tandem with other institutions, we are attempting to illustrate the importance of developing skills that allow one to work effectively across institutional boundaries.

The increased focus in current curriculum debates on national priorities makes it even more imperative for education professionals to develop these boundary-spanning skills. For example, if content-based national professional organizations, such as the National Council of Teachers of Mathematics, are going to play a more prominent role in articulating standards and expectations for good curriculum and instruction, then someone has to explain these standards to state and local policymakers, teachers, and the public. Simply having professional agreement on what good curriculum is doesn't mean that agreement will be translated into any meaningful policy or action. On the other hand, professional agreement on good curriculum and instruction can be a powerful force in influencing policy and practice if it is specifically linked to policymakers and classroom practitioners. As we begin to focus increasingly on national issues of quality and performance, it is increasingly important for knowledgeable professionals to be able to explain to people in diverse settings what good curriculum is.

Institutional and Individual Capacity

A fourth cross-cutting theme in this yearbook is the importance of institutional and individual capacity in shaping the outcomes of curriculum policy. Recent changes in policy at the federal, state, and local levels all share the common objectives of raising the quality of academic content to which students are exposed, improving the quality of instruction that teachers deliver, and increasing expectations for the level and type of performance that students will demonstrate. These changes are heavily dependent on the capacities of institutions and individuals at all levels. Policymakers—legislators, governors, local board members, and high-level state and local administrators—depend heavily on expert advice to make good decisions. Several chapters in this book describe how these various policymakers have begun to develop and extend their institutional capacities—by hiring expert staffs, by establishing networks with others who confront the same issues, and by collecting intelligence about the effects of policy decisions. Likewise, those closer to the delivery of educational services—curriculum specialists, district administrators, principals, and teachers—depend heavily on access to new knowledge to be responsive to changes in policy. Several chapters describe how schools and districts are grappling with the problem of how to move new knowledge into practice.

Under the best of circumstances, these capacity problems are extraordinarily difficult. Political pressures often outstrip the capacities of policymakers, so that they often find themselves having to make decisions without having access to the right kind of expertise. Policies often change in response to political pressures, without regard for the difficulties they pose for practice. And local educators find themselves in the position of responding to policy directives from higher levels without adequate preparation or resources. At all levels, the big ideas of policy are vulnerable to the capacities of the people and institutions that implement them.

Because current reforms reach so deeply into the core processes of schooling, these reforms are more vulnerable than past policies to these capacity problems. There is a danger that, as the implementation problems of current reforms begin to surface, policymakers and practitioners will conclude that the reforms are simply too complex and ambitious for existing schools to absorb. This conclusion would almost certainly be true, if we were to take the existing institutional and individual capacities in the system as a given. But if we see the implementation of ambitious reforms as an opportunity to focus on capacity problems and make dramatic improvements in capacity, the prognosis could be more optimistic.

Solutions to capacity problems depend heavily on the skills that are the stock in trade of educational professionals. Many of the problems involved in implementing ambitious education reforms are essentially problems of knowledge development and learning. The audiences for new knowledge in education reform are diverse, their roles differ, and their needs vary by their roles; but the central problem for the whole system is not dramatically different from the problem that education professionals confront daily in their work. That problem is how to get the right knowledge in the heads and hands of the right people and how to get them to use it imaginatively.

The success of the current generation of ambitious education reforms, then, depends heavily on our willingness to treat the problems of reform as problems of learning—on a broader, more systemic basis than we have done with previous reforms. Legislators and governors need more opportunities to learn about the consequences of policies in schools and classrooms. Those opportunities need to be heavily influenced by education professionals, whose firsthand knowledge of the challenges of implementing complex policies is an important complement to the perspective of policymakers. Likewise, teachers and principals need access to new ideas and to concrete examples of practices that will help them respond to new policies. Between these two levels are a vast number of people whose responsibilities are (or should be) largely to mobilize the knowledge and resources needed for both policymakers and practitioners.

Reference

Tyack, D., and E. Hansot. (1982). *Managers of Virtue*. New York: Basic Books.

I

Policy Development at the National and State Levels

2

National Curriculum Standards: Are They Desirable and Feasible?

Marshall S. Smith, Susan H. Fuhrman, and Jennifer O'Day

U.S. educators are developing voluntary national education standards, or explicit expectations of what students should know and be able to do. Professional associations in each of the key subject areas have established processes to devise standards, supported by U.S. Department of Education grants. Not surprisingly, considerable debate has arisen about whether such standards are a good idea and whether there should be a more official governmental role in their creation. Legislation now in Congress would expand the National Educational Goals Panel (NEGP) and authorize a National Educational Standards and Improvement Council to certify standards. Much of the discussion around this legislation has focused on such questions as: What might such standards look like and how would they be established? What effect might they have on teachers, principals, and other educational personnel? How would they affect students' achievement and educational opportunity? Are national standards even feasible in a nation as diverse as the United States and in an educational system with such a long history of local control?

That such questions both abound and engender heated controversy is hardly surprising. The establishment of standards represents a profound and unprecedented shift in educational practice in this country. In its two and a quarter centuries, the United States has never had explicit education

---

Authors' Note: This chapter is adapted from the report written by the authors for the National Council on Educational Standards and Testing (NCEST) concerning the desirability and feasibility of establishing national education goals. This chapter focuses on the potential effects of national educational standards on student achievement, the quality of teachers and schools, and educational equity; the appropriateness of establishing national standards, given the characteristics of the current system; and the feasibility of establishing national education standards. The authors acknowledge the intellectual contributions of other task force members and the staff of NCEST.

content or performance goals. Nor, until very recently, have the individual states advanced challenging, absolute standards for their students to target and surpass. Instead of having challenging content expectations, instead of determining what level of performance represents a high level of mastery of content, we have relied on *relative* comparisons among schools, districts, and states to give us an indication of how well we are doing. Our standardized tests generally tell us whether our students are above or below the average in the nation or in the state, but not whether their performance is superior either when compared to a national standard or to some a priori absolute standard.

Of course, the absence of common standards has not prevented some schools from setting their own ambitious expectations. Unfortunately, most schools set their sights on the basement rather than the rooftop. In the absence of common, well-specified, demanding content standards and high expectations for students, our schools and our nation have gravitated toward a minimum competency curriculum. Indeed, this trend has been so marked that some observers have suggested we now have a de facto national curriculum of basic skills. This national focus on basic skills reflects both intentional policy at the state and local levels and the indirect influence of other forces—including textbook publishers who cater to the lowest common denominator in content, test developers, educational administrators who use standardized tests that reinforce this focus, and teachers who have had neither adequate training nor appropriate role models in their own educational experience (Tyson-Bernstein 1988, Smith and O'Day 1991b). In addition, some evidence indicates that teachers tend to focus their teaching on maximizing student performance on tests used for accountability purposes, which have typically emphasized basic competencies (Madaus 1991, Shepard 1991).

Public expectations for student performance are also sadly low. As parents, as voters, and as members of the community, we settle for far less than do our counterparts in other developed nations (Cohen and Spillane 1993). Most state standards, where they exist, provide a floor, not a goal, for practice. High, or leading edge, requirements for education practice and student performance mean that for some period of time, perhaps a lengthy one, most schools would be below standard, a situation typically viewed as politically intolerable. Moreover, when high standards are proposed, they are likely to be followed by educator requests for more resources, making policymakers wary of initiating the cycle. This condition is beginning to change in a few states, such as Kentucky and Vermont; but the fact is that in a tight economy, the battle for higher education standards is generally difficult to win. Typically, voters are only lukewarm, and this makes policymakers legitimately cautious.

The quality of our school resources too often reflects our minimal expectations. With the general exception of schools in affluent areas, many of our youth attend institutions that lack the human and material capacity to deliver to their students a curriculum based on a challenging conception of content. In too many schools, there is no science lab; students are not allowed to take home textbooks or other books to do their homework; and, of most concern, teachers are not trained well enough to understand, much less to teach, the kind of demanding material envisioned in the new content standards (Kozol 1991, Taylor and Piche 1990).

What effect has the low quality of our standards and our schools had on student achievement? Over the past 20 years, student achievement has remained relatively flat or very slightly improved at best, with the exception that minority groups, particularly African Americans, have improved in basic skills areas. On the one hand, this trend suggests that the national emphasis in the 1970s and 1980s on de facto basic skills standards—spurred and reinforced by direct state and local policy activity—had a distinct and positive effect on student achievement for those who could most benefit from it (Smith and O'Day 1991a). On the other hand, the data indicate that our overall level of student achievement remains low to mediocre when compared with that of other developed nations (NEGP 1992).

Given these effects, we as a nation are faced with a choice. One alternative is to either ignore or reject outright the challenge of setting higher and more challenging standards for the content of instruction, for student performance, and for school quality. This course of action is clearly the easiest and least controversial. It is also, we argue, the least prudent, for it would perpetuate a national conception of scholastic achievement distinctly inferior to that of other developed nations and well below the capabilities of our youth. Under such conditions, it is difficult to imagine that our level of student performance or our international standing will improve greatly. We believe it wise to seek an alternative, that of setting challenging national standards for all our students.

Defining National Education Standards

The purpose of education standards, as we discuss them here, is to respond with appropriate direction and specificity to the fundamental questions: What should schools teach? What should students learn and how well should they learn it? And, what is the school's capacity to ensure that all students have an opportunity to learn the standards? The term *education standards* is generic—it is important to develop a set of specific definitions for responding to the important questions posed in this discussion. Within the context of a defined subject matter area, the Standards Task Force of the National Council on Educational Standards and Testing (NCEST 1992) suggested several components designed to flesh out an overall definition of education standards: the overarching statement, content standards, student performance standards, school delivery standards, and system delivery standards.

• **Overarching Statement**. This statement should describe briefly and in general terms a vision of the nature of the education standards for the content area. It should emphasize a theoretically and pedagogically coherent and engaging presentation of up-to-date subject matter and high expectations for all students, including an ultimate goal of world-class achievement. The description of "Mathematical Power" in the new California Mathematics Framework is an example. The California Overarching Statement on Mathematics states: "Mathematical power, which involves the ability to discern mathematical relationships, reason logically, and use mathematical techniques effectively, must be the central concern of mathematics education and must be the context in which skills are developed" (California State Department of Education 1985).

• **Content Standards**. Content standards should set out the knowledge, skills, and other necessary understandings that schools should teach to ensure that all U.S. students attain high levels of competency in the subject matter. Generally, for our purposes, what schools are expected to teach is equivalent to the knowledge, skills, and other understandings that students are expected to learn in schools. The National Council of Teachers of Mathematics (NCTM 1989) *Curriculum and Evaluation Standards for School Mathematics*, the California Frameworks, the Syllabuses for Advanced Placement Tests of the College Board, and the *Course of Study for Lower Secondary Schools* in Japan (UNESCO 1983) are all examples of content standards. Content standards should cover the entire range of precollegiate formal schooling (grades K–12), as do the NCTM *Curriculum and Evaluation Standards for School Mathematics* and the California Frameworks (NCTM 1989, California State Department of Education 1985). Figure 2.1 shows NCTM's standard for high school algebra.

• **Student Performance Standards**. These standards should establish the degree or quality of student performance in the challenging subject matter set out in the content standards. In general, the development of such standards will require examples of a range of professionally judged student

---

Figure 2.1
NCTM Standard 5: Algebra

In grades 9–12, the mathematics curriculum should include the continued study of algebraic concepts and methods so that all students can—

- represent situations that involve variable quantities with expressions, equations, inequalities, and matrices;
- use tables and graphs as tools to interpret expressions, equations, and inequalities;
- operate on expressions and matrices, and solve equations and inequalities;
- appreciate the power of mathematical abstraction and symbolism;
- and so that, in addition, college-intending students can—
- use matrices to solve linear systems;
- demonstrate technical facility with algebraic transformations, including techniques based on theory of equations.

Source: National Council of Teachers of Mathematics. (1985). *Curriculum and Evaluation Standards for School Mathematics.* Reston, Va.: Author.

---

performances to serve as benchmarks for assessing the quality of a new student's performance. For example, the College Board Advanced Placement (AP) Tests are scored from 1 to 5. Typically, a score of 3 indicates that a student has performed well enough to pass a college-level examination on the subject, a score of 4 indicates the student would have gotten a B in a college course examination, and a score of 5 is superior performance equating to an A in college. The assignment of a level of performance on an AP Test requires an explicit comparison of the examination performance (e.g., essays, analyses of text, record of how different calculus problems are solved) with the prior performance of successful and unsuccessful college students on "equivalent" tests.

Undoubtedly, whether there should be one or multiple performance standards will be a matter of some debate. The Standards Task Force recommended that at least a three-level scale of student performance standards be used for grading assessments based on the content standards. These levels might be labeled "competent performance," "excellent performance," and "world-class performance" standards. To establish the criteria for the final level, "world-class standards," we will need to gather information about the quality of the best student work in other nations.

• **School Delivery Standards**. These standards, referred to as "opportunity to learn" standards in proposed federal legislation, should set out criteria to enable local and state educators, policymakers, parents, and the public to assess the quality of a school's capacity and performance in educating their students in the challenging subject matter set out by the content standards. School delivery standards should provide a metric for determining whether a school "delivers" to the students the opportunity to learn the material in the content standards. Are the teachers in the school trained to teach the content of the standards? Does the school have appropriate and high-quality instructional materials that reflect the content standards? Does the actual curriculum of the school reflect the content standards in sufficient depth for the students to master it to a high standard of performance? These conditions are fundamental to providing all children the opportunity to learn the material of the content standards (Porter 1992, Darling-Hammond 1992, O'Day and Smith 1993). Finally, on the outcome side, does the performance of the students in the school indicate that the school is successfully providing all students the opportunity to learn.

• **System Delivery Standards**. These standards should set out criteria for establishing the quality of a school system's (local, state, or national) capacity and performance in educating all students in the subject matter set out in the content standards. To some degree, U.S. performance standards have already been developed by the NEGP and the President in Goals 3 and 4, which establish targets for students for the year 2000.

Goal 3 states: "By the year 2000, American students will leave grades four, eight, and twelve having demonstrated competency in challenging subject matter including English, mathematics, science, history and geography; and every school in America will ensure that all students learn to use their minds well, so they may be prepared for responsible citizenship, further learning, and productive employment in our modern economy."

Goal 4 states: "By the year 2000, U.S. students will be first in the world in science and mathematics achievement."

Each state and local district might establish their own achievement targets that, when summed, would enable the nation to reach the national goals.

THE GOVERNANCE OF CURRICULUM

Are National Standards a Good Idea?

Even though professional associations have forged ahead, there is still considerable controversy over whether national standards are a good idea. Many arguments exist both supporting and contesting their desirability.

Pros

One typical argument used to support the establishment of national education standards is that the international standing of the United States and the competitiveness of the U.S. economy, system of security, and diplomatic influence are national, not state or local, concerns and therefore require national attention to the development of the nation's human capital. National educational standards could help ensure that our increasingly diverse and mobile population will have the shared knowledge and values necessary to make our democracy work on a national level. Another common argument is that many states have insufficient resources, both human and fiscal, to establish their own standards and assessment systems; it would thus be far more efficient for states and localities to cooperate in a national approach than to create their own standards and assessment systems separately. Other arguments in favor of national standards include the assertions that the establishment of challenging national standards will encourage states and localities to raise their educational expectations; that such standards will help improve the quality of schools and of teacher professional development by providing a clear, common set of challenging goals and criteria for the allocation of scarce resources; and that national standards, applicable for *all* children, will help provide the impetus for realizing equality of educational opportunity across the nation.

Cons

A prevalent argument against establishing national education standards is that our nation's experience with centrally established standards (e.g., at the state level in education and at the state and national levels in other sectors) has not been promising. Standards are generally "minimum standards" that serve to drag down the entire system; if such were the case with national education standards, the entire nation would suffer. Related concerns are that the establishment of national standards would draw attention and resources away from the many very positive state and local reforms that are now underway, and that if challenging national standards are established but the strategies and resources for enabling students and schools to meet them are not put into place, the result will be a disservice to our students. Other arguments depict national standards as too narrow and restrictive. They assert that national standards will lead to a national curriculum, which will inhibit local and state creativity and initiative, and that the great diversity of the nation—culturally, ethnically, and regionally—makes it impossible to have a common set of educational standards that would have widespread acceptance.

Assumptions

In examining the pros and cons of national standards, we make three important assumptions about the characteristics of the proposed standards. First, we assume that the education standards are to be national rather than federal. We take this to mean that although the process for establishing and implementing the standards will be national in scope, it will not and should not be under the control of the federal government. We assume that the professional associations would continue to play a leadership role in standards development, and that any body created to certify or approve standards would be represent the various levels of government and the broader public.

Second, we assume that standards are "voluntary" for the states. Only the federal government could have the authority to require states to use national education standards—and even that is unlikely in light of the language of the Constitution. Discretion for the adoption of the standards would continue to rest with the states, providing an important balance of power and responsibility. This is an extremely important point. It addresses questions concerning what the effects would be of imposing national standards in an education system where curriculum is traditionally controlled at the state and local level. The position taken here is that "education standards" would be voluntary, not mandatory or imposed nationally. Being voluntary nationally, however, would not stop individual states from making the standards mandatory for the school districts within their borders.

Third, we assume that these would be challenging, not minimal education standards. Undergirding the interest in national education standards is the idea that the content of the present curriculum in most U.S. schools lacks coherence, depth, and quality. We assume that national education standards will legitimately be "world class" in scope and quality. The initial efforts of the various professional associations indicate similar ambitious goals. The standards must reflect high, not minimal expectations for all of our students. If standards are not challenging and of the highest quality, they are guaranteed to do more harm than good.

Questions

Arguments for and against national standards are captured by three overarching questions:

1. Will national standards have a positive influence on student achievement and the quality of teachers and schools?
2. What is the potential effect of national standards on educational equity?
3. Are national standards appropriate given the American tradition of local control of curriculum and the existing wide variations in state and local resources for education?

Let's look first at the effect of national standards on student achievement.

Student Achievement. What might happen to student achievement and teacher behavior if there were challenging, voluntary national education standards? One obvious desired outcome would be to produce a ripple effect throughout the entire system by stimulating improvements in state and local content and performance standards and expectations. This stimulus, in turn, could have a positive effect on education practice in local schools and classrooms. The content and teaching standards developed by NCTM have had a great influence on the policies and practices of state and local boards of education as these groups have established the curriculums of their jurisdictions (Hayes 1992). Similarly, though to a lesser extent, state and local communities have drawn from the work of the American Association for the Advancement of Science (AAAS) *Project 2061* (AAAS 1989).

Content and performance standards *alone*, however, cannot change student achievement and teacher performance. To be fully effective, the standards must be part of a coherent, systemic approach to improving instruction in the schools (Smith and O'Day 1991b, Cohen and Spillane 1993). Education policy efforts aimed at changing the status quo are generally short term, unconnected to other policies and overall goals of the system, limited to a small set of schools or grades, and focused on particular problem areas rather than on the entire system. Consequently, policy efforts rarely have a sustaining effect. National standards could lay the foundation for a different approach.

Challenging national standards could set expectations for all schools and grades in key content areas, signalling the type of substantive changes we need systemwide in all our schools and classrooms. The content and performance standards could form the basis for other state policies, such as those dealing with adoption of instructional materials, teacher licensing, and professional development. We could then have several interconnected policy efforts giving coherent guidance about teaching and learning around ambitious, not basic skills, outcomes.

Most important, student achievement and teacher performance will change in a dramatic way only if existing and future teachers are trained to be able to teach the challenging content in the new national standards (Darling-Hammond 1990, Murray 1992, David 1993). Though it would be important that new instructional materials based on the new standards be developed and that schools have the other material resources necessary to teach the content standards, none of this will help unless there is a dramatic effort to prepare teachers to teach the new content. Most public school teachers do not have the deep, sophisticated understanding of the subject matter required to teach the content indicated by the kind of education standards proposed here. The new content expectations would also call for new ways of teaching, for strategies that actively engage students. Most teachers are not used to teaching in such ways. They have few opportunities and little time to learn on the job. Nor does preservice professional development meet these challenges. If national standards are to spur improved teaching and learning, they will need reinforcement from extensive and carefully developed professional development activities (Cohen and Ball 1990; Cohen and Spillane 1993; Smith, O'Day, and Cohen 1991).

Evidence about the effect of ambitious, coherent instructional reforms on teaching and student achievement is positive, if not abundant. Some states, notably California, New York, Vermont, Kentucky, Arizona, and Delaware, are aligning challenging content objectives and assessment. However, almost all these efforts are very recent; most do not yet tie teacher professional development and instructional materials policies to the curriculum/assessment strategies. In many other developed nations, however, coherent policy systems link content standards to instructional materials, examination systems, and professional development (Smith, O'Day, and Cohen 1991; Cohen and Spillane 1993).

Some evidence suggests that ambitious content standards reinforced by assessment and other policies have the potential to improve schooling. Preliminary data indicate that the California Mathematics Framework actively influences local policy and instruction (Cohen and Ball 1990). A study using the International Education Assessment's Second International Mathematics Study (SIMS) found that teachers in nations with more coherent curricular guidance were more consistent and more alike in the topics they covered, indicating an influence of the common focus (Stevenson and Baker 1991). Analyses of national survey data indicate that secondary schools that have coherent approaches, such as common curriculums and shared goals, tend to be somewhat more successful in limiting absenteeism and student dropouts, improving achievement performance, and reducing performance differences among students (Bryk and Thum 1989; Bryk, Lee, and Smith 1990).

The next question concerns the success of schools in promoting equity in opportunities to learn.

Educational Equity. What would be the potential effect of national education standards on educational equity? A major part of the justification for national education standards must rest on their promise for improving the quality of the educational experiences of the most needy in our society. During the 1970s and throughout the 1980s, the achievement gap between majority and minority and rich and poor narrowed substantially. In the past 25 years, African-American, Hispanic-American, and low-income children have made gains in partially closing the achievement gap with middle-income whites; these gains have resulted both from changes in social and economic conditions and from a national focus on basic skills, which sought to equalize the quality of education offered to students of different backgrounds. The test scores of minorities and low-income students rose, while the scores of the middle income and majority students have stayed essentially level (Smith and O'Day 1991a).

Under present conditions, however, this trend is unlikely to continue. Over the past decade, the social, political, and economic circumstances of many low-income and minority families have worsened. Moreover, the basic skills emphasis in school is being legitimately criticized for its failure to develop in all students the higher levels of learning and more complex skills necessary in a technologically advanced society. As a consequence, many local districts and schools have instituted reforms that attempt to emphasize higher-order thinking and a more challenging curriculum (O'Day and Smith 1993).

Ironically, such locally initiated reforms might actually widen the gap between low-income and minority students and middle-income and majority students. As educationally progressive as the local reforms to improve the quality of the curriculum may be, they could also place many minorities and the poor at a new disadvantage because the poor and minorities in the society are typically the last to benefit from locally generated reforms—if they benefit at all. Districts and schools with large numbers of poor and minority students often have less discretionary money to stimulate reform, fewer well-trained teachers, and more day-to-day problems that drain administrative energy away from constructive reforms. In conjunction with the increasing numbers of children in poverty and the depressingly bad economic condition of many cities, the new reforms may already be leading to substantial new increases in the achievement gap.

This outcome will almost certainly occur if the changes in the schools are initiated one school and one district at a time. If, however, the changes were expected to apply roughly equally across the schools within a very large district or across the schools and districts within a state, there is some hope that greater equality of opportunity would result.

Common, challenging standards and high expectations could serve equity well. The opportunity for a condition of equal expectations could be enhanced under a system (large district, state, or nation) that had a common set of challenging content standards and high performance standards for all of its students. Within such a system, the nature of inequalities in resources necessary for preparing students to reach the common standards would be more easily exposed than under the present system—where the expectations differ across schools and districts. Educators and policymakers in a large system would be more likely to spot differences in the capacity (knowledge and experience) of teachers to teach the common material and differences in the quality of textbooks and school resources to support teaching the common material.

Exposing such differences, however, will not be enough; national content and performance standards must also be accompanied by measures to ensure equal opportunity to learn. Without such measures, national standards could actually help to widen and legitimize the achievement gap between the advantaged and disadvantaged in this country. Standards and assessments must be accompanied by policies that provide access for all students to high-quality resources, including appropriate instructional materials and well-prepared teachers. Demanding content and performance standards can be used to challenge all students with the same expectations, but high expectations will result in common high performance only if all schools provide high-quality instruction designed to meet these expectations (O'Day and Smith 1993).

School delivery standards could be an important mechanism for helping to ensure that all students have access to this high-quality instruction. Delivery standards could provide targets and guidance for school improvement efforts by amplifying the vision and structure provided by the content standards and reform strategy. This process could be particularly effective if incorporated into a democratically developed and professionally monitored system of school improvement. The next question, concerning local control of schooling, addresses this process.

Local Control of Schooling. What are the benefits and liabilities of imposing uniform national standards on an educational system where curriculum is traditionally controlled at the state and local level? We have already discussed the issue of "imposing" national standards in our earlier discussion of "voluntary versus mandatory" education standards. Here we assume that the standards would be voluntary but consider the desirability of national certification or recommendation of standards, rather than leaving this task solely to the states and localities.

What would be the effect on our educational system of a national consensus around education standards? Such a consensus could enhance the sense of national identity and community we need as our nation becomes increasingly diverse. Given such a consensus and system, we as a nation could accommodate diversity and still have a means of achieving a prime purpose of public schooling: creating an informed citizenry that shares underlying values about democracy.

Of course, there is a danger and counterargument: national standards might be too centralizing and might in fact constrain states, communities, and schools from responding effectively to the diverse goals and needs of their constituents. Several safeguards could prevent such a situation from materializing. First, as stated previously, the standards should be national and voluntary, not federal or mandatory.

Second, the standards should be developed and viewed as a common core that, where adopted, would be enhanced through considerable state and local flexibility. For example, while national standards should be detailed enough to avoid being vague, they should be general enough to permit schools and teachers to develop their own detailed curriculums. One form that this flexibility might take would be to build in state and local choices and options, as in the sequencing of subjects or in the choice of literature within each genre. Another form would be the addition by states and localities of their own unique content and performance expectations to reflect their own histories and populations. This notion of flexibility within a common core is supported by a variety of evidence. Research in the United States, for example, shows that central curriculums are only one of the many influences on teaching; and the ambitious new state content frameworks are being interpreted by teachers in a variety of ways (Floden et al. 1988, Archbald and Porter 1992). At the same time, experiences from other countries provide practical models for building local flexibility into a national framework.

A third factor mitigating against overcentralization is that national standards could build on the already significant work done by a number of states in reaching a consensus about ambitious student outcomes. California, New York, Kentucky, Vermont, South Carolina, and other states have developed or are beginning to develop standards that national groups could adapt, adopt, mirror, or borrow from (Fuhrman and Massell 1992, Massell, this volume). By building on more locally derived consensus, the national standards would not prescribe as much as they would reinforce what states and communities have already developed.

The Feasibility of National Standards

Having addressed the desirability of national education standards, we must now ask whether developing such standards is possible. Can the United States develop high-quality content, performance, and delivery standards? Isn't the nation too ethically and culturally diverse and too rooted in traditions of state and local governance and control? Can we reach the national "consensus" over content and performance standards that would make their development ultimately worthwhile?

One worry is that national standards, developed by consensus, will not be challenging. Experience in education and in other sectors teaches us that standards set by governments are likely to be set at minimum levels, the lowest common denominator. One approach to answering the question is to examine examples of activities that offer proof of the existence of high-level national standards. The NCTM standards are a clear illustration. Professional associations and groups of experts are now undertaking standard-setting activities in science, history, geography, the arts, and English. The California Frameworks are examples of high-quality content standards for our most populous and diverse state. The performance standards for the AP examinations are also an example of demanding performance standards in the United States. At the same time as various organizations are developing standards for student knowledge, the National Board for Professional Teaching Standards (NBPTS 1991), an independent body composed primarily of teachers, is defining high-level competencies for distinguished teachers in some thirty areas of expertise. The expectations for what teachers should know are predicated on reaching consensus on what students should know.

Although there is little relevant experience in delivery standards in the United States, we believe that appropriate delivery standards could also be developed for meeting the demands of challenging content and performance standards. In the United States, delivery standards (i.e., accreditation standards) have typically been developed independently of the curriculum because there have been no common content standards. The specification and use of delivery standards associated with common content standards (e.g., high-quality curricular materials and professional development programs based on the content standards) would be breaking new ground. A few partial models exist, however, including the guidelines for instruction developed by NCTM to be used with its curriculum standards and the materials associated with the AP courses and the International Baccalaureate. One key will be to develop a system of implementing delivery standards that relies on and enhances professional judgment. In this way, we would be more likely to avoid the tendency to reduce such standards to bureaucratic checklists and more able instead to use them to foster professional development and real school improvement.

Another concern is raised by current debates over the extent to which content must reflect the racial and ethnic diversity of the nation and over the extent to which each school's focus must reflect its own racial and ethnic makeup. The debates underscore the challenge of reaching consensus, except at a superficial level. In addition, consensus—and therefore acceptance and ownership—is endangered by disagreement over controversial curriculum issues, like the teaching of evolution. However, a variety of experiences provides counterexamples to these arguments.

For example, one highly diverse state, California, has developed challenging and high-quality content standards, even in sensitive and particularly complex areas such as science and history/social studies. This accomplishment indicates that the challenge of diverse opinions can be overcome by hard work and careful attention and respect for differences in opinion among various interests. California has been able to adopt sophisticated and complex curriculum frameworks in mathematics, social studies, and science. We are not suggesting that the task will be easy or quick, but we believe that it is feasible.

The fact that the NCTM as a professional group has reached national consensus on content standards is a positive though not entirely convincing argument for our ability to bridge strong state and local traditions. The nationwide agreement among professionals in mathematics and mathematics teaching reached by the NCTM on very challenging content expectations is echoed by the experiences of several area standards Task Forces formed by the NBPTS. Neither of these efforts reflects any watering down of content or avoidance of controversial issues. As the NCTM standards or closely cloned versions of the standards are adopted by more and more state boards of education, the argument for the power of compelling, high-quality, yet voluntary national standards becomes more convincing.

These examples (and others, such as the National Assessment of Educational Progress) show that it is feasible to develop voluntary, national education standards that are far more challenging than the minimal, basic skills standards that currently drive much of American education. Even with these examples, however, we do not know the extent to which the standards will be embraced by the public and thus the extent to which they will ultimately effect our schools. The extent of the influence of these standards will largely depend on the level of ownership of the new standards felt by the nation's education profession, federal, local, and state policymakers, parents of all children, and the public. Ownership of the new national education standards by these various constituents will be an essential cornerstone of our commitment to change the content and quality of instruction in our schools. Moreover, ownership of the new national standards will generate a vision to guide the actions of state and local policymakers, to focus reform and the use of resources in schools, and to provide purpose and content to teacher professional development.

How can we create a standards-developing process that will ensure that all interested participants, including teachers, have an opportunity to be heard? If national standards are to form the basis of a shared national vision of what schools can provide to students, the standards must accurately reflect what we as a nation want schools to achieve. They must represent a true, shared understanding of our goals for student academic achievement. Yet, how can we expect policymakers, the public, and many education professionals to aspire to new and challenging standards if they have not had the opportunity to be exposed to them? The public will embrace challenging national standards of "world-class" quality only if people are given the opportunity to engage in a national discussion, with concrete examples of high-quality content and student performance. People must be encouraged to discuss, debate, and refine expert judgment on national education standards. We should enlist parents, business leaders, citizens, political leaders, university educators, and even students throughout the nation in this important effort, which will require time, commitment, and effort of all concerned. We should view setting national standards not as an educational get-rich-quick scheme, but as a long-term strategy for upgrading the expectations we hold for our youth and transforming the entire educational enterprise.

Currently, U.S. schools operate under a de facto national system of basic skills competencies and minimal expectations. Consequently, our schools and the outcomes they produce are not of the same caliber as the educational systems of other developed nations. One solution to this problem is to develop national content standards and performance standards for students and schools. Although such standards are currently under development by professional associations, there is continuing debate about a more formal governmental role in certifying, recommending, and supporting standards. Arguments against the establishment of such standards center on concerns that they would be minimal and drag down or draw attention and resources away from currently successful programs and that national standards would not respond to the diversity of our nation. We could avoid these problems, however, if we were to develop and implement challenging standards through a national (not federal) and voluntary (not mandatory) process that allowed for flexibility at the state and local level. Evidence suggests that if standards are properly implemented, challenging and high-quality national standards could potentially have a substantial positive effect on student achievement, the quality of teachers and schools, and educational equity in our nation.

References

American Association for the Advancement of Science. (1989). *Science for All Americans*. A Project 2061 report on Literacy Goals in Science, Mathematics, and Technology. Washington. D.C.: Author.

Archbald, D.A., and A.C. Porter. (in press). "Curriculum Control and Teachers' Perceptions of Autonomy and Satisfaction." *Education Evaluation and Policy Analysis*.

Bryk, T., V. Lee, and J. Smith. (1990). "High School Organization and Its Effects on Teachers and Students: An Interpretive Summary of the Research." In *Choice and Control in American Education, Vol. 1*, edited by W. Clune and J.F. Witte. Philadelphia: Falmer Press.

Bryk, A.S., and Y.M. Thum. (1989). *The Effects of High School Organization on Dropping Out: An Exploratory Investigation*. New Brunswick, N.J.: Rutgers University, Center for Policy Research in Education.

California State Department of Education. (1985). *Mathematics Curriculum Framework for California Public Schools*. Sacramento, Calif.: Author.

Cohen, D., and D. Ball. (1990). "Relations Between Policy and Practice: A Commentary." *Educational Evaluation and Policy Analysis* 12, 3: 331–338.

Cohen, D.K., and J.P. Spillane. (1993). "Policy and Practice: The Relations Between Governance and Instruction." In *Designing Coherent Policy: Improving the System* (pp. 35–95), edited by S. Fuhrman. San Francisco: Jossey-Bass.

Darling-Hammond, L. (1990). "Instructional Policy into Practice: The Power of the Bottom Over the Top." *Educational Evaluation and Policy Analysis* 12, 3: 339–348.

Darling-Hammond, L. (1992). "Creating Standards of Practice and Delivery for Learner Centered Schools." *Stanford Law and Policy Review* 4: 37–52.

David, J.L. (1993). "Systemic Reform: Creating the Capacity for Change." Unpublished manuscript. New Brunswick, N.J.: Consortium for Policy Research in Education.

Floden, R., A. Porter, L. Alford, D. Freeman, S. Irwin, W. Schmidt, and J. Schwille. (1988). "Instructional Leadership at the District Level: A Closer Look at Autonomy and Control." *Educational Administration Quarterly* 24: 96–124.

Fuhrman, S., and D. Massell. (1992). *Issues and Strategies in Systemic Reform*. New Brunswick, N.J.: Consortium for Policy Research in Education.

Hayes, L. (1992). "News and Views." *Phi Delta Kappan* 73, 10: 806–807.

Kozol, J. (1991). *Savage Inequalities*. New York: Crown.

Madaus, G. (1991). "The Effects of Important Tests on Students." *Phi Delta Kappan* 73, 3: 226–231.

Murray, C.E. (1992). "Rochester's Reforms: The Teachers' Perspective." *Educational Policy* 6, 1: 55–71.

National Board for Professional Teaching Standards. (1991). *Towards High and Rigorous Standards for the Teaching Profession*. 3rd ed. Detroit, MI: Author.

National Council of Teachers of Mathematics. (1989). *Curriculum and Evaluation Standards for School Mathematics*. Reston, Va.: Author.

National Council on Education Standards and Testing. (January 24, 1992). *Raising Standards for American Education*. Washington, D.C.: Author.

National Education Goals Panel. (1992). *Building a Nation of Learners*. Washington, D.C.: U.S. Government Printing Office.

O'Day, J., and M.S. Smith. (1993). "Systemic School Reform and Educational Opportunity." In *Designing Coherent Education Policy: Improving the System* (pp. 250–312), edited by S. Fuhrman. San Francisco: Jossey-Bass.

Porter, A. (1992). "School Delivery Standards." Paper prepared for the meeting of the National Governors' Association, Washington, D.C.

Shepard, L. (1991). "Will National Tests Improve Student Learning?" *Phi Delta Kappan* 73, 3: 232–238.

Smith, M.S., and J. O'Day. (1991a). "Educational Equality: 1966 and Now." In *The 1990 American Finance Association Yearbook: Spheres of Justice in Education* (pp. 53–100), edited by D.A. Verstegen and J.G. Ward. New York: Harper-Collins.

Smith, M.S., and J. O'Day. (1991b). "Systemic School Reform." In *The Politics of Curriculum and Testing* (pp. 233–267), edited by S. Fuhrman and B. Malen. Bristol, Pa.: Falmer Press.

Smith, M.S., J. O'Day, and D.K. Cohen. (September 1991). "A National Curriculum in the United States?" *Educational Leadership* 49, 1: 74–81.

Stevenson, D., and D. Baker. (1991). "State Control of the Curriculum and Classroom Instruction." *Sociology of Education* 64, 1: 1–10.

Taylor, W., and D. Piche. (December 1990). *A Report on Shortchanging Children: The Impact of Fiscal Inequity on the Education of Students at Risk*. Staff Report for House of Representatives Committee on Education and Labor, U.S. Congress. Washington, D.C.: U.S. Government Printing Office.

Tyson-Bernstein, H. (1988). "The Academy's Contribution to the Impoverishment of America's Textbooks." *Phi Delta Kappan* 70: 194–198.

UNESCO. (1983). *Course of Study for Lower Secondary Schools in Japan*. Tokyo: Author, Education and Cultural Exchange Division.

3

Legislatures and Education Policy

Susan H. Fuhrman

The mid-1990s is an appropriate time to examine the role of state legislatures in making education policy. From some perspectives, legislatures have been eminently successful in facing up to the challenges of improving education. They have consistently devoted attention to education issues for the past twenty-five years. They have been at the forefront of educational policymaking, often taking the initiative in crafting new approaches. However, from other perspectives, legislatures have been less successful. Serious education problems remain, problems that increasingly seem beyond the scope of traditional legislative approaches. Furthermore, changing perspectives on educational improvement appear to call for new responses on the part of legislatures, responses that may be difficult for them to make.

Legislatures as Education Policy Leaders: The 1970s Through the Mid-1980s

During the '70s and '80s, legislatures generated volumes of statutes related to education. In the 1970s, they revised school financing statutes to address wealth-related disparities among local districts; and they provided special programs, such as compensatory education, for the neediest students. In the early 1980s, they turned their attention to the performance of

---

Author's Note: This chapter draws on research conducted by the Consortium for Policy Research in Education (CPRE), a consortium of Rutgers University, the University of Southern California, Harvard University, Michigan State University, Stanford University, and the University of Wisconsin-Madison. CPRE is funded by the Office of Educational Research and Improvement, U.S. Department of Education. The views expressed are those of the author and do not represent endorsement by the sponsoring institutions. The chapter also benefitted from support by the Eagleton Institute of Politics' Symposium on the Legislature in the 21st Century.

all students, increasing standards for high school graduation and mandating more testing to assess student progress. They also addressed the need to attract and retain quality teachers through salary increases, higher standards for teacher education and certification, and provisions for continuing professional development. Throughout the latter period, they kept up their commitment to finance educational improvement; state funding for education rose 21.3 percent in real terms between 1982–83 and 1986–87 (Firestone, Fuhrman, and Kirst 1989).

Unprecedented Educational Initiatives

The volume of statutory accomplishment is extremely impressive. Twenty-eight states enacted school finance reform measures between 1971 and 1981 (Brown and Elmore 1982). By 1979–80, twenty-three states provided funds to local districts to support services for disadvantaged students; the same number offered financial assistance for instruction of limited-English-proficient students; and all fifty states had enacted special education programs that conformed to Public Law 94-142, although they varied in financing mechanisms (Winslow and Peterson 1982). In the early and mid-1980s, education reform spread so rapidly from state to state that some elements of reform were addressed by virtually every state. For example, forty-five states modified high school graduation requirements, generally by increasing the number of required courses in mathematics and science. More than forty new state testing programs were put in place between 1980 and 1988.

Within specific areas of reform, there was unprecedented legislative activity. Between 1980 and 1986, for example, more than 1,000 pieces of legislation regarding teacher certification and compensation were introduced (Darling-Hammond and Berry 1988). Many states, including California, Florida, Georgia, Indiana, Mississippi, South Carolina, and Texas, approached reform through comprehensive packages that bundled tens of separate items together into omnibus bills. At the decade's end, some states, like South Carolina, enacted comprehensive reform measures for a second time. By the early 1990s, there were still examples of legislative overhauls of education. For example, Kentucky revised its entire system through a major reform act in 1991.

Also impressive is the degree to which legislative action focused on the most serious problems of the time. Despite long traditions in most states of local control, legislatures were able in the 1970s to specify minimum and maximum amounts of local spending when they perceived the degree to which spending disparities made a child's education dependent on accidents of geography. When legislators saw that substantially equal spending would not be fair to districts especially burdened by large numbers of students with special needs, they created programs that targeted extra funds and services to such districts. In the 1980s, legislatures correctly diagnosed the question to be one of student performance, realizing that the issue was not solely one of enabling districts to spend adequately but of challenging them to provide ambitious programs for all children. To do this, legislatures had to move beyond traditional definitions of the legislative role in education into core issues of what should be taught and who should teach it. The emphasis on teaching and learning continues into the 1990s.

Finally, the degree to which legislatures took the initiative, as opposed to a more reactive stance, in addressing these problems is also impressive. In every state undergoing school finance reform, legislative leaders masterminded and executed a strategy of reform, resorting to various compromise and persuasion tactics to convince their colleagues (Fuhrman 1982). Legislatures were also at the forefront of the reform movement of the past decade. For example, a study of reform in six states found that legislative chairs and leaders shaped and shepherded reform packages in five states. In the sixth, legislators pressured the state board to ensure that their reform goals were met. There were other key players in each of the states, including governors and business leaders, but legislators were active pilots at each stage of the education reform process. Even before reform bill introduction, legislators often served as members of gubernatorial task forces and commissions and convened their own studies (Fuhrman, Clune, and Elmore 1988; Firestone et al. 1989; Firestone, Rosenblum, Bader, and Massell 1991).

Legislative Response to Social Pressure

Legislative leadership is in part a reflection of outside forces. In the 1970s, many legislatures were responding to court orders declaring financing systems unconstitutional; others were acting in anticipation of court suits. They were also urged on by a national network of experts and citizen groups that pressured—and assisted—them in reaching their goals. In the 1980s, the state education reform movement was given energy and momentum by the perception of an educational crisis, best expressed in the stirring words of the National Commission on Excellence in Education's *A Nation at Risk* (NCEE 1983); the withdrawal of the federal government from programmatic leadership and its resort to putting pressure on states through the bully pulpit; and the active interest in education of business elites.

These pressures were so strong that legislatures were at greater risk by not enacting education reforms than they were by acting, even though such action meant unprecedented extension into issues of school performance (McDonnell and Fuhrman 1985). Moreover, legislative activity in both decades was dependent on the availability of resources. In the late 1970s, the very early 1980s, and the early 1990s, when there was little fiscal slack, legislatures did not maintain the high profile they assumed both earlier and later over the twenty-five-year period.

However, legislative leadership in education also reflects the strengthened capacity of legislatures as institutions. The increase in staff resources, including staff who specialize in education, the more professional stance of legislatures, and the increased time devoted to legislative duties all prepared legislatures to assume leadership over a function that commanded the largest share of state budgets (Rosenthal and Fuhrman 1981). The activity of legislatures in the school finance reforms of the 1970s in some senses made their leadership in the substantive reforms of the 1980s inevitable; as the state share of the education dollar grew so did the need for accountability and the interest of legislatures in promoting and assessing school performance.

Factors Influencing Legislative Leadership

Whatever the source of legislative leadership in education, the decades of proactivity leave legislatures accustomed to a commanding presence in the field. Their own internal structures have developed in ways that facilitate and support a leadership role. These include highly sophisticated education committees composed of members who have developed expertise in education over a long period. Simultaneously, as the state share of education spending continued to rise, appropriations committees were increasingly disposed to education deliberations (Rosenthal and Fuhrman 1981). In many states, legislatures have come to believe in the importance of making their mark on education (National Conference of State Legislatures, NCSL, 1990). Moreover, having crossed customary boundaries of local control and educator dominance of education, legislatures are not likely to retreat. They are highly unlikely to return to the pattern prevalent through the mid-1960s of responding fairly mechanically to an agenda set by state departments of education and education associations (Bailey, Frost, Marsh, and Wood 1962).

Acclimated to a leadership role, legislatures now face the task of assessing the contributions of their accomplishments and determining what next steps are necessary. Planning for future educational reform is likely to become an even more salient activity as the national goals and the developing national standards put pressure on states to improve further.

Assessing the Accomplishments of Legislative Leadership: Implications for the 1990s and Beyond

Whereas legislatures can be applauded for their commitment, initiative, and willingness to break with tradition in addressing educational problems, the approbation should not preclude serious scrutiny. Such examination reveals that serious educational problems remain, despite unprecedented legislative attention. Even more damning, some aspects of the solutions crafted by legislatures may themselves be impeding educational progress. A look at student performance, social problems, and school structures, for example, reveals the complexities involved.

Student Performance

If the effectiveness of legislative educational policymaking over the past twenty-five years is to be judged by student performance, the picture is quite discouraging. Although educational achievement increased slightly in the 1980s, the gains have not been dramatic; and they have primarily concerned mastery of basic skills, not improvement in analytic and reasoning skills. For example, Scholastic Aptitude Test (SAT) average total scores increased 16 points between 1980 and 1985 (an upward trend that fought against years of steady decreases); but then, between 1987 and 1991, the scores declined 10 points (NCES 1992). National Assessment of Educational Progress (NAEP) scores remained relatively stable for all students on average reading and writing proficiencies[1] between 1984 and 1990, and the scores that were achieved on writing in particular were poor. At grade 11, the average writing score was 212; a score of 200 is a minimal level of proficiency (National Education Goals Panel 1992). Although U.S. 9- and 14-year-olds compare favorably with their cohorts in other industrialized nations on basic reading, our students fall behind on comprehending complex passages and in comparisons of math and science achievement (Elley 1992, Organisation for Economic Cooperation and Development 1992, Kirst 1993).

It seems that virtually every day we discover that American youth suffer from some basic form of illiteracy—cultural, numeric, or geographic. Businesses worry about the work force of the 21st century, and national political leaders fault the education system for failure to maintain the economic competitiveness of the United States.

Social Problems and Cultural Norms

The sources of America's educational shortcomings are multifold: they include the overwhelming effects of social problems, particularly in inner cities; the relative lack of respect accorded the teaching profession; and a culture that does not place sufficient priority on achievement in school. Some of these problems are beyond legislative influence; others may be chipped away by legislative efforts, like providing higher salaries for teachers. It will be many years, however, before such activities result in measurable educational improvement.

Structure and Function of Schools

At least part of the educational deficit relates directly to the structure and functioning of schools, and these were the aspects legislatures sought to reform. They sought to enable districts to spend adequately, to halt a drift toward relevancy at the expense of academics, and to make schools more accountable. Their efforts met with only mixed success. Financing disparities remain and have grown or reappeared in some states—like Texas and New Jersey—sufficiently to require renewed court action. Statutes to increase high school graduation requirements did lead to more academic coursetaking, but much of the enrollment increases were in basic or general courses, not in more challenging courses (Clune 1989, Hanson 1989). Increased testing to provide accountability led in some instances to explicit teaching to the test—cheating, both narrowly and broadly defined. In most instances, increased testing led to more emphasis on the currently measurable, narrow basic skills, rather than on the kind of problem-solving skills needed by the work force of the next century (Koretz 1988, Richards and Shujaa 1988, Madaus 1991).

Some of the efforts legislatures undertook may be considered building blocks in longer-term improvement efforts (Firestone et al. 1989). For example, mandating more math and science coursetaking in itself was insufficient to guarantee the quality of the courses; but now states are developing new and more challenging curriculum frameworks to be coupled with more sophisticated assessments and efforts to train teachers in new content (Smith and O'Day 1991; Massell, this volume). These next steps make the course requirements appear to be first efforts toward more academic content.

Mandating more assessment and evaluation for teachers sets in place a structure for the introduction of better assessment systems that more adequately capture good teaching than do current pencil-and-paper tests. The same can be said about student assessment. Current standardized tests do little to lead practice toward more ambitious notions of teaching and learning, but newer tests, seen in prototype in several states, may provide such impetus.

However, even if one forbids mixed success to date to stand in the way of optimistic assessment of legislative reform efforts, it is hard to escape the conclusion that some of those efforts were at best weak and that elements of reform were, in fact, impediments to progress.

Problems in Translating Policy into Practice

Policy typically has less effect on practice than policymakers desire because education works through the interplay of policy, administration, and practice. While policy can set the conditions for effective administration and practice, it cannot prescribe solutions to problems that need to be addressed at those levels (Elmore and McLaughlin 1988, Darling-Hammond 1990).

Some of the recent reforms were particularly weak in that they didn't do enough to encourage appropriate conditions for translation into practice. For example, as we have seen, the graduation requirements led to lower-quality academic coursetaking than reformers might have envisioned. In part, this result reflects the bluntness of the requirements; they simply called for more credits in key subjects and were not typically coupled with other mechanisms, such as challenging learner outcomes and assessments and high-quality technical assistance, to encourage schools to create more ambitious courses (Clune 1989).

Another major problem is that legislative policymaking in education has been fragmented and, therefore, sometimes contradictory. A clear example of ambiguous and contradictory policy exists within the field of teacher policy, where many states simultaneously raised standards for teacher education and for certification and created or permitted loopholes to ensure an adequate teacher supply. States used one or more of the following mechanisms to increase the quality of the teaching force: increased entrance requirements for teacher education; tightened requirements for teacher education programs; more specific grade-level or subject-matter credentials; new or expanded teacher competency tests in basic skills, subject matter knowledge, and professional knowledge; special support programs for beginning teachers; and more stringent standards for continuing certification.

At the same time, states left in place or created measures to avert shortages. Some were carefully designed alternative routes aimed at recruiting individuals with nontraditional backgrounds to education, but many were simply escape routes, such as emergency certification or condoning teaching out-of-field (Darling-Hammond and Berry 1988, American Association of Colleges for Teacher Education 1985).

If it was difficult to make coherent policy within a single policy area like teacher certification, it was even harder to coordinate policies addressing different aspects of education policy. States mandated more credit hours in liberal arts subjects for prospective teachers, particularly for secondary school teachers; they also developed new curriculum materials and requirements for schoolchildren. Few attempts were made to explore the match between the jumble of credits taken by teachers and the actual content they would be expected to teach (Smith and O'Day 1991). Similarly, some states, particularly in the South, developed new statewide teacher evaluation systems at the same time they were dealing with curricular content for children. Typically these activities proceeded on parallel paths that never crossed, and the ability to teach the newly required content did not make it to the list of the competencies on which teachers were to be evaluated.

Some of these individual policies, of course, were effective—and some were not. Success often depended on the context and the specific design of the policies. The point I wish to make is that legislators and educators have missed opportunities to multiply policy effects through coherent approaches to problems. In the worst cases, parallel policies were so contradictory as to raise the risk that they might cancel each other out. When policies send conflicting signals, the ambiguity is deferred to the field, where local districts sort out what the policies actually mean. The variation in district response that typically occurs in reaction to state policy is likely to be magnified when the policies themselves are unclear (McLaughlin 1987).

To some extent, fragmented policymaking reflects the reality of legislative life. Short electoral cycles and competition with the governor for the policy limelight create incentives for new policymaking, because new initiatives bring more visibility than either restraint or refinement of existing measures (Mayhew 1974, Fuhrman 1993). New policies often mean new directions, rather than consistent attempts to build on the past, for several reasons. The legislature—and sources on which it relies—may lack capacity for study and reflection on the effectiveness of past policy, and new directions often have more political currency because they signify creativity and innovation. Governors interested in education tend to propose new policy directions for many of the same reasons, and legislatures must respond in some fashion to these new proposals. Simply debating them gives them salience. Finally, the very inability of policy to directly affect some of the most serious problems of educational practice and performance may suggest, misleadingly, that the problem lies not in the limits of policy but in failure to yet identify the new policy or set of policies—the magic bullet—that will actually work.

The fast succession and sheer volume of policy initiatives emanating from legislatures may be questioned for reasons other than the obvious relationship between rapid-fire policymaking and frequent shifts in direction. At least two problems are posed by quick layering of policy initiatives: The system has no time to absorb them, and it is impossible to sort out the effects of any one policy to determine the value of the approach.

Many analysts were skeptical about the capacity of local districts and schools to absorb and make sense of the barrage of legislative initiatives, particularly in the 1980s. Some researchers predicted local problems in implementation—and even massive local resistance (Killian 1984, Anderson and Pipho 1984, Cuban 1984). In fact, local response turned out to be surprisingly positive; many local districts seized on the new state policies readily, orchestrating them around their own needs (Fuhrman et al. 1988, Fuhrman and Elmore 1990, Firestone et al. 1991).

However, ready implementation does not necessarily mean long-term absorption and institutionalization of new policy initiatives. Nor does it mean that the true goals of the policy are being met. As we have seen, new courses in academic subjects for high school students are in place; but more challenging content is frequently not being provided to the students affected. When graduation requirements were rapidly followed by special dropout-prevention programs admirably aimed at helping at-risk students meet the new requirements, the easiest response by schools was to develop remedial programs around the new courses. The end result appears to be remediation to meet remedial courses—not more thoughtful approaches that would place a greater priority on the education of at-risk students than on their graduation (Patterson 1991, Williams 1989).

Further, even though the response of districts to reforms was more positive than predicted, there remain large variations in the capacity of districts that affect their ability to absorb the new policies. Not all districts were able to rapidly retrain teachers, design new curriculums and adopt new tests at the state's behest, and supplement or stretch facilities to provide sufficient laboratory space. When capacity is limited, even one major change can be difficult; several changes in rapid succession can be impossible.

Differences in local capacity can be somewhat compensated for by state technical assistance; however, state agencies were themselves overwhelmed by the volume of new statutes. Most statutes imposed regulations; presented guidelines; and required implementing activities, such as developing new assessments and writing model curriculums. Technical assistance often fell by the wayside; the available assistance was largely restricted to interpretation of compliance requirements and was rarely concerned with the substance of the new policies (Fuhrman and Elmore 1990, Fuhrman 1989, U.S. General Accounting Office 1993).

The volume of policy makes it difficult to sort out the effects of any one policy to guide future efforts. Where achievement increases have occurred, as they have in some states with consistent data over the period, it is impossible to tell which improvement resulted from which policy. For example:

- Did improvements in student test scores result from more emphasis on the content to be tested?
- Did improved teacher engagement with students and the subject matter result from higher salaries, mentoring programs, or enhanced professional opportunities?
- Did increased parent and student engagement in schoolwork result from policy or from the increased visibility of education in general?

From one viewpoint, such analytic distinctions may not matter. As long as we see improvement, it may not be important whether the specific policies or the climate of attention to education they engendered deserve credit. However, such a conclusion provides little guidance about which policy mechanisms to employ in the future. And improvement on available measures may also result from less promising practices, like teaching to the test. Studies are needed to assess the relationship between reforms and educational improvement, but an atmosphere of rapid-fire policymaking inhibits reflection and puts a premium on new programs over experience-based revisions of older programs.

Recent legislative policymaking has been characterized by reliance on two primary instruments: mandates and incentives, to the exclusion of other possible approaches (McDonnell and Elmore 1987). Specifically, legislatures did little on the whole to build long-term capacity in districts and schools, through extensive staff development, for example (Little 1993). Most legislatures generated requirements, and sometimes they offered inducements (McDonnell 1987). Most of the mandates set requirements at minimum levels so that the districts at the bottom of the barrel would be brought up, but only to the middle of the barrel (Bardach and Kagan 1982). For example, high school graduation requirements set by state legislatures were exceeded by the majority of districts in most states before their enactment (Clune 1989, Firestone et al. 1989). Nor were the inducements generally designed to spur large-scale improvements in practice.

A skeptic would say that inducements or incentives were used most often not because legislators thought they were a better approach than mandates, but because funds were available only for activities in a subset of districts. Better to embark on an endeavor like supporting mentor teachers or dropout prevention with volunteers on a small scale than to mandate such programs statewide without funds to support it. Moreover, inducements often ended up with lots of strings, looking very much like mandates. For fiscally pressed districts that were searching for funds from any source, the decision to participate in an incentive program often did not appear much of a choice (McDonnell 1987).

Need for Innovative and Supportive Policies

Neither of the two major approaches, mandates or inducements, as they were used over the past two decades, appears sufficient for achieving educational excellence as we now understand it. We have learned that there are many excellent, ambitious approaches to teaching and learning being practiced in schools, including some in the most difficult learning environments. These experiments have flourished *despite*, not because of, state regulation and have occurred where people at the school site—teachers, administrators, and parents—felt free enough to design approaches that best met their needs (David 1989; Elmore 1988, 1990; Firestone and Bader 1992). It would appear that legislatures could best encourage, propagate, and sustain such activities through fiscal support and technical assistance—through building capacity in the system—rather than through regulation or incentives burdened by strings.

Mandating school-level improvement is inappropriate because the changes required cannot take place in the absence of local ownership, initiative, or capacity, regardless of how stringent the state is. Moreover, school-level solutions are likely to be very different from place to place, reflecting the needs of the local faculty, students, and parents. The increasingly popular saying, "You can't mandate excellence," captures this understanding of educational improvement, an understanding supported by numerous national commissions and task forces (Carnegie Forum on Education and the Economy 1986; Holmes Group Executive Board 1985; National Governors' Association, NGA, 1986).

Achieving excellence does not mean turning every educational decision over to schools. There continues to be an important state role—particularly in expressing a core body of content students need to know. As both national and state policymakers talk about educational goals, it is clear that those who carry a heavy financial burden for schooling should and will want to make sure that students are taught and learn the content necessary for work force and citizenship participation.

State policymakers, including legislatures, are likely to continue to express desired content through their assessment systems, curriculum guides, and development of model instructional materials. And this is not incompatible with school-level improvement. In fact, it can be argued that consensus at higher levels about core content and good ways of measuring achievement of that content can provide secure underpinnings for school experimentation in structure, governance, the organization of students into grades and groups, and pedagogy (Smith and O'Day 1991, Cohen and Spillane 1993).

Given the likely strong role of the state in expressing desires about educational content, mandates and inducements are apt to remain popular approaches. The criticisms cited here are not to say that there is no place for mandates and inducements, only that they are often insufficient and sometimes impeding as they are currently used. In addition to building local capacity, school improvement may require more sophisticated versions of the traditional approaches—mandates that lead practice rather than set minimums, for example. Challenging assessment systems that encourage problem solving, rather than mastery of basic skills, are mandates that might encourage improvement in local practice. Yet, such mandates might still leave school personnel free to design instructional delivery systems and explore pedagogical approaches that best support mastery of the content required by the assessments.

A critical review of legislative policymaking in education, then, finds that legislatures have acted courageously to address educational problems, but that their efforts fell short of the mark. What seems to be required is less volume and more coherence—more emphasis on clear, ambitious, state-level explication of what students should know and willingness to delegate to the schools many decisions about how students should be taught. School-based improvement requires state support through capacity-building efforts, such as sustained technical assistance and enhanced professional development. Whether legislatures can face up to these challenges depends on how they address a series of factors related to the politics of education and their own functioning.

Meeting the Challenges of the Next Century: Four Issues to Be Addressed

If legislatures are to turn to more coherent policy that promises true educational improvement, they will have to address four issues to improve their current functioning. First, they will have to take a longer time frame than the biennium, because school improvement is a long-term proposition that is not served by frequent shifts in direction. Second, they will have to exhibit more trust—particularly with regard to local school personnel—than they have previously exhibited. Third, they need to attend to the state's own capacity for education policymaking. Fourth, they may need to improve mechanisms for coordination among policymakers to encourage coherent policymaking, within education and among human services more generally.

Taking a Long-Term Perspective

If state policymakers are to encourage school improvement, they must understand the long-term nature of that endeavor. The policies they enact require time to exert their effects. First, the policies must be implemented by local districts and schools; and wise policymakers must recognize the busyness of American educators by providing realistic implementation schedules. As noted previously, local educators can be swamped by new policy initiatives that follow rapidly upon one another.

Translating a new state policy into practice is not a simple endeavor. It requires a review of local policy to determine the consistency of the new policy with current practice; changes in local policy if the new state initiative is inconsistent with current operations; and, typically, amplifications of local policy to accommodate the specifics of the state policy, even if the new policy is consonant with current district directions.

Putting a new policy into place often requires resource shifts, sometimes means changes in facility use, and very often means altered roles for local personnel who may require training or assistance. Moreover, the variation among districts in capacity and in willingness to respond to new state policy means that no new state policy will result in uniform effects on practice. Rather, there will be a range of results. Even if all districts move in good faith and with deliberate speed, some districts will take much longer than others to set policy into place—and some may not get there without intensive encouragement and assistance.

Anticipating the lag between policy and practice is only part of the problem. There is likely to be an even longer gap between changes in practice and results, particularly with respect to effects on student learning.

Many policies only indirectly exert an effect on student learning because they focus on conditions of schooling that are not tightly linked to student achievement. For example, changing school organization by encouraging school-site management and shared decision-making will not directly affect student achievement (Malen, Ogawa, and Kranz 1990; Wohlstetter 1993). Such changes may be worthwhile in themselves and may influence factors more closely linked to student achievement, such as teacher engagement, but the paths between such policy changes and improved learning are long and complicated.

Even when policies directly affect factors clearly linked to learning, such as the provision of specific subject matter deemed important, learning is a joint production between student and teacher and is a function of many factors other than required content. Certainly students are *more likely* to learn something they are taught, but whether they *will* learn it depends a great deal on how they are taught and the skills, predispositions, and enthusiasm they bring to the task. Some of these factors are beyond policy influence; others can be affected by policy, but not simply by the one policy that affects content.

Noting the influence of diverse factors on learning reinforces the imperative that policies to affect achievement need to be coherent. Because many factors that affect learning are beyond the direct influence of policy, policymakers need to build in a consistent direction. Frequent shifts in direction or failure to coordinate various curriculum policies or to coordinate those with teacher policies and governance policies do not serve that goal. Making coherent policy also requires a long-term perspective; it requires deliberate efforts to build on past policy where it is worthy, extensive review of the fit of any new policy with other state policies, and willingness to delay any one initiative until others that affect it can be modified if necessary.

Too often, the political will exists to support a change in one aspect of policy but not in others (Fuhrman 1993). A legislature may decide to tackle course requirements or to mandate that the state board of education determine core learner outcomes; it may not anticipate the need to also review teacher education for its consistency with the new learner outcomes, or it may decide that the moment is not opportune for movement on both student and teacher issues. However, when the time comes to revisit teacher education, the institutional memory to ensure coherence with the earlier student initiatives may be lacking. Or the political factors may have changed so that other directions take the fore.

For legislators to take the long-term perspective, they will need to display restraint and courage. They will have to educate the public to understand that legislative interest in education should not be measured by the volume or rapid production of policy. They will have to resist the political forces that suggest that action is better than inaction and that getting on the record is a more important goal than wise, deliberate policymaking. Clearly the need to stand for election every two years and demonstrate tangible evidence of attention to education policy makes it difficult for legislative education leaders to display the restraint suggested.

Some legislatures have created structures that assist them in maintaining the long-term perspective and weathering momentary political pressures. For example, South Carolina's legislature created a Business-Education subcommittee, a stable group of political, business, and education leaders that oversees the state's reform efforts. The subcommittee reviews progress toward policy goals, determines necessary adjustments or improvements, and keeps the momentum focused on educational improvement. The subcommittee also reports to the public on progress, demonstrating that improvement takes place incrementally over a period of time. Its very existence and its charge to monitor progress signals that legislative interest in education need not be gauged by new policymaking.

Trusting Others in the Educational Policy Community

Just as the politics of running for legislative office make it difficult to take a long-term perspective, the political climate also stands in the way of a second theme required for educational policymaking in the 1990s and beyond: trust. It may seem naive to argue for trust at a time when election campaigns are increasingly negative and when ethics scandals dominate the headlines. It may seem especially naive to argue for trust in the field of education policy. After all, legislative interest in education reform over the past ten years was spurred by widespread signs of failure of the education system, leading many legislators to the conclusion that local educators would not improve in the absence of stringent state standards and severe sanctions, such as state takeover of local districts.

Unfortunately, the absence of significant improvement over the past several years is more likely to be taken as a sign that local educators need still more controls, rather than as a sign that we have not yet found the formula for systemic improvement at either level.

In addition, the politics surrounding education at the state level are likely to be contentious, mitigating against trust. It has been many years since education groups presented a united front on anything but increased funding. Legislators are accustomed to differences among education associations and unions. They know, for example, that teachers support overall salary increases over merit-based pay schemes, and they know that local boards and superintendents may resist state-mandated salary increases on the grounds of local control or fiscal limitations. However, recently the political alignments may seem particularly confusing. Both the American Federation of Teachers and the National Education Association speak of radical reform, including significantly enhanced roles for teachers in determining policy at the school level. But state-level affiliates of the national organizations are slower to call for drastic change and wary that moves to school autonomy may imperil rights hard won at the district level (McDonnell and Pascal 1988). For example, school staff authority to hire and fire teachers and peer evaluation of teachers threaten carefully worked out procedures on supervision and evaluation.

Although some individual teachers and local associations may be amenable to changes toward local autonomy, other local associations may resist, forcing the state association to take a conservative stance. Similarly, local boards of education may support moves toward more school autonomy in principle; but board members may be confused about their own roles in a system marked by simultaneous increases in the roles of the state and of individual schools. Such layers of contradiction may result in mixed signals to legislators.

Legislatures face increasingly acrimonious electoral politics and confusing education politics. Certainly these factors are not conducive to displaying trust in the education system. Yet trust is precisely what is needed right now. We have learned that state standards are only a part of approach to educational improvement. Much of the solution requires actions that can only be achieved at the school level: developing school-specific goal consensus about instruction; changing the organization and structure of schools so they focus on teaching and learning; enhancing student and teacher engagement; and supporting all actions with appropriate governance and management structures. State policy can encourage these school-level changes, but primarily through approaches that build local capacity to make them rather than through approaches that require them.

Building local capacity means acting out of trust. In specific policy terms, it may mean additional aid to districts to use for teacher planning time or staff development without a great many strings that constrain the school's own initiative. It means permitting schools to generate many of their own goals and giving them time to reach them, as well as leeway to experiment and falter along the way. It means expressing trust in public statements and restraining from generating policies that may inhibit schools from finding their way toward the improvement process. It means avoiding standards and attendant regulations that treat all districts as if they were compliance-shirkers seeking to avoid or frustrate state policy objectives. It also means tolerance for variation among districts (Fuhrman and Elmore 1992).

Anticipating variation means providing some districts and schools considerable leeway in their conformation to the letter of state standards, as long as it is clear that they are progressing in ways that meet the spirit of state objectives. States are increasingly interested in granting waivers of regulation to encourage local innovation. For example, South Carolina and North Carolina give blanket waivers that provide considerable regulatory flexibility up front to participating schools. Blanket waivers may avoid some of the problems apparent in rule-by-rule waiver approaches that depend on local request. The rule-by-rule approaches do not engender a great deal of local interest, perhaps because schools are not yet envisioning doing things differently enough to find that state regulation impedes their efforts. Many schools have found that the intersection of many rules—or the mindset created by the intersection of rules—forms the barrier. Sometimes local overinterpretation of state regulation, rather than the regulation itself, impedes progress. Many local schools do not trust the state to forswear from ultimate insistence on compliance to the waived rules. Unfortunately, many state policymakers think that waivers should be available only to schools or districts that are already doing very well on available performance measures. Perceiving regulatory flexibility as a reward is not consonant with what we know about school improvement. School-level discretion is a likely precursor of school improvement, not a condition that appropriately comes after schools have already improved. The essence of trust may lie in letting schools that are not doing well find their own paths to improvement, without restrictive state regulation (Fuhrman 1989, Fuhrman and Elmore 1992).

Enhancing Capacity at the State Level

State policymakers cannot appropriately enhance local capacity without attending to the state's own capacity in education. Legislatures need to turn their attention to the state-level system for delivering education policy, an issue they have virtually neglected over all the years of active education policymaking.

State education departments have for some years been mistrusted by legislators (Rosenthal and Fuhrman 1981). State agencies are often seen as self-interested bureaucracies, composed primarily of people who have entered state government after failing at the local level. This distrust, as well as the fact that political benefit comes from placing scarce dollars in local schools rather than in state agencies, has led to a vicious cycle, in which state department jobs often carry lower salaries than local education positions and fail to attract highly qualified people. As noted previously, state agency resources have not kept pace with the challenges of implementing education reform. In fact, numerous agencies report actual cuts in positions over the past ten years, despite many added responsibilities (Fuhrman 1989, Massell and Fuhrman, in press).

Failure to enhance capacity at the state level has serious consequences for the implementation and effects of education policy. First, *technical assistance suffers*. State agencies are increasingly finding that they must target technical assistance to the neediest districts. This is a worthy and appropriate goal, but it means that states can not offer widespread assistance on new policy initiatives, such as new curricular frameworks, where even the most capable districts might benefit from help and substantive understanding of state intentions. Moreover, even the targeted assistance falls short. It is generally insufficient for the most troubled districts, and the squeeze on agency capacity means that agencies are having difficulty separating their compliance and assistance functions in such districts. For example, in states with academic bankruptcy programs, the people who are charged with assisting troubled districts to avoid takeover may well be the very same people who have consistently failed the district in monitoring visits over the years. These monitors are not likely to have developed a high degree of trust among educators.

Second, *development of curriculum and instruction suffers*. When staff resources are stretched, state agencies cannot pay much attention to coherence, to developing coordinated curriculum and staff development policies. Even more critically, most states lack the capacity for serious research and development in areas where technical advances are required (Kaagan 1988). We know, as a nation, that we must place priority on developing assessment mechanisms that go beyond basic skills and adequately tap the ability of students to understand the structure of a discipline, to solve problems, and to conceptualize. Such mechanisms would not only provide us with better, truer accountability for a high-quality education system, but would also encourage, rather than discourage as current standardized tests do, ambitious notions of teaching and learning. However, only a handful of states have seriously invested in the development of more sophisticated assessment.

Not much progress is apparent on other measures of educational well-being. No state has a fully developed system of indicators that relate educational inputs, processes, and outcomes (Kaagan and Coley 1989). Hence, we are hindered in our efforts to describe the educational system (e.g., to assess the quality of teachers), to measure progress toward policy objectives (e.g., to tell how much and what kind of math students are taking in response to graduation requirements) and to examine interrelationships between policy and outcomes (e.g., to tell if increased coursetaking is associated with student achievement).

Many states collect volumes of data, but many fail to integrate it in a meaningful way. For example, states may have data on graduates of teacher education programs and on teachers who are certified—but these data are not integrated in ways that permit examination of the steps between graduation and certification and comparison of teachers from out of state or from nontraditional routes. Few states extend their data collection to permit determination of the characteristics of certified teachers that then seek employment and the characteristics of those who are actually hired out of the pool seeking to teach.

Even less progress is being made on developing new types of data. Measures like the numbers of credits in a subject or even the course titles of classes students are taking tell little about the content and quality of that coursework. Developing measures of course quality, however, are expensive and technically difficult.

Though indicator research and development are sorely needed to create better measures of student outcomes and educational quality, even if we had much better and complete indicator sets, we would be unable to determine the effects of policy sufficiently to inform future policy. That purpose is best served by *policy research/evaluation*, a third function that suffers from inadequate state-level capacity. Indicator systems can raise questions about the relationship of policy to student achievement. For example, if a state had appropriate measures of the implementation of a new math curriculum, policymakers could track the relationship between implementation and student achievement. They could learn that students do better in math where the curriculum is implemented. However, without learning why it was implemented better in some places than others, the kind of barriers to implementation that exist, or how other state and local policies or school conditions support or hinder implementation, policymakers will not know how to encourage wider implementation. They will not learn whether the curriculum is most appropriately mandated, offered to districts voluntarily, or best supported by a certain kind of technical assistance or staff development. They will not learn from an indicator system alone how to best design policy to support learning. Those questions require in-depth studies in a well-constructed sample of schools and districts (Goertz et al. 1989); but few states have such analytic capacity available or are willing to purchase sufficient amounts of it.

Of course, states do conduct evaluations, and legislatures do perform oversight. However, evaluations are too often contracted to outfits like national accounting firms with little in-depth knowledge of the state's education system or the other policies that may interact with the one under study. And legislative oversight is typically a relatively low priority of legislatures, ranking well behind policymaking. Moreover, studies of how well programs or policies are working are just a part of the responsibilities of legislative audit-evaluation staff. These studies also focus to a large degree on agency management and structure; even studies termed *program evaluations* sometimes center as much on agency operations, such as reporting and information-management procedures, as on program effectiveness (Rosenthal 1981).

The lack of attention to assistance, development, and policy analysis may suggest that state agencies are appropriately focusing on a function increasingly central to state policymaker concerns: accountability. It is true that agencies are directing more efforts toward accountability—continuing to monitor for compliance, developing increasingly elaborate reports of performance measures for policymakers and the public, and implementing programs that attach rewards and sanctions to various levels of performance (OERI Study Group 1988, Fuhrman 1989). However, true accountability is illusive, without really good measures of performance, quality efforts to assist those who are not performing well, or analysis of how policy exerts its influence on performance.

In the absence of good measures, we do not really know if students are performing sufficiently well to meet the challenges of the future; in the absence of sufficient support or assistance, we may be holding low-capacity schools and districts unfairly accountable; in the absence of policy analysis, we do not know how much or little state policy is contributing to performance, and we cannot hold state policymakers accountable.

A final point related to capacity is that all the capacity the state needs to implement and understand education policy need not be housed in the state education agency. Legislators may prefer that some functions, such as evaluation, remain separate to ensure objectivity. Legislators may also determine that some functions, like assistance, may be conducted by a number of organizations. Among the institutions that can provide necessary state-level functions are regional service units, universities, and state policy research centers housed at universities or at nonprofit research firms. Approximately half the states now have university-based education policy research centers that conduct research on indicator development and study the implementation and effects of state policies. Some state legislatures may desire to enhance their own capacity for policy research by vesting broader responsibility in and shoring up the staff of oversight committees and agencies. Finally, states can share capacity by joining consortia to pool forces with other states. The New Standards Project, for instance, has eighteen state partners and seven local partners working together to develop alternative assessments and content standards.

Coordinating with Other Policymakers

Achieving coherent education policy has obvious implications for coordination among branches and levels of government. What is becoming increasingly apparent is that addressing education improvement also depends on progress in other areas of state policy and on coordinated approaches to problems (Kirst 1992). Legislators will need to work more closely with the executive branch, in particular. Legislative education leaders will need to work with their colleagues who specialize in other human service areas. Legislative leadership will need to assure that such coordination happens.

Legislative concern about its own prerogative may hinder attempts to coordinate policy with the executive branch. Legislators have correctly viewed themselves as trustees of state constitutional responsibility for education because statute defines the dimensions and the funding of the educational system. Certainly, as indicated previously, legislatures have exerted their prerogative through aggressive policymaking. However, the very visibility of education, given further momentum by unceasing legislative attention, means that other state-level policymakers also need to make their mark in this field. Governors, in particular, have felt this imperative. Both the school finance movement in the 1970s and the education reform movement of the 1980s were marked by the emergence of the education governor. Examples are plentiful: Askew of Florida, Milliken of Michigan, and Anderson of Minnesota in the 1970s; and Clinton of Arkansas, Kean of New Jersey, Riley of South Carolina, and Alexander of Tennessee in the 1980s. These governors have gained national prominence through attention to education.

Gubernatorial interest in developing education policy is driven by more than the prominence of education. The nature of the governor's office is changing in the direction of more policy development. As state government becomes increasingly complex and difficult to manage from the governor's office, governors are downplaying their role as managers. They find more incentives in "formulating policy, steering programs through the legislature, building popularity and support among the public, helping develop the state economy, and engaging in a host of entrepreneurial activities" (Rosenthal 1990, p. 170). Hence governors are likely to show their attention to education by proposing and popularizing more new initiatives.

Coherence in education policy requires that legislators and governors find ways to share credit for education policy, exhibit restraint even if it means looking less active by comparison to the other branch, and avoid policy bidding wars where each branch tries to outdo the other. But coordination with the governor is important for another reason, aside from achieving coherence within education: The governor's leadership is the key to more coherent policies across programs that affect children and youth. Increasingly, education improvement hinges on overcoming many of the societal problems that have invaded schools: the health and nutritional problems students bring to school; the environment of drugs and violence that surrounds schools, particularly in the inner cities; and poverty and family instability. All these societal problems create challenges for schools that cannot be handled by education policymakers alone. Educators, business leaders, and other reformers argue that coordination among the social services is essential, that health, social services, employment training, and education programs must work together to attend to children's needs (Committee for Economic Development 1987, Carnegie Council on Adolescent Development 1989).

A key barrier to achieving greater coordination among social service efforts is the functional division among state agencies. Gubernatorial establishment of interagency task forces or councils seems to be a first step toward integration. Coordination at the district and school level is a function of legislative leadership, as well as agency guidance and flexibility, however. Legislatures can provide incentives for joint service provision, authorize waivers of statutes that interfere, and attend to both state and local capacity and resources for designing integrated delivery systems.

Legislators may find that current committee structures impede policy development in the area of coordinated services. A first step would be a review of structure to determine if that is the case; a second step would be revisions of jurisdictions or the establishment of special committees to promote integration. Legislative leadership must take the initiative in such internal evaluation.

The considerable achievements that legislatures have made in the field of education should neither obscure the challenges that remain nor constrain creative thinking about the future. Improving education will require more coherent policymaking that accounts for appropriate delegations of authority among states, districts, and schools. Such delegations may differ from state to state; but all state policymakers need to find a balance between the state's constitutional responsibility and the school community's ability to shape programs responsive to local context and student needs.

Developing coherent policy and appropriate delegations of authority requires a long-term perspective toward improving education. This perspective includes trust in educators that supports efforts to build capacity at the school and district level; attention to the state's own capacity for technical assistance, development, research, and accountability; and coordination among state policymakers. Calls for coherent and restrained policymaking that acknowledges local variability are not new (Elmore 1979)—but the juxtaposition of persisting, serious educational problems and the recent explosion of state education policymaking lend new force to such a plea.

Endnote

[1]The one exception was on average writing proficiency scores for grade 8, which showed a statistically significant improvement between 1984 and 1990.

References

American Association of Colleges for Teacher Education. (1985). *Teacher Education Policy in the States: 50-State Survey of Legislative and Administrative Actions*. Washington, D.C.: Author.

Anderson, B., and C. Pipho. (1984). "State-Mandated Testing and the Fate of Local Control." *Phi Delta Kappan* 66: 208–212.

Bailey, S., R. Frost, P. Marsh, and R. Wood. (1962). *Schoolmen and Politics*. Syracuse, N.Y.: Syracuse University Press.

Bardach, E., and R. Kagan. (1982). *Going by the Book: The Problem of Regulatory Unreasonableness*. Philadelphia: Temple University Press.

Brown, P.R., and R.F. Elmore. (1982). "Analyzing the Impact of School Finance Reform." In *The Changing Politics of School Finance* (pp. 107–138), edited by N.H. Cambron-McCabe and A. Odden. Cambridge, Mass.: Ballinger.

Carnegie Council on Adolescent Development. (1989). *Turning Points: Preparing American Youth for the 21st Century*. New York: Carnegie Corporation.

Carnegie Forum on Education and the Economy. (1986). *A Nation Prepared: Teachers for the 21st Century*. N.Y.: Author.

Clune, W.H., with P. White and J. Patterson. (1989). *The Implementation and Effects of High School Graduation Requirements: First Steps Toward Curricular Reform*. New Brunswick, N.J.: Rutgers University, Center for Policy Research in Education.

Cohen, D.K., and J.P. Spillane. (1993). "Policy and Practice: The Relations Between Governance and Instruction." In *Designing Coherent Education Policy: Improving the System* (pp. 35–95), edited by S.H. Fuhrman. San Francisco: Jossey-Bass.

Committee for Economic Development, Research and Policy Committee. (1987). *Children in Need: Investment Strategies for the Educationally Disadvantaged*. New York: Author.

Cuban, L. (1984). "School Reform by Remote Control: SB813 in California." *Phi Delta Kappan* 66: 213–215.

Darling-Hammond, L. (1990). "Instructional Policy into Practice: The Power of the Bottom Over the Top." *Educational Evaluation and Policy Analysis* 12, 3: 339–348.

Darling-Hammond, L., and B. Berry. (1988). *The Evolution of Teacher Policy.* (Prepared for the Center for Policy Research in Education.) Santa Monica, Calif.: RAND Corporation.

David, J.L. (1989). *Restructuring in Progress: Lessons from Pioneering Districts.* Washington, D.C.: National Governors' Association.

Elley, W.B. (July 1992). *How in the World Do Students Read?* N.Y.: International Association for the Evaluation of Educational Achievement.

Elmore, R.F. (1979). *Complexity and Control: What Legislators and Administrators Can Do About Implementation.* Public Policy Paper No. 11. Seattle: University of Washington, Institute of Governmental Research.

Elmore, R.F. (1988). *Early Experience in Restructuring Schools: Voices from the Field.* Washington, D.C.: National Governors' Association.

Elmore, R.F. (1990). *Working Models of Choice in Public Education.* New Brunswick, N.J.: Rutgers University, Center for Policy Research in Education.

Elmore, R.F., and M.W. McLaughlin. (1988). *Steady Work: Policy, Practice and the Reform of American Education* (R-3574-NIE/RC). Santa Monica, Calif.: RAND Corporation.

Firestone, W., and B. Bader. (1992). *Redesigning Teaching: Bureaucracy and Professionalism.* Albany: SUNY Press.

Firestone, W.A., S.H. Fuhrman, and M.W. Kirst. (1989). *The Progress of Reform: An Appraisal of State Education Initiatives.* New Brunswick, N.J.: Rutgers University, Center for Policy Research in Education.

Firestone, W.A., S. Rosenblum, B.D. Bader, and D. Massell. (1991). *Education Reform from 1983 to 1990: State Action and District Response.* New Brunswick, N.J.: Consortium for Policy Research in Education.

Fuhrman, S.H. (1982). "State-Level Politics and School Financing." In *The Changing Politics of School Finance* (pp. 53–70), edited by N.H. Cambron-McCabe and A. Odden. Cambridge, Mass.: Ballinger.

Fuhrman, S.H., ed. (1993). "The Politics of Coherence." *Designing Coherent Policy: Improving the System* (pp. 1–34). San Francisco: Jossey-Bass.

Fuhrman, S.H., H.W. Clune, and R.F. Elmore. (1988). "Research on Education Reform: Lessons on the Implementation of Policy." *Teachers College Record* 90, 2: 237–58.

Fuhrman, S.H., and R.F. Elmore. (1992). *Takeover and Deregulation: Working Models of New State and Local Regulatory Relationships.* New Brunswick, N.J.: Consortium for Policy Research in Education.

Fuhrman, S.H., and R.F. Elmore. (1990). "Understanding Local Control." *Educational Evaluation and Policy Analysis* 12, 1: In Press.

Fuhrman, S.H., with P. Fry. (1989). *Diversity Amidst Standardization: State Differential Treatment of Districts.* New Brunswick, N.J.: Rutgers University, Center for Policy Research in Education.

Goertz, M.E., B.F. King, R.J. Coley, G.Z. Wilder, S.S. Kaagan, and G. Sykes. (1989). "Missouri Education Indicators Development Project Final Report." Unpublished manuscript, Center for Policy Research in Education, Rutgers University, New Brunswick, N.J., and Educational Testing Service, Princeton, N.J.

Hanson, T.L. (1989). *Curricular Change in Dade County 1982–83 to 1986–87: A Replication of the PACE Study.* New Brunswick, N.J.: Rutgers University, Center for Policy Research in Education.

Holmes Group Executive Board. (1985). *Tomorrow's Teachers: A Report of the Holmes Group.* East Lansing, Mich.: Author.

Kaagan, S.S. (1988). "State Education Agencies: Above or Beneath the Waves of Reform." Unpublished manuscript, Center for Policy Research in Education, Rutgers University, New Brunswick, N.J.

Kaagan, S.S., and R.J. Coley. (1989). *State Education Indicators: Measured Strides, Missing Steps.* (Co-sponsored by the Center for Policy Research in Education.) Princeton, N.J.: Educational Testing Service.

Killian, M.G. (1984). "Local Control—The Vanishing Myth in Texas." *Phi Delta Kappan* 66: 192–195.

Kirst, M.W. (1992). *Financing School-Linked Services. USC Center for Education Finance (CREF) Policy Brief.* Los Angeles, Calif.: University of Southern California.

Kirst, M.W. (1993). "Strengths and Weaknesses of American Education." *Phi Delta Kappan* 74: 613–618.

Koretz, D. (1988). "Arriving in Lake Woebegone: Are Standardized Tests Exaggerating Achievement and Distorting Instruction?" *American Educator* 12, 2: 8–15.

Little, J.W. (1993). "Teachers' Professional Development in a Climate of Educational Reform." *Educational Evaluation and Policy Analysis*, forthcoming.

Madaus, G. (1991). "The Effects of Important Tests on Students." *Phi Delta Kappan* 73, 3: 226–231.

Malen, B., R. Ogawa, and J. Kranz. (1990). "What Do We Know About School-Based Management: A Case Study of the Literature," In *Choice and Control in American Education, Volume 2* (pp. 289–342), edited by W.H. Clune and J.F. Witte. Philadelphia: Falmer Press.

Massell, D., and S.H. Fuhrman. (in press). *Ten Years of State Education Reform: Update with Four Case Studies.* New Brunswick, N.J.: Consortium for Policy Research in Education.

Mayhew, D. (1974). *The Electoral Connection.* New Haven, Conn.: Yale University Press.

McDonnell, L.M. (March 1987). "The Instruments of State Education Reform." Paper presented at the Western Political Science Association annual meeting, Anaheim, Calif.

McDonnell, L.M., and R.F. Elmore. (1987). *Alternative Policy Instruments.* (Prepared for the Center for Policy Research in Education). Santa Monica, Calif.: RAND Corporation.

McDonnell, L.M., and S.H. Fuhrman. (1985). "The Political Context of Reform." In *The Fiscal, Legal and Political Aspects of State Reform of Elementary and Secondary Education* (pp. 43–46), edited by V.D. Mueller and M.P. McKeown. Cambridge, Mass.: Ballinger.

McDonnell, L.M., and A. Pascal. (1988). *Teacher Unions and Educational Reform.* (Prepared for the Center for Policy Research in Education.) Santa Monica, Calif.: RAND Corporation.

McLaughlin, M.W. (1987). "Lessons from Past Implementation Research." *Educational Evaluation and Policy Analysis* 9, 2: 171–178.

National Center for Education Statistics. (1992). *The Condition of Education.* Washington, D.C.: U.S. Government Printing Office.

National Commission on Excellence in Education. (1983). *A Nation at Risk: The Imperative for Educational Reform.* Washington, D.C.: U.S. Government Printing Office.

National Conference of State Legislatures. (1990). *State Issues 1990: A Survey of Priority Issues for State Legislatures.* Denver, Colo.: Author.

National Educational Goals Panel. (1992). *Building a Nation of Learners.* Washington, D.C.: U.S. Government Printing Office.

National Governors' Association. (1986). *Time for Results: The Governors' 1991 Report on Education.* Washington, D.C.: Author.

OERI Study Group on State Accountability. (1988). *Creating Responsible and Responsive Accountability Systems.* Washington, D.C.: Office of Educational Research and Information, U.S. Department of Education.

Organisation for Economic Cooperation and Development. (1992). *Education at a Glance.* Paris: Author.

Patterson, J. (1991). "Graduation vs. Education: Reform Effect for Youth at Risk." In *The Politics of Curriculum and Testing* (pp. 81–101), edited by S. Fuhrman and B. Malen. Philadelphia: Falmer Press.

Richards, C.E., and M.J. Shujaa. (1988). "The State Education Accountability Movement: Impact on the Schools?" Unpublished manuscript prepared for the U.S. Department of Education OERI Study Group on State Accountability, Washington, D.C.

Rosenthal, A. (1981). *Legislative Life*. New York: Harper and Row.

Shepard, L. (1991). "Will National Tests Improve Student Learning?" *Phi Delta Kappan* 73, 3: 232–238.

Rosenthal, A. (1990). *Governors and Legislatures: Contending Powers*. Washington, D.C.: Congressional Quarterly Press.

Rosenthal, A., and S. Fuhrman. (1981). *Legislative Education Leadership in the States*. Washington, D.C.: Institute for Educational Leadership.

Smith, M., and J. O'Day. (1991). "Systemic School Reform." In *The Politics of Curriculum and Testing* (pp. 233–267), edited by S. Fuhrman and B. Malen. Philadelphia: Falmer Press.

U.S. General Accounting Office. (1993). *Systemwide Education Reform*. Washington, D.C.: U.S. Government Printing Office.

Williams, P.A. (1989). "School Level Response to At-Risk Students." Unpublished manuscript, Center for Policy Research in Education, Rutgers University, New Brunswick, N.J.

Winslow, H.R., and S.M. Peterson. (1982). "State Initiatives for Special Needs Students." In *New Dimensions of the Federal-State Partnership in Education* (pp. 46–62), edited by J.D. Sherman, M.A. Kutner, and K.J. Small. Washington, D.C.: Institute for Educational Leadership.

Wohlstetter, P. (1993). *School-Based Management: Strategies for Success*. New Brunswick, N.J.: CPRE Finance Brief.

4

Governors and Education Policy in the 1990s

Susan H. Fuhrman and Richard F. Elmore

Today, governors act as leaders in educational policymaking. Historically, however, they have not always taken that role. Despite the states' formal responsibility for education, governors have shown only modest interest and little sustained influence over educational policy. What explains their growing assertiveness in this arena? What role might they play over the longer term?

In this chapter, we first describe the emergence of governors as educational policy leaders in the 1970s and their broadening influence in the 1980s and '90s. We then explore four factors that affect governors' influence on educational policy. One factor is a constraint on their influence—the traditional institutional limits on governors' direct control of education. Balanced against this constraint are two factors drawing governors into greater involvement in educational policymaking—the increasing volume and political salience of policy-making activity that surrounds education and the increasing presence of governors as a collective, organized national force in shaping the education reform agenda. The final factor affecting governors' influence is more uncertain. It is the present fragmentation and incoherence of state-level education policy. In some respects, this factor may be seen as a threat to gubernatorial influence, or a threat to state influence in educational policy as a whole. We argue, however, that the fragmentation and incoherence of state educational policy offers governors an opportunity to assert a kind of policy leadership that is well suited to their institutional and political position.

Authors' Note: This chapter draws on research conducted by the Consortium for Policy Research in Education (CPRE)—a consortium of Rutgers University, the University of Southern California, Harvard University, Michigan State University, Stanford University, and the University of Wisconsin-Madison—funded by the Office of Educational Research and Improvement (OERI), U.S. Department of Education. The opinions expressed are those of the authors and are not necessarily shared by OERI, CPRE, or its institutional partners.

The Emergence of Governors as Education Leaders

Governors did not begin to play a visible, leading role in educational policy until the 1970s. In that decade, many governors became leaders in school finance reform—

- Creating study commissions to assess funding equity and recommend solutions;
- Crafting proposals to respond to real or anticipated court orders to reform unconstitutionally inequitable systems; and
- Most courageously, proposing tax increases or new revenue sources to fund a higher state share of educational spending (Fuhrman 1979).

Governors Anderson of Minnesota, Askew of Florida, and Milliken of Michigan, among others, made school finance reform a major state political issue. Several factors contributed to gubernatorial interest in the issue. First, because education consumed the major portion of state budgets, state leaders had to pay attention to major shifts in education spending. Second, the prominence of school finance reform coincided with significant improvements in the capacity of state governments for policy leadership. Finally, strengthened through constitutional reforms in the 1960s—longer gubernatorial terms and enhanced veto power—governors' offices, like legislatures, became modern and professional (Sabato 1983). By one estimate, governors' office staff almost tripled on average between 1956 and 1976 (Beyle 1989).

In the 1980s, a major educational reform movement swept through the states. Governors' roles in educational policymaking expanded as well. The states saw a high volume of statutory and regulatory changes and a further increase in their share of education spending. By mid-decade, virtually every state had enacted versions of several popular reform approaches—increased high school graduation requirements, more student testing, and changes in teacher certification and compensation (Firestone, Fuhrman, and Kirst 1989). By the decade's end, states were still initiating new educational reform policies, embarking on revisions in accountability systems, new ways of assessing student performance, and efforts to encourage school-based innovation (OERI 1988; Fuhrman 1989; David, Cohen, Honetschlager, and Traiman 1990; Kirst 1990).

In the 1980s, gubernatorial leadership took several forms. Some governors, like Riley of South Carolina, Harris of Georgia, Graham of Florida, and Alexander of Tennessee established commissions or blue-ribbon committees to recommend comprehensive reform approaches, placed the full prestige of their office behind the packages, and took the lead in generating public and legislative support. Georgia's Harris took pride in the fact that there were no amendments to his initial proposal and that it was passed unanimously by the legislature. Others, like Florida's Graham, skillfully merged their own programs with recommendations from the legislature. Still other governors, like Kean of New Jersey and Clinton of Arkansas, made education a consistent focus throughout their multiple terms, relying on successive reform bills.

Whatever approach governors took, their influence was apparent. Several major reform initiatives became known throughout the nation by the name of the governor who initially sponsored them. Hence, "Alexander's Career Ladder Program," a merit pay plan for teachers; "Kean's Alternate Route," a certification program for prospective teachers without a teacher education background; and Booth Gardner's "Schools for the Twenty-First Century Program" in Washington, a grant program for school restructuring, have all emerged as major reform initiatives.

In the early 1990s, governors began to broaden their interests beyond education to the relationship between education and other social services. For example, Governor Wilson in California created a cabinet position for education and children's issues; Governor Chiles of Florida continued the work he had done in the U.S. Senate in the areas of infant mortality and the coordination of health and human services; and Governor Miller of Georgia launched a pilot program called "Family Connection" to link education and human service agencies to provide comprehensive medical screening and follow-up services. Chiles, Miller, and others, like Florio of New Jersey, have also actively protected education from budget cuts during the recent recession (Massell and Fuhrman in press).

The interest of the governors in education in the 1980s and 1990s is not simply a natural extension of their leadership in the field in the 1970s, although it can be argued that the enlarged state role in school finance made an expanded concern with the substance of education, with what state dollars were buying, inevitable (Fuhrman 1987). The governors' concern also reflects the perception of a national crisis in education. The early 1980s saw some stemming of a national decline in test scores and other aspects of performance that had occurred in the 1970s, but the publication of *A Nation at Risk* (National Commission on Excellence in Education 1983) spurred widespread belief in the need for dramatic improvement measures. As business elites and the public placed a priority on improving education, governors who did *not* become active education leaders incurred significant political risk (McDonnell and Fuhrman 1985).

Business interest was particularly persuasive. Business leaders drew explicit links between education and the quality of the work force; clearly, no state could compete unless it improved its education system. The link between education and economic development grew stronger as the decade progressed. Not only were states attending to their relative rankings on educational measures, but state leaders and those who influence them became increasingly concerned about how the nation's performance as a whole spoke to our competitiveness in a global economy.[1] As a result, the decade ended with the governors taking the lead, along with the president, in establishing national expectations for educational improvement, expectations that could only be met if each state continued reform efforts.

In the 1980s, then, governors maneuvered themselves, or were pushed, into a more prominent role in educational policy. Also during this period, the federal government withdrew its leadership in educational policymaking (Clark and Astuto 1990, Elmore and Fuhrman 1990). And between 1983 and 1989, most states had available resources generated by strong state economies to devote to education.

In their new roles, governors have typically relied more on policy leadership rather than on their managerial influence. In the parlance of research on executive leadership, governors' interest in education is expressed through their "political" and "legislative" roles rather than their "managerial" role (Beyle and Muchmore 1983), through their role as "chief legislator" rather than their role as "manager" (Rosenthal 1990). For a governor to be "active" in education has meant focusing on new policy initiatives rather than managing existing policy—in part because education is, like any other state policy area, too complex and sprawling for governors to actually manage directly (Rosenthal 1990, p. 170) and, in part, because education is, unlike other state policy areas, formally insulated from the governor's direct control.

Further analyses of gubernatorial strategies would be valuable. For example, how and why do education governors draw on their various policy leadership strengths, like their professional reputations and public prestige, to borrow Neustadt's (1960) terms for presidential advantages? And we would benefit from comparative studies of state-level factors that affect the tools of gubernatorial leadership. However, our purpose here is to understand the context that affects gubernatorial leadership *across* the states, to examine the limits and opportunities that present themselves to governors, and the implications for educational policy.

We turn first to limitations on the exercise of gubernatorial leadership, beginning with the formal barriers to gubernatorial control over education.

Formal Constraints on the Governors' Role in Education

Despite the strong pressures promoting gubernatorial interest in education over the past twenty years, governors' willingness to invest significant political capital in educational improvement is remarkable. In the past, the relatively weak formal controls governors can exert over education have reduced their attention to the field. Still today, we find the same barriers that have historically restricted governors' role in education.

A major barrier to gubernatorial leadership in education is its fragmented structure at the state level. Late 19th century and early 20th century reformers argued that, with the minds of children at stake, the corrupting influences of partisan politics had to be kept at bay. Educators of the "administrative progressive" stripe supported establishing separate policy and administrative structures—elected, often nonpartisan, chief state school officers and state boards of education, for example—that they hoped would reinforce professional influence (see, e.g., Tyack and Hansot 1982). Those structures, established over a century ago in many states, still exist.

Governors and legislatures can, and do, ignore those structures in making educational policy. For example, they produce statutes that direct boards and agencies to implement specific policy decisions of their own making. But the boards and chiefs serve as a separate policy voice in education, not just as implementors that political leaders must rely on, as they must with any state agency. They must be accounted for—persuaded to join the administration's team or publicly debated if they cannot be so persuaded—especially where they have mobilized their own constituencies. Elected chiefs are most likely to have built a following of their own that strengthens their hand with governors, but even appointed chiefs must typically mobilize constituencies to demonstrate their attractiveness as appointees. And just as all agencies develop ties with their constituency groups, chiefs and boards are often in a better position than the governor to marshall the political support of educational interest groups that typically have large memberships—there are more teachers than doctors or dentists—and are frequently among the most powerful lobbies at the state level. The expectation among constituencies that state boards of education and chief state school officers will exert policy leadership remains strong, even in the face of the growing body of gubernatorial and legislatively initiated policy over the past twenty years. In fact, much discussion of the relationship of the education reform movement to education governance cast the increasing role of general government in terms of a "preemption" of the role of boards and chiefs.

In most states, strong traditions of local control over education have also limited governors' influence over educational policy. Historically, states have delegated the provision, as well as much of the financing and policy control, of education to local school districts, which themselves are separate in structure from municipalities. For governors to exert policy leadership, they must assert an increasing state role in education, not just an increasing role for the top state official. Governors have not been shy in that regard, but their new leadership posture runs counter to two strong traditions: both insulation of state-level policy from political influence and insulation of local governance from state direction. Local school officials are likely to resist governors' initiatives for two reasons, as well: They see their own autonomy threatened by state direction; and they have closer ties to and more sympathetic masters in state boards, chiefs, and agencies (the latter are generally primarily staffed by former local school personnel) than in governors and legislatures.

Another barrier to gubernatorial control is the system of financing education itself. In the aggregate, half of the spending for education comes from the states, and that average percentage is a recent high. As recently as 1979, states contributed an average of about 45 percent of total school spending (NCES 1989, p. 98). These averages conceal a lot of variation. Half the states contributed significantly less than 50 percent of school revenues in 1988–89 (NEA 1989); local revenues and federal dollars made up the balance. Therefore, any control the governor can exert through the state budget affects only a portion of education spending. And so, the larger the share of spending absorbed by the state, the more the state budget will be a useful educational policy tool for the governor.

However, as state shares have been increasing, so too has earmarking of specific revenue sources for education. In at least nine states, lottery receipts support education (ACIR 1989); in at least fourteen states, certain income or sales tax revenue is so earmarked. In several states, a host of other revenues—severance, insurance, and sin-tax receipts—are also earmarked for K–12 schools (Fabricius and Sneel 1990).

California embarked on a new approach to earmarking five years ago. In 1988, voters approved a constitutional amendment, Proposition 98, mandating that a minimum percentage of the state's budget be spent for schools.

In keeping with the local-control tradition, most state money is distributed as general aid, with few restrictions about how local districts may apply the receipts. In fact, depending on the specifics of the finance formula, districts are often free to use state money for tax relief, reducing their own share of education spending accordingly. Governors and legislatures have initiated numerous mandates influencing local activities that significantly affect local expenditure decisions, but it remains true that budgetary control in and of itself only indirectly influences local practice. An enduring challenge concerns the design of school finance systems that promote good practice; we have yet to figure out how to use formula aid to create incentives for needed policy directions.

One Voice Among the Many, and Increasing Complexity

The educational governance system, fragmented by design, is even more fragmented in practice. Governors seeking to exert educational leadership quickly find that they are only one voice among many seeking to influence what occurs in schools. The entrance of a powerful actor like the governor does not still the other voices; educational governance is not a zero-sum game. Furthermore, the "busyness" of educational policy can tip over into acrimony. And finally, educational improvement is a complex undertaking; policy, no matter who makes it, plays only a partial role. These factors can serve as incentives for governors to exert leadership through dramatic new policy initiatives that distinguish their voice from the rest and offer the allure of cutting through the complexity to achieve striking results.

Separate structures and multiple levels of governance are designed to insulate professionals who work with children from direct political interference and to be responsive to the needs of their communities. The central idea behind these constraints was to limit policy interference by limiting the scope and authority of the actors, by creating an elaborate system of checks and balances within and across levels of government. But each structure and actor with a purchase on educational policymaking exercises that purchase. And as the arena becomes more crowded, each actor feels the need to contribute distinctly, perhaps even dramatically, with policies that are highly visible and stand out from the field. The more actors, the more policy. The more policy, the more contradictions, missed signals, and confusion. There is an ever busier policy landscape (Cohen 1982, Fuhrman and Elmore 1990). Each policy promulgated by each separate structure can lead to a separate program at the local level, with attendant local bureaucracies, fiscal accounting mechanisms, and school staffs.

For example, teachers wanting to coordinate services for children with special needs, integrate subject matters, or design programs that cross grade levels are often stymied by the regulatory or procedural complications. Gubernatorial leadership has the potential of rationalizing this mess, but so far it has mainly just added another prominent actor, with a distinct set of policies, to the mix. Governors get active, and so do legislatures. But boards, chiefs, and agencies remain active, and so do local school districts. Activity breeds more activity, but not necessarily more concerted activity.

The crowded field of educational policy means that there is a great deal of turf to protect. Turf battles can quickly become rancorous; and, unfortunately, educational policy has become much more acrimonious as the stakes have escalated. In 1979, at the close of ten years of intense activity around school finance, legislative education committee chairs reported that infighting between and among interest groups and educators at the state and local levels made it difficult to recruit new legislators to their committees (Rosenthal and Fuhrman 1981). Over the more recent period of state education reform, issues such as differentiated pay for teachers, accountability reporting of school test scores, testing of teachers, and certification of teachers who have not participated in traditional teacher education programs have proved extremely divisive in some states. Such issues represent radical departures from past practice, threatening traditions, such as local control, or the province of established interests, such as teacher education institutions.

A final influence on gubernatorial policy leadership concerns the very nature of education as an endeavor. As important as education is, politicians who want to see short-term results in student learning do not find the field immediately attractive. Policy only indirectly affects student learning for three major reasons.

First, any given policy is but one influence on practice. New policies are surrounded by existing and other new state and local policies and join a host of administrative arrangements, traditions, and practitioner inclinations in shaping what occurs in the classroom (Cohen 1982, 1990; Cohen and Spillane 1993; Cuban 1984; Elmore and McLaughlin 1988). With more actors interested in educational policy and more resulting policy volume, the chances that policies coordinate and integrate diminish. During the educational reform of the 1980s, state policymakers made policies that directly contradicted one another—for example, simultaneously raising standards for entry into teaching and creating loopholes to ensure a sufficient supply of teachers (Darling-Hammond and Berry 1988). In addition, the policymakers failed to attend to potential links between policy areas that might contribute to a more coherent approach to educational policy. For example, although some states reformed the curriculums for elementary and secondary students, they did little to coordinate those changes with the content of teacher education (Smith and O'Day 1988, 1991).

Second, various implementation issues influence how policy links to practice—the type of policy instrument used, state and local capacity, and educators' orientations (Berman and McLaughlin 1975, 1978; Elmore 1978; Bardach 1980; Fullan 1982; Hargrove 1983; Pressman and Wildavsky 1984; McDonnell and Elmore 1987; Elmore 1987). As a result, the effects of policy vary greatly, from district to district, from school to school, and from classroom to classroom.

Finally, many factors besides school practice influence student learning—family background and student activities outside of school (Coleman et al. 1966; Jencks et al. 1972; Keith, Reimers, Fehrmann, Pottebaum, and Aubey 1986; Milne, Myers, Rosenthal, and Ginsburg 1986).

The best policy—one negotiated across the complex set of interests and actors, designed with the incentives of implementors in mind, and with widespread support and adequate funding—cannot, alone, produce increased student achievement. As we stated previously, education can be a low-payoff endeavor for policymakers who want fast improvement. Policymakers cope, of course. They identify and look for intermediate measures of success. They keep chipping away at problems with multiple policies. Those most attuned to the realities of the classroom realize that their job is not just to increase learning but to influence the conditions of teaching and learning through a supportive policy environment.

If we move away from the proposition that the job of policy is to improve learning and toward the proposition that the job of policy is to improve the conditions affecting learning, then the attractiveness of single, dramatic policy initiatives diminishes greatly. Governors can contribute more by overseeing consistent policy development that supports good practice than by initiating new policies designed to distinguish their voice from the field. In this light, the tools that governors possess seem much stronger.

In striving for educational policy leadership, governors have a strong and relatively new set of allies, their forty-nine compatriots. In the next section, we turn to the third factor shaping the context of gubernatorial education policymaking in the 1990s, the emergence of collective leadership by the nation's governors.

The Nation's Governors and Education

Over the past decade, governors have collectively endorsed the importance of educational reform. The National Governors' Association (NGA) made education a top priority in the 1980s.[2]

NGA took a major role in educational reform. First, NGA was influential in shaping the substance of the state reforms of the past decade. Second, NGA's role in educational reform during the 1980s reflected changes in its stance toward state policy and in its operations. Third, NGA's larger leadership role marked a shift in how governors think about educational leadership. This shift may have implications for other state policies, as well.

NGA's 1986 report, *A Time for Results: The Governors' 1991 Report on Education*, marked a turning point in educational reform. It called on NGA members to move away from the current policy preoccupation with increasing standards for students and teachers toward a "second wave of reform in American public education," one focused less on regulation and more on school-based change. As NGA Chairman Alexander wrote in his summary of the report:

> First, the Governors want to help establish clear goals and better report cards, ways to measure what students know and can do. Then, we're ready to give up a lot of state regulatory control—even to fight for changes in the law to make that happen—*if* schools and districts will be accountable for results (NGA 1986, p. 4).

The call for a "second wave" of reform had powerful results. According to subsequent NGA follow-ups, at least twenty-five states supported (with funding or technical assistance) efforts for schools to redesign or restructure the organization and delivery of instruction; twenty-one states planned to offer waivers of regulations; and nine states instituted severe sanctions for troubled districts (NGA 1989). At least eleven states offer, or plan to offer, monetary incentives for school improvement (Richards and Shujaa 1990).

NGA was certainly not the sole source of these ideas. Two other major reports issued in 1986 contained similar language about school change and shifts in state policy to support restructuring (Carnegie Forum 1986, Holmes Group 1986). All three reports drew on business analogies about unit discretion and administrative simplicity, reflecting the heightened interest of business leaders in education. However, the NGA report gave particular impetus and political legitimacy to those new reform ideas.

First, the NGA effort involved all the nation's governors for the first time; each governor served on one of the six task forces responsible for the report. Second, *Time for Results* found a way to urge a new wave of reform without denigrating the standards and regulation that had characterized reform to date. It provided language and a set of ideas about building on what had already been accomplished and moving beyond standards without making it seem as if embracing the new agenda meant scrapping the old. That was important for reform governors who had invested considerable energy and reform capital in the old agenda. Third, NGA followed up on the report with competitive grants to states to undertake parts of the new agenda and with annual status reports that indicated how states were making progress on various elements of the new ideas. Because NGA took on the education issue in *Time for Results*, ideas that were already circulating through other influential forums became the property and responsibility of the governors.

In 1989 and 1990, NGA joined President Bush in calling for, establishing, and promoting a set of national education goals. The idea had antecedents in NGA publications that called for state goals, following up on the *Time for Results* emphasis on educational outcomes. If outcomes were to form the basis of accountability systems, then leaders needed to determine which outcomes were desirable. The discussion around goal setting laid the groundwork for national goals, making them an appropriate topic for President Bush's Education Summit of 1989.

NGA's leadership was critical in several respects. The goals shifted the nation's attention to high performance in key subject areas and to challenging concepts of content in those areas. They created expectations that the federal government will assume more leadership and responsibility, particularly in the area of school readiness. They also fixed collective and individual responsibility on top political leadership for educational improvement.

NGA's leadership in education marks a change in the organization's stance that we can trace to the convergence of several forces. First appearing as "The Governors' Conference" in 1966, the organization focused primarily on lobbying the federal government on behalf of the states. During the 1970s, it began to focus more on improving governors' performance within their states through workshops and publications on the process of governing (Beyle 1989). Throughout the late 1970s, several governors began pressing the association to broaden its activities even further to provide substantive assistance on state government issues. According to Joan Wills, former director of NGA's Center for Policy Research:

> Governors' offices were bigger and tougher and the governors were increasingly disenchanted with Washington being the source of policy solutions. They were expecting the NGA to provide more substance in support of state-based initiatives. Each year in the early 1980s saw more pressure for

the association to focus on state government issues (Interview with J. Wills, September 27, 1990).

Internally, the NGA research staff had been pushing for more support and for equal footing with the federal relations staff. They received support when a new executive director, Ray Scheppach, was hired with the same agenda. Finally, when Lamar Alexander became NGA chair in 1985, he chose for the first time to have a substantive chair's agenda that involved every governor. This effort, which led to the formation of task forces and the *Time for Results* report, set a precedent for subsequent chairs to select a state-based policy issue for the focus of their leadership year.

To some extent, it was coincidental to NGA's emergence into state policy leadership that education happened to be the first focus chosen. However, Alexander's choice of education was a popular one that capitalized on the governors' emerging roles within their own states, and the perception of the urgency surrounding educational reform made education a good starting point for a new NGA role. Furthermore, education was a subject that was particularly amenable to promoting a several-year focus for the association. Chairs that followed Alexander picked themes like economic development and federalism that were closely tied to education and gave added impetus to a continued emphasis on the field. The educational initiatives of the initial NGA report and subsequent follow-ups set the stage for long-term efforts that would persist beyond the initiating chair's term. NGA will most certainly continue to study and recommend education policy approaches for state issues and will keep attention focused on states' progress in these areas.

NGA leadership in education may have a lasting influence on how state policy innovation occurs. Traditionally, we have seen the diffusion of policy innovation among the states as a function of emulation and competition within regional groupings and, for a small group of highly visible innovators, competition with regional leaders from across the country. Professional associations of state officials have eased the spread of ideas. Those associations provide forums for exchanging information, assist job seekers in moving from state to state, and help build consensus around desirable policy options (Walker 1971). NGA's entry into state issues provides a consensus-building mechanism for the highest state policymakers—state officials, as well as national political figures. NGA's positions carry high visibility; they draw authority not only from their own validity but from the political power they represent. NGA can take ideas in good currency among policy specialists and professionals and grant them widespread political legitimacy.

In the future, governors may increasingly turn to NGA for a stamp of approval for policy innovation; the association's role may replace or eclipse traditional patterns of state-to-state emulation. If that happens, we may see more innovation at the state level than ever before because an association can promote ideas not yet in place in any state. Further, the association may become a new structure for policy entrepreneurship among the governors. Through NGA, governors can make a name for themselves within a policy area that extends beyond what they achieve within their own state. We might argue that Clinton's presidential bid was significantly enhanced by his NGA leadership, which earned him influential friends and followers beyond the boundaries of Arkansas.

Governors and the Movement Toward More Coherent Policy

If governors are to exert leadership in an environment of increasing complexity and incoherence, they will have to exert influence consistent with their position and direct that influence more coherently. Governors can use the particular strengths of their positions as leverage to promote more coherent policy aimed at broader, more systemic educational improvement. Systemic reform is the most promising response to the increasing incoherence of state-level educational policy, and governors are particularly well situated to encourage it.

The fragmented governance of education and the growing incoherence of policy would not be the problems they are if everything were fine in the classroom. If every classroom were a warm, happy place where children were fully engaged and challenged to their potential with deep understanding of subject matter, we would not care so much that there are too many new policies or that they are often contradictory. In some senses, the confusion might protect the classroom from inconsistent direction because the warring policies might cancel one another out or permit practitioners to disregard them. However, only some classrooms approach our vision of good schooling. Many classrooms either are dull places where bored children drill in basic skills or are substandard in basic conditions for teaching and learning.

By virtually all aggregate indexes of performance, schools have shown little improvement since the beginning of the current reform period. Academic achievement does not seem to have improved significantly over the past several decades (NCES 1992). Even on measures of academic achievement where some groups of students have shown improvement on basic skills, performance is extremely weak on the higher-level, problem-solving tasks that reformers value. Dropout rates and rates of retention in grade have been stuck at unacceptably high levels (NCES 1989, pp. 24–25; Frase 1989; Shepard and Smith 1989; O'Day and Smith 1990). Indexes of students' attachment to school, such as engagement and membership in school activities and work-force participation, show a high level of alienation among many groups of school-aged children (Wehlage 1989; Wehlage, Rutter, Smith, Lesko, and Fernandez 1989).

The incapacity of educational governance structures to encourage, sustain, and propagate exceptional classrooms relates directly to the fragmented policy system in which schools operate. The barrage of inconsistent signals has three major effects:

- It drains the energy of school personnel who are responding to contending pressures.
- It reinforces the basic conservatism inherent in any large governmental system, in this case leading to the lowest common denominator of a "basic skills" curriculum.
- It inhibits concerted improvement around a coherent vision of reform (Smith and O'Day 1991, O'Day and Smith 1993).

If we were to attempt systemwide reform to make the exceptional classroom the norm, we might start with proactive state leadership around the goals of education, coupled with encouragement of school-level reform in organizing and providing instruction. As Smith and O'Day argue:

> The first prong of the strategy is to establish a coherent system of instructional guidance whose purpose is to ensure that all students have the opportunity to acquire a core body of challenging and engaging knowledge, skills, and problem-solving capacities. This will require overcoming the fragmentation of the system through coordination of the key functions affecting instruction: curriculum, teacher training, and assessment. The actual coordination of these functions, we argue, can best be handled on the state level, but it must be linked to the second prong of the strategy: a complete overhaul of the governance structure at all levels and a careful and coherent delineation of the responsibilities of different parts of the political and administrative system. Only in this way can we ensure that "bottom-up" initiative and teachers' professional discretion are at the heart of what happens at the school site while at the same time reducing the fragmentation that has been so detrimental in the past (1991, p. 247).

Many states are acting on these notions and focusing on educational outcomes. Forty-five states report that they are at least in the beginning stage of designing more coherent instructional guidance systems that include curriculum frameworks built around challenging concepts of subject matter, sophisticated assessments tied to those frameworks, and teacher professional development programs built around the same content students need to know (Pechman and LaGuarda 1993). At the same time, state policymakers are experimenting with ways to reduce the amount of regulation that deals with educational processes, seeing *practice* issues as best left to the school (Fuhrman 1989, Fuhrman and Elmore in press).

Governors may be particularly well suited to exert influence for more streamlined, coherent policies that promote challenging outcomes. Because of their electoral constituencies, governors have a broader perspective on the diverse interests and actors who would need to participate in crafting such policies and can energize them around a common vision. Governors can convene interests and build coalitions through structures like commissions or interagency task forces and through public outreach and rhetoric. Because of their overarching responsibility for elementary, secondary, and higher education, governors have a legitimate role in assembling the varied constituencies that would have to contribute to a broader, systemic solution: for example, K–12 policymakers and higher education policymakers; education policymakers and policymakers for related children's services; subject area specialists and the public, university, and school faculty.

The characteristics of the gubernatorial office also lend themselves to a broader, more coherent view of policy leadership. As Rosenthal notes, governors take a statewide perspective (1990, pp. 52–54). They must articulate a public interest that is greater than the sum of parochial interests, accept responsibility for policy and for state progress, and take a broad and long-term view. Rosenthal contrasts those aspects of gubernatorial leadership with the orientations of legislators who are more likely to take district, subgroup, or special interest perspectives; share diffuse responsibility for policy; and take a shorter-term view bounded by policy enactment or the end of session. Of all state-level educational policymakers, only the legislature shares with the governor responsibility for the entire education system—elementary and secondary through adult—and for the integration of other children's services in support of education. Yet the legislature is less likely to coordinate and lead an effort to promote coherent policy. The governor has both the perspective and the responsibility for all the aspects of educational policy that must come together for the system to improve.

In suggesting that the governors have a special role to play in promoting coherent educational policy, we are not arguing that they necessarily must initiate or develop the component pieces. In fact, the governor's office is clearly not the best point of origin for many specific elements of reform, such as new curriculum frameworks, but is the best point of origin for a statewide effort to coordinate educational policy so that the specific elements fit together. The governor must articulate a vision of coherent policy for successful schools to set the process in motion.

We have shown that the fragmented nature of the educational governance system acts both as a barrier to gubernatorial leadership and as an incentive for governors to stake out their piece of an increasingly complex landscape with distinct policies that redound to their credit. The vicious cycle of fragmented governance leading to more and more fragmented policy inhibits any concerted effort to improve education systemwide.

We have also argued that, because of their broad responsibilities and perspectives, governors are particularly well suited to break the cycle. They are appropriately positioned to stop the pattern in which each policy actor offers more and more policy ideas that fail to add up to an integrated whole. Moreover, an increasingly powerful association, NGA, supports them in that effort. NGA brings political legitimacy to the notion of coherent policy leadership. Its recent reports, *Educating America: State Strategies for Achieving the National Education Goals* (1990) and *From Rhetoric to Action: State Progress in Restructuring the Education System* (1991), support more coherent policy approaches. The service of prominent governors and NGA leaders, like Romer and Campbell on the National Educational Goals Panel and the National Council on Educational Standards and Testing, secures the links between the systemic reform strategy and the leadership of the nation's governors.[3] NGA reinforces the notion that governors must take primary responsibility for the progress of education. They can best do that by providing the kind of coherent policy leadership that systemic educational improvement requires.

Endnotes

[1]Since 1984, the U.S. Department of Education has published an annual "wall chart" comparing states on several performance indicators, including high school graduation rates and college admission test scores.

[2]Much of the information in this section derives from interviews with Michael Cohen (education director of NGA at the time of the interview) on September 21, 1990, and with Joan Wills, former director of NGA's Center for Policy Research, on September 27, 1990.

[3]For a discussion of the recommendations of the National Council on Educational Standards and Testing, see Smith, Fuhrman, and O'Day, in this yearbook.

References

Advisory Commission on Intergovernmental Relations (ACIR). (1989). *Significant Features of Fiscal Federalism*. Washington, D.C.: Author.

Bardach, E. (1980). "Implementation Studies and the Study of Implements." Paper presented at the annual meeting of the American Political Science Association.

Berman, P., and M.W. McLaughlin. (1975). "The Findings in Review." *Federal Programs Supporting Educational Change, Vol. 4*. Santa Monica, Calif.: Rand Corporation.

Berman, P., and M.W. McLaughlin. (1978). "Implementing and Sustaining Innovations." *Federal Programs Supporting Educational Change, Vol. 7*. Santa Monica, Calif.: Rand Corporation.

Beyle, T.L. (1989). "From Governor to Governors." In *The State of the States* (pp. 33–68), edited by C.E. Van Horn. Washington, D.C.: Congressional Quarterly Press.

Beyle, T., and L. Muchmore, eds. (1983). *Being Governor: The View from the Office*. Durham, N.C.: Duke University Press.

Carnegie Forum on Education and the Economy. (1986). *A Nation Prepared: Teachers for the 21st Century*. New York: Author.

Clark, D.L., and T.A. Astuto. (1990). "The Disjunction of Federal Education Policy and Educational Needs in the 1990s." In *Education Politics for the New Century* (pp. 11–26), edited by D.E. Mitchell and M.E. Goertz. London: Falmer Press.

Cohen, D.K. (1982). "Policy and Organization: The Impact of State and Federal Educational Policy in School Governance." *Harvard Educational Review* 52, 4: 474–499.

Cohen, D.K. (1990). "Governance and Instruction: The Promise of Decentralization and Choice." In *Choice and Control in American Education*, edited by W.H. Clune and J. Witte. Philadelphia: Falmer Press.

Cohen, D.K., and J. Spillane. (1993). "Policy and Practice: The Relations Between Governance and Instruction." In *Designing Coherent Education Policy: Improving the System* (pp. 35–95), edited by S.H. Fuhrman. San Francisco: Jossey-Bass.

Coleman, J.S., E. Campbell, C. Hobson, J. McPortland, A. Mood, F. Weinfeld, and R. York. (1966). *Equality of Educational Opportunity*. Washington, D.C.: U.S. Government Printing Office.

Cuban, L. (1984). *How Teachers Taught: Constancy and Change in American Classrooms, 1890–1980*. New York: Longman.

Darling-Hammond, L., and B. Berry. (1988). *The Evolution of Teacher Policy*. Prepared for the Center for Policy Research in Education. Santa Monica, Calif.: Rand Corporation.

David, J.L., M.K. Cohen, D. Honetschlager, and S. Traiman. (1990). *State Actions to Restructure Schools: First Steps*. Washington, D.C.: National Governors' Association.

Elmore, R.F. (1978). "Organizational Models of Social Program Implementation." *Public Policy* 26: 185–228.

Elmore, R.F. (1987). "Instruments and Strategy in Public Policy." *Policy Studies Review* 7, 1: 174–186.

Elmore, R.F., and S.H. Fuhrman. (Summer 1990). "The National Interest and the Federal Role in Education." *Publius: The Journal of American Federalism* 20, 3.

Elmore, R.F., and M.W. Mclaughlin. (1988). *Steady Work: Policy, Practice, and the Reform of American Education*. Santa Monica, Calif.: Rand Corporation.

Fabricius, M., and R.K. Sneel. (1990). *Earmarking State Taxes*. Denver: National Conference of State Legislatures.

Firestone, W.A., S.H. Fuhrman, and M.W. Kirst. (1989). *The Progress of Reform: An Appraisal of State Education Initiatives*. New Brunswick, N.J.: Rutgers University, Center for Policy Research in Education.

Frase, M.J. (1989). *Dropout Rates in the United States: 1988.* NCES 89–609. Washington, D.C.: U.S. Government Printing Office.

Fuhrman, S.H. (December 1979). *State Education Politics: The Case of School Finance Reform* (monograph, pp. 87–95), with contributions by M. Kirst, J. Berke, and M. Usdan. Denver: Education Commission of the States.

Fuhrman, S.H. (Summer 1987). "Education Policy: A New Context for Governance." *Publius: 1986 Annual Review of Federalism* 17, 3: 131–144.

Fuhrman, S.H., and R.F. Elmore. (1990). "Understanding Local Control in the Wake of State Education Reform." *Educational Evaluation and Policy Analysis* 12, 1: 82–96.

Fuhrman, S.H., and R.F. Elmore. (in press). *Opportunity to Learn and the State Role in Education.* Washington, D.C.: National Governors' Association.

Fuhrman, S.H., with P. Fry. (1989). *Diversity Amidst Standardization: State Differential Treatment of Districts.* New Brunswick, N.J.: Rutgers University, Center for Policy Research in Education.

Fullan, M. (1982). *The Meaning of Educational Change.* New York: Teachers College Press.

Hargrove, E.C. (1983). "The Search for Implementation Theory." In *What Role for Government?* edited by R.K. Zeckhauser and D. Leebaert. Durham, S.C.: Duke University Press.

The Holmes Group, Inc. (1986). *Tomorrow's Teachers: A Report of the Holmes Group.* East Lansing, Mich.: Author.

Jencks, C.S., M. Smith, H. Acland, M.J. Bane, D. Cohen, H. Gintis, B. Heyns, and S. Michaelson. (1972). *Inequality: A Reassessment of the Effect of Family and Schooling in America.* New York: Basic Books.

Keith, T.Z., T.M. Reimers, P.G. Fehrmann, S.M. Pottebaum, and L.W. Aubey. (1986). "Parental Involvement, Homework, and TV Time: Direct and Indirect Effects on High School Achievement." *Journal of Educational Psychology* 78: 373–380.

Kirst, M.W. (1990). *Accountability: Implications for State and Local Policy Makers.* Policy Perspectives Series. Washington, D.C.: U.S. Department of Education, Office of Educational Research and Improvement.

Massell, D., and S. Fuhrman. (in press). *Ten Years of State Education Reform: Update with Four Case Studies.* New Brunswick, N.J.: Consortium for Policy Research in Education.

McDonnell, L.M., and R.F. Elmore. (1987). *Alternative Policy Instruments.* Prepared for the Center for Policy Research in Education. Santa Monica, Calif.: Rand Corporation.

McDonnell, L., and S.H. Fuhrman. (1985). "The Political Context of Education Reform." In *The Fiscal, Legal, and Political Aspects of State Reform of Elementary and Secondary Education* (pp. 43–64), edited by V.D. Mueller and M.P. McKeown. Cambridge, Mass.: Ballinger.

Milne, A.M., D.W. Myers, S. Rosenthal, and A. Ginsburg. (1986). "Single Parents, Working Mothers, and the Educational Achievement of School Children." *Sociology of Education* 59: 125–139.

National Education Association. (1989). *Estimates of School Statistics.* Washington, D.C.: Author.

National Center for Education Statistics. (1989). *The Condition of Education 1989: Vol. 1. Elementary and Secondary Education.* Washington, D.C.: U.S. Government Printing Office.

National Center for Education Statistics. (1992). *The Condition of Education 1992.* Washington, D.C.: U.S. Government Printing Office.

National Commission on Excellence in Education. (1983). *A Nation at Risk: The Imperative for Education Reform.* Washington, D.C.: U.S. Department of Education.

National Governors' Association. (1986). *Time for Results: The Governors' 1991 Report on Education*. Washington, D.C.: Author.
National Governors' Association. (1989). *Results in Education 1989: The Governors' 1991 Report on Education*. Washington, D.C.: Author.
National Governors' Association. (1990). *Educating America: State Strategies for Achieving the National Education Goals*. Washington, D.C.: Author.
National Governors' Association. (1991). *From Rhetoric to Action: State Progress in Restructuring the Education System*. Washington, D.C.: Author.
Neustadt, R.E. (1960). *Presidential Power: The Politics of Leadership from FDR to Carter*. New York: Wiley & Sons.
O'Day, J., and M.S. Smith. (1990). *Retention Policies in U.S. Schools*. New Brunswick, N.J.: Rutgers University, Center for Policy Research in Education.
O'Day, J., and M.S. Smith. (1993). "Systemic Reform and Educational Opportunity." In *Designing Coherent Education Policy: Improving the System* (pp. 250–312), edited by S.H. Fuhrman. San Francisco: Jossey-Bass.
Office of Educational Research and Improvement (OERI). (1988). *Creating Responsible and Responsive Accountability Systems*. Washington, D.C.: U.S. Department of Education, OERI.
Pechman, E., and K. LaGuarda. (1993). *Status of New Curriculum Frameworks, Standards, Assessments, and Monitoring Systems*. Washington, D.C.: Policy Studies Associates.
Pressman, J., and A. Wildavsky. (1984). *Implementation*. 3rd ed. Berkeley: University of California Press.
Richards, C.E., and M.J. Shujaa. (Spring 1990). "State-Sponsored School Performance Incentive Plans: A Policy Review." *Educational Considerations* 17, 2: 42–52.
Rosenthal, A. (1990). *Governors and Legislatures: Contending Powers*. Washington, D.C.: Congressional Quarterly Press.
Rosenthal, A., and S.H. Fuhrman. (1981). *Legislative Education Leadership in the States*. Washington, D.C.: Institute for Educational Leadership.
Sabato, L. (1983). *Goodbye to Good-Time Charlie: The American Governorship Transformed*. Washington, D.C.: Congressional Quarterly Press.
Shepard, L.A., and M.S. Smith. (1989). *Flunking Grades: Research and Policies on Retention*. New York: Falmer Press.
Smith, M.S., and J. O'Day. (1988). "Teaching Policy and Research on Teaching." Unpublished manuscript. Center for Policy Research in Education, Rutgers University, New Brunswick, N.J.
Smith, M., and J. O'Day. (1991). "Systemic School Reform." In *The Politics of Curriculum and Testing* (pp. 233–267), edited by S. Fuhrman and B. Malen. Philadelphia: Falmer Press.
Tyack, D., and E. Hansot. (1982). *Managers of Virtue: Public School Leadership in America, 1820–1980*. New York: Basic Books.
Walker, J.L. (1971). "Innovation in State Politics." In *Politics in the American States*, edited by H. Jacobs and K.N. Vines. Boston: Little, Brown.
Wehlage, G.G. (1989). "Engagement, Not Remediation or Higher Standards." In *Children at Risk* (pp. 57–73), edited by J. Lakebrink. Springfield, Ill.: Charles C Thomas.
Wehlage, G.G., R.A. Rutter, G.A. Smith, N.L. Lesko, and R.R. Fernandez. (1989). *Reducing the Risk: Schools as Communities of Support*. Philadelphia: Falmer Press.

5

Commentary on National and State Education Policy Developments: A State Legislator's Perspective

Ken Nelson

The Governance of Curriculum is an unusual, if not provocative, title for a book. It sounds like an incongruous alliance between two nonconsenting institutional bodies, for example, state government and K–12 public education. Educators have repeatedly told me there is too much government intervention in the classroom. Therefore, during the past decade, as chair of the Minnesota House Education Finance Committee, I spent significant effort and political capital trying to restrain my colleagues and myself from legislating the daily activities of educators.

Such governmental intervention reminds me of the frontier sheriff who swaggered into the saloon to shoot bullets at the patrons' feet, making them dance to his gunblast tune. Governors and legislators frequently shoot their "silver bullet" projects and policies at educators, making them dance to their mandated tune. But wouldn't educators rather be teaching?

What do we mean by governing curriculum? I suspect that curriculum is already being governed by, among other influences, textbook publishers, status quo inertia, serendipitous activity, and incoherent decision making. So the relevant question is, How can curriculum be governed in a thoughtful, participative manner that enables educators to best educate our children? This question reflects the current systemic struggle to improve U.S. public education within our democratic context. I address this uneasy alliance between governing and practicing from my perspective as a former state legislator by commenting on the need for educational standards and the respective roles of legislators and governors in educational policy. Three chapters in this yearbook are particularly relevant to these issues: Chapter 2, "National Curriculum Standards: Are They Desirable and Feasible?" by

Marshall Smith, Susan Fuhrman, and Jennifer O'Day; Chapter 3, "Legislatures and Education Policy," by Susan Fuhrman; and Chapter 4, "Governors and Education Policy in the 1990s," by Susan Fuhrman and Richard Elmore.

National Standards

I thoroughly enjoyed Chapter 2, by Smith, Fuhrman, and O'Day. Wasn't it Alice in Wonderland who said if we don't know where we are going, any path will get us there? Since the publication of *A Nation at Risk* (National Commission on Excellence in Education 1983), education improvement initiatives have been everywhere on the reform landscape, frequently lost without a systemic reform compass. Having been one of those policymakers who wandered in the education reform wilderness of the 1980s, I am hopeful that the policymakers, practitioners, and students of the 1990s will instead be guided by clear and thoughtful educational and system performance indicators.

Perhaps the diversity of standards as characterized by Smith et al. can provide the conceptual framework for such indicators. Judging from my legislative experience, mutually developed performance standards have the ability to energize students, education practitioners, and policymakers by focusing a common vision on the achievement of challenging results. At the same time, such standards must allow a rich diversity of local, district, and state options to achieve the respective goals. They should not become externally imposed mandates that divert energy from results, inputs that overshadow outcomes, or rules that restrict education entrepreneurs. People are not as energized or creative if they have less freedom of action, especially if they are prescriptively ordered by those less informed. Students, practitioners, and policymakers can achieve more if the following occur:

- The educational objectives are collaboratively developed and clearly communicated;
  - Resources and strategies are provided that are adequate to the task;
  - Quality assessment and feedback are used for course correction; and
  - A trusting environment of risk-taking is encouraged.

Two paradigms are shifted by Smith et al. Much of the standards debate of the 1980s focused on student performance. But the 1990s debate makes it clear that standards aren't just for students anymore—they are for all education stakeholders and systems. In addition, the new purpose of standards is not to expose failure, as it frequently did in the past, but to leverage continuous improvement for all people and parts of the education system. Therefore, standards become indicators of progress, not judgments of failure.

This, I believe, is a healthy use of standards; not characterized as mandates, rules, or regulations, but as statements of results, expected outcomes, or performance indicators. Once collaboratively developed and applied, they enable all of us to measure how well the total system and our part in it are performing and where we can continuously improve.

Such applied standards can provide a multifaceted tool for systemic transformation in the 1990s. It's what we were lacking in the 1970s and 1980s.

Each type of standard characterized by Smith et al. provides a unique interdependent dimension to the systemic reform whole. Content standards provide the opportunity for challenging, synergistic alignment of curriculum, pedagogy, and assessment at all learning levels. Student performance standards can determine the degree and nature of learner success and provide feedback for greater learning. School delivery standards will be able to assess the capacity of the classroom and school site for greater student learning. System delivery standards can hold state and district policymakers accountable for effective, long-term, coherent direction and infrastructure. My legislative experience suggests that without such comprehensive standards, we will continue to blame each other for our lack of educational quality.

Content Standards

Content standards are the keystone of systemic reform efforts. The other standards (student, site, system) cannot grasp beyond the reach of content standards. My Minnesota experience teaches me that content standards will not be challenging enough if exclusively designed by school districts or sites. Local control is frequently an excuse for the status quo, and we have taken false comfort in comparisons between local schools, districts, or states. In addition, multiple interpretations of these comparisons have allowed us to convince our constituencies that we are improving, when such improvement is minimal or nonexistent. Therefore, parents and communities become complacent, believing that their schools and students are doing well compared to others. Instead, comparisons should be made to world class standards. National, state, or local standards will not be challenging enough without world class comparability. Fortunately, the proposed national math and science standards offer us exciting prototypical examples of high content standards.

Student Performance Standards

Student performance indicators are being developed and clarified by many states, including Minnesota. It became clear to us in the 1980s that all students needed a clear and consistent statement of learner outcome expectations to challenge them to greater learning each step of the way. This began our Minnesota commitment to move the entire public education system toward learner outcomes. I call it "reform at the core" of the system, while many of our "choice" initiatives, as valuable as they are, are "reform at the margin." After all, greater learner achievement is the central purpose of the system. I am convinced we can best accomplish this with clear outcome expectations clearly communicated to each student, parent, and teacher at each step on the learning way.

In 1991 the Minnesota Legislature, working with the Department of Education, provided this statutory definition, which links content and performance:

> Outcome-based education is a pupil-centered, results-oriented system premised on the belief that all individuals can learn. In this system: (1) what a pupil is to learn is clearly identified; (2) each pupil's progress is based on the pupil's demonstrated achievement; (3) each pupil's needs are accommodated through multiple instructional strategies and assessment tools; and (4) each pupil is provided time and assistance to realize her or his potential (Minnesota Statute 126.661).

By this definition, we attempted to provide a student-centered focus to bring pedagogy, curriculum, and assessment in alignment toward greater learning for each individual.

The 1992 Legislature tied learner outcomes to graduation requirements:

> The Legislature is committed to establishing rigorous, results-oriented graduation rule for Minnesota's public school students. To that end, the State Board of Education shall use its rulemaking authority to adopt a statewide, results-oriented graduation rule (1992 Laws, Chap. 499, Art. 8, Sect. 32).

These outcomes are to be a blend of general top-down and specific bottom-up standards that will be periodically updated to match the best student performance in other nations. They are developed by education practitioners in consultation with the students' future employers and the post-secondary system. Because many employers are engaged in international competition, this helps to assure world class comparability.

School and System Performance Standards

Smith et al. emphasize establishing school-site and system (district, state, national) standards for capacity and performance. It's tragic that in the past we have failed students, but not systems or institutions. And yet, W. Edwards Deming claims that 85 percent of the problem of low-performance systems is not people, but structure and process. Students or educators are not the problem; it's the way we have structured the process of public education. Another way of saying it: "Every organization is perfectly designed to get the results it gets." If we don't like our education results, then obviously we need to change the learning organization. School and system delivery standards can give us a mechanism for continuous improvement.

There is an additional domain to which the education community should apply standards. To be coherent and productive, we must also have indicators for holding educational policies and policymakers accountable. Are state and local policies consistently guided by a unifying vision and goals? Do they best support and encourage the performance and content standards? Are policymakers' decisions long-term and not episodic—systemic and not situational? Probably not. State legislators and school board members have been renowned for incoherent decisions and micromanagement. Yet if other components (such as schools and students) are held accountable by challenging educational indicators, then so should the policies and policymakers. It's all interconnected.

Legislatures and Governors: Policymaking at the Top

In Chapters 3 and 4, Fuhrman and Elmore illustrate the difficulty of our present political process to effectively govern and guide education improvement. Fuhrman's multistate research and analysis of the 1970s and 1980s corroborates my own experience as a legislator who served on the House Education Committee from 1972 to 1992. I concur with her assessment: "Legislatures have acted courageously to address education problems, but their efforts fall short of the mark." Elmore and Fuhrman see a positive but slowly evolving trend toward coherence by legislators and governors from the 1970s and 1980s to the 1990s. Fuhrman summarizes her suggestions for the legislators of the 1990s. I believe her suggestions are also relevant for governors:

> Take a long-term perspective, trust local educators, build the state's capacity, and collaborate with other policymakers.

Beyond Patchwork Legislation

Episodic decision making has frequently characterized the 1970-1980 state legislative/executive process, driven by two- or four-year election cycles and partisan activity. It's ironic that in a democracy, the reelection incentives for our political decision makers are often contrary to the long-term objectives of our major institutions. It's a double irony when reelection incentives (including campaign contributions from education groups) are not based on reform accomplishments, but more of the status quo. Consequently, legislators, governors, and school board members become victims and victimizers of quick fixes and handy mandates in an attempt to please an impatient electorate or special interest constituencies. These are inept tools for transforming an education system that has been constructed like a patchwork quilt for more than 200 years. It will take longer than a few election cycles to peel the patches from K–12 education.

Our nation's political saint, Thomas Jefferson, spoke of needing a revolution every generation to keep a democracy vibrant and responsive. If he were here today, perhaps he would speak of the enemy within our public institutions: not educators or legislators or governors or parents or students, but structures and processes and systems. It's what Peter Senge (1990) in *The Fifth Discipline* calls old "mental models." These hierarchical and centralized methods of decision making have prevented us from revitalizing public education.

But Fuhrman and Elmore anticipate a new future for educational improvement, allowing educators to teach and legislators and governors to be Jeffersonian: "What seems to be required is less volume and more coherence; more emphasis on clear, ambitious, state-level explications of what students should know and willingness to delegate many decisions about how they should be taught to schools."

Mission Statements and Alliances

Some of the 1984 members of the Minnesota Legislature and the Commissioner of Education criss-crossed the state to talk with Minnesotans about what they wanted from public education. From these conversations and hearings, the 1985 Legislature drafted, refined, and adopted a mission statement. It became a unifying vision for the Department of Education, state policymakers, and school districts. It provided a conceptual infrastructure for the development of learner outcomes and other initiatives consistent with the mission.

It had become apparent that Minnesota's education stakeholders needed a common vision to lift us above the traditional session-by-session fray if we were going to transform public education. We could then use our respective professional strengths to enrich the common enterprise. Otherwise, we were like the Minnesota Democrats, characterized by their political saint, Hubert Humphrey. He said that they would traditionally form a circle, not for protection from outsiders, but to shoot inward at each other. That seems to be similar to our education reform efforts of the 1970s and 1980s, pointing at each other with fingers of blame.

Fuhrman and Elmore suggest that the 1990s policymaking will have to be different to achieve systemic educational reform. State policymakers can enrich their decision making and the state public education system by supporting collaborative strategies, including the development of a unifying vision and new, long-term forums of decision making. The National Goals statement provides a comprehensive, unifying mission for all states and districts to translate into their own objectives and strategies. And the future role of governors and legislators will be enhanced by aligning with national organizations like the National Governors' Association, the National Conference of State Legislators, and the Education Commission of the States, as well as developing state coalitions such as South Carolina's Business-Education Alliance. Such coalitions provide forums for reform and accountability that bridge beyond two- and four-year election cycles and partisan activity. When practitioners and policymakers link the Fuhrman and Elmore suggestions with the new use of standards, coherent policy and systemic reform will be made possible in the 1990s.

References

National Commission on Excellence in Education. (1983). *A Nation at Risk: The Imperative for Educational Reform.* Washington, D.C.: U.S. Government Printing Office.

Senge, P. (1990). *The Fifth Discipline.* New York: Doubleday.

II

State Curriculum Reform Development and Management

6

Achieving Consensus: Setting the Agenda for State Curriculum Reform

Diane Massell

Policymakers at every level of the educational system are currently developing standards that specify "what students should know and be able to do." At the national level, professional subject-matter organizations are following the lead taken in the 1980s by the National Council of Teachers of Mathematics (NCTM) and the American Association for the Advancement of Science (AAAS) to set high academic standards for their fields. In a recent survey, forty-five states reported that they were developing or implementing new curriculum frameworks (Pechman and Laguarda 1993). Existing state agencies or newly created task forces are identifying content standards, student outcomes, performance standards, or new assessments. Many districts around the country are attending to these changes at the state and national levels, and specifying their own curriculum guidelines and materials accordingly.

Critical to all these endeavors is the notion that the adopted standards must achieve broad consensus across professional and public groups. The idea of establishing agreement on challenging expectations for student learning is a new one for American schools (NCEST 1992, Cohen and Spillane 1993, Fuhrman 1993). Because states are critical in the governance of public schooling—indeed, they have Constitutional authority over education—this chapter focuses on their efforts. Directly or indirectly, national or local standards will be filtered through states' policies. Thus state agendas in this sphere will be pivotal.

Why is developing standards seen as a key policy solution today? Remedies to the crisis of low academic standards outlined by the National Commission on Excellence in Education's 1983 report, *A Nation at Risk*, encouraged states to establish or expand many familiar policy solutions, such as increased graduation credit requirements, assessment programs for students and teachers, a longer school day and year, and incentive and reward programs (Murphy 1990). However, these earlier "excellence" reforms, which often imposed *more* requirements without specifying *what*, in particular, the content should be, were found to lack the substantive grist necessary for meaningful school-based change. Raising graduation credit requirements, for instance, did little to ensure more rigorous content in the delivered curriculum. Research found evidence that higher credit requirements could simply lead to more seat time in relabeled, lower-level courses (Firestone, Rosenblum, Bader, and Massell 1991). Previous state curriculum frameworks attempting to more directly influence course content were sharply criticized as providing little more than lengthy lists of behavioral objectives and laundry lists of isolated "factoids" (Bartels, quoted by Curry and Temple 1992).

In addition, although the reforms of the 1980s focused public attention on academic learning, they have done little to decrease the conflicting policy demands that operate on schools. In fact, they have often contributed to an increasing incoherence in the policy environment because different policies are frequently designed for different sets of standards and objectives.

Current standards are, then, an attempt to improve both the quality and the coherence of the delivered curriculum. They have become the heart of a new overall strategy of coordinated, systemic reform (Smith and O'Day 1991). Although many versions of systemic reform have emerged in the states (see Fuhrman and Massell 1992), at a minimum two or more components of the policy system—assessment, textbooks and instructional materials, or staff development—are keyed to a common set of curricular and instructional standards.

Previous efforts by the National Science Foundation to upgrade science and mathematics curriculums have failed because they neglected the importance of gaining broad understanding and support. In many respects, there is already remarkable consensus on the broad substance and direction of content reform today. Most educational policymakers and school professionals agree, for example, on the need to encourage "higher-order thinking"; more interdisciplinary learning and understanding; active, student-centered learning; more in-depth explorations of less content rather than superficial coverage of a broader range of content (dubbed the "less is more" or "depth over breadth" goal); and curriculums that meet the needs of diverse student populations. They also agree that these reforms should be appropriate for all students, not just the college-bound, the gifted and talented, the educationally disadvantaged, or other special needs students (Curry and Temple 1992).

And yet, the problem of how to approach these ideas and operationalize them into standards raises many questions and many contentious professional and public debates. For example, if all students should receive the same content, does this mean that tracking and special programs for at-risk or gifted and talented students should be abolished? Certainly the prospect of these more dramatic organizational changes prompts pedagogical disputes and equity concerns (see, e.g., Hoffmeister, in press), in addition to posing political challenges to established interest groups. With a "less is more" objective, decisions must be made about precisely what content should be trimmed down or eliminated. These decisions can threaten obsolescence for subject-matter areas or topics in K–12 education. In curriculum policy, it is always easier to appease interests by adding rather than taking away; in public education this has resulted in the "shopping mall high school" (Powell, Farrar, and Cohen 1985). Furthermore, content in certain subject areas like science or social studies inevitably features such controversial issues as evolution or multiculturalism (Massell 1993b).

Consequently, specifying these broad goals is an enterprise laden with powerful consequences that can galvanize opposition from many sides of the political, social, and professional spectrums (see Massell, Kirst, Kelley, and Yee 1993). As a result, states and others engaged in the standard-setting effort are taking care to launch strategies that build consensus across professional and lay citizen communities. State policymakers are keenly aware that their approach to agenda-setting may improve the legitimacy as well as the quality of their new leadership, ease the thorny disputes that arise, and facilitate local implementation.

This chapter examines the approaches that four states—California, Vermont, South Carolina, and Kentucky—are taking to set their standards agenda. I focus chiefly on the states' efforts to establish student content and learning standards and create curriculum frameworks or similar documents. (I use the term *documents* to refer to the written products that states are using: curriculum frameworks, guidelines, written statements about expected student learning goals and outcomes, reports on model instructional practices, and other such materials.) The study was exploratory because very little has been written on this topic.

My research is based on pertinent documents and on 1992 telephone interviews of key staff members within each state department of education, as well as interviews of externally based participants or outside observers. It must be noted, however, that states' strategies are continually adjusted to respond to various political, pedagogical, or other considerations; thus certain features of these processes may have already been altered. Moreover, in California many modifications were made to the process of creating each framework, so the portrait presented here is generic and may not fit each framework exactly. Together, however, the cases do illustrate the kinds of concerns and issues that emerge around agenda-setting activities; help us to conceptualize the process; and provide insight into how the states might better chart a course through the as yet murky waters of curriculum reform.

Conceptual Tools for Understanding Agenda-Setting

Before describing the agenda-setting procedures in these states, let me first offer a few conceptual tools that will help identify the salient differences in standards and state strategies.

First, the ways standards are operationalized and deployed in the four states differ along many dimensions. Standards vary according to whether they:

1. Offer a more abstract or precise level of detail;

2. Are anchored in a particular subject-matter perspective, or are skill based and not necessarily linked to any one discipline; and

3. Focus on content, outcomes, performance standards, or teaching pedagogy.

Decisions on these three issues reflect different assumptions about how specific and prescriptive state leadership should be; how best to achieve integrated, interdisciplinary teaching; how to provide sufficient detail for the coordination of other policy instruments; and how best to accomplish learning that "matters" for students both in school and in the world of work.

Kentucky's learner goals and "valued outcomes" (see the next section, "Agenda-Setting in the Four States") illustrate abstract, skill-based objectives that emphasize the outcomes (rather than the curricular inputs) of schooling. For example, their learner goals state that students should learn to "demonstrate self-sufficiency" and "think and solve problems" (Council on School Performance Standards 1991). Kentucky's curriculum framework discusses skills and content-related concepts in the context of different subject-matter areas, although at a relatively abstract level of detail. By contrast, California's frameworks begin with the disciplines. The science framework provides precise, subject-matter based standards, such as: "It is essential to show that classification of living things is based on evolution, because evolution explains both the similarities among living things and the diverse paths taken by different groups through geologic time" (California Department of Education 1990). (One can also find examples of abstract, subject-matter goals, or precisely detailed skill-based goals.)

Strong debates are emerging within national professional associations about whether standards should identify pedagogy and performance standards as well as content and outcomes. Thus far, states have responded differently to these issues; some, like California, have identified pedagogical approaches within the context of their curriculum frameworks. Others, like Vermont and Kentucky, are planning to engage in a separate effort to identify important pedagogical principles that will facilitate their overall reform programs. Although it is too early to tell how these documents will evolve and what shape they will take, a key decision will be whether the pedagogy is (1) grounded in particular subject-matter disciplines or student skills or (2) presented as a distinct and generic set of principles.

In addition, the standards are embedded in different types of policy instruments. Although many states are using curriculum frameworks, they are also using course content guidelines, core course proficiencies, general goal statements, and other mechanisms to carry their new standards. The *scope* of these instruments, and the *sequencing*, also varies across states. Kentucky, for example, developed several standards documents, beginning with more abstract goals and refining them with several subsequent documents to a more specific level of detail. California, by contrast, defines its content standards primarily within its curriculum frameworks, although these are bolstered by a wide array of more finely detailed documents such as videotapes, brochures, and other curriculum guidelines.

It is helpful to think of the process of setting standards as an iterative, tripartite one that looks, roughly, like that in Figure 6.1.

One important difference is the extent to which states articulate the standard-setting part (I) of the process as a separate activity carried out by individuals other than those who draft the documents (II).

Finally, and most important, the states' approaches to agenda-setting reflect two general styles, which I call *populist* and *professional elite*. One

Figure 6.1
Tripartite Model of Agenda-Setting

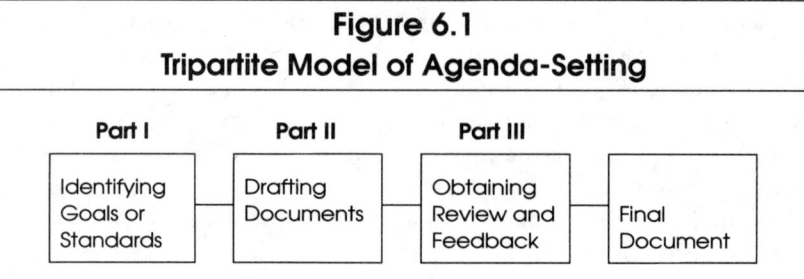

of the critical differences between the two styles is who participates, and when, in the three stages of agenda setting. Participants range across groups of professional educators (university academics, content specialists, teachers, curriculum supervisors) and lay citizens (parents, business and industry elites, elected officials, students). Although at some point both professionals and lay citizens are involved in the agenda-setting process of each state discussed in this chapter, the scope of their representation varies markedly—that is, the extent to which the process is opened up to the broad "grassroots" of lay citizens and professionals, or to smaller, more elite groups.

A populist agenda-setting strategy tends to maximize representation of the lay public and professionals in all three components of the process and to create special institutional structures or mechanisms to encourage broad involvement. A professional elite model, by contrast, places stronger emphasis on professional participation and tends to be more selective about who in this community becomes involved.

The participation strategies, as well as other managerial aspects of the process in the two models, reflect fundamentally different *ideologies of authority* (Elmore, Sykes, and Spillane 1992). In a populist effort, the legitimacy of state content leadership is achieved by an agenda-setting process that attempts to reflect the popular will. As such, the process relies on inductive, grassroots strategies at the front end; and public and professional participation is maximized. Standards developed in a professional elite model move more deductively; that is, the state begins with and relies heavily on a core of professional educators to give shape to the standards, and turns to broader involvement (again, primarily of professionals) to review the documents and provide feedback to the drafting committees. Here the belief is that the legitimacy of the state's enterprise will be leveraged through the quality of the documents and their reflection of cutting-edge, professional knowledge.

With these conceptual tools in mind, let us now turn to the four case studies.

Agenda-Setting in the Four States

California and Vermont provide the purest illustrations of the professional elite and populist models of agenda-setting, respectively.

California

California was an early leader in states' efforts to shape the core curriculum around more challenging content standards. In 1982 Bill Honig was elected state Superintendent of Public Instruction on a platform that promised a more academic, "traditional education." To fulfill this pledge, he and his staff seized on curriculum frameworks as the key instrument to leverage these standards. The frameworks became the centerpiece of a long-term strategy for coordinated change, a forerunner of what we would now call *systemic reform*.

Although subject-matter frameworks had been used in the state since 1972 to guide textbook adoption, Honig and others perceived the existing documents as little more than "good doorstops"—symbolic, vague statements with only a minor impact on the actual curriculum and instruction of classrooms. Over the next ten years, the new administration dramatically altered both the form and function of the frameworks. For instance, whereas the older frameworks offered lengthy lists of the content and behavioral objectives to be covered, the newer initiatives provide conceptual roadmaps that highlight the "big ideas" of the field, written in a literary, narrative style to convey the information in a more compelling and understandable way. They are not highly detailed documents that a teacher can use directly in the classroom, but they do offer general pedagogical advice. Just as important, the newer frameworks attempt to take more decisive stances on professional or public controversies in particular fields. The 1987 history-social science framework, for example, reinserts the teaching of religion as an important factor in world history. And although the older frameworks focused only on providing guidance for statewide textbook and instructional materials selection, the new frameworks provide the intellectual foundation for the state's staff development agenda, teacher certification, student assessments, and accountability. The frameworks also serve as the touchstone for the more detailed curricular materials that the state provides to districts, such as course models for particular grades or recommended reading lists.

Agenda-setting takes place under the aegis of the Curriculum Development and Supplemental Materials Commission, an advisory body to the State Board of Education. When a framework comes up for review, the Commission recommends and the Board appoints a Curriculum Framework and Criteria Committee to serve for the length of time it takes to review and, if necessary, craft a new document. The frameworks are revisited on a staggered, eight-year cycle.[1]

To elevate the frameworks from doorstop status, state policymakers wanted to create documents that would reflect cutting-edge positions within the particular subject-matter areas and provide strong leadership to the field. As one staff member said, "Consensus is a great goal, but if you put consensus above a high quality goal—a powerful statement—then it is going to hurt you." Policymakers emphasize professional participation, selecting university faculty, teachers, and other educators with strong expertise in the particular subject-matter field. Even though selecting framework writers on this basis might seem an obvious choice, it was an unusual notion in the early 1980s. Selection strategies for statewide committees of this sort typically focused on obtaining a balance of people from different geographic regions; racial, gender, or ethnic backgrounds; and established interest groups like teacher unions, special education lobbies, and others. California continues to balance its committees using representational matrixes; however, policymakers believed that relying *primarily* on these selection practices generated a politics of compromise between vested interest groups. To paraphrase one former key staff member, "If a committee is representative in the broadest sense, what you get is the status quo enshrined." As a result, formal rules of procedure in California now state that leading professionals must be given priority in selection to these committees (California Department of Education 1988). In addition, to a certain extent the state engages in what Walker (1990) calls "limited deliberation" by at times eliminating candidates for the writing committees from the extremes of the political or pedagogical spectrum. After the document is drafted, however, it is circulated through a broader network of teachers and other education professionals for critical review and feedback.

Although lay citizens do have some access to the standard-setting process, California clearly emphasizes professional participation and control over the majority of the developmental process. Unlike other states, it does not articulate a distinct, early phase in which standards are first identified by a lay public or others outside the writing team.[2] Although sunshine laws require all meetings to be open to the public, and the Curriculum Commission and the State Board of Education[3] hold public hearings prior to adoption, California has no special strategy for soliciting and sustaining broad, lay citizen input during review and feedback (see Figure 6.2 for a summary of comparisons of the four states). As a consequence, existing mechanisms for access at the state level tend to involve organized public interests rather than the "average" citizen or teacher. After the frameworks are drafted, the state holds a series of regional "awareness" conferences that the lay public may attend, but again, most participants are professional educators.

Figure 6.2
A Summary of Agenda-Setting Strategies

	California and South Carolina	
	Part I and Part II	**Part III**
	Identifying Standards and Drafting Documents	**Obtaining Review and Feedback**
CA	Committee of professional educators appointed under the Curriculum Commission, an advisory body to the State Board of Education to produce content-based curriculum frameworks	Networks of professional educators, with public access to framework meetings and hearings
SC	Professionals on framework writing teams with input from Curriculum Congresses to produce content-based curriculum frameworks	Extremely broad distribution to grassroots professionals and the public, including the Congresses

	Vermont and Kentucky		
	Part I	**Part II**	**Part III**
	Identifying Standards	**Drafting Documents**	**Obtaining Review and Feedback**
VT	1. Common Core of Learning (CCL) with input from Focus Forum (public and local school professionals) identified what students should know and do; 2. State Department of Education (SDE) elaborating CCL to create interdisciplinary framework matrixes; and 3. Three academic commissions to identify content, student performance standards.	1. For CCL, Common Core "Corp" within the SDE, composed of lay citizens and education professionals including SDE staff; 2. Interdisciplinary matrixes by SDE staff; and 3. Three academic commissions will draft frameworks.	Focus Forums, teachers throughout the state
KY	Interconnected, 2-step process under Council for School Performance Standards: 1. 6 learning goals, developed with public and professional input; and 2. 75 valued outcomes, developed by specially convened committees of education professionals	All documents drafted by professional committees, including curriculum framework based on the goals and standards documents	No formal review process for goal and standards documents; review of curriculum framework by district curriculum supervisors primarily, with input from professional advisory groups

Vermont

The centerpiece of Vermont's efforts to set student standards is its Common Core of Learning (CCL), initiated by the Vermont Department of Education (VDE) in 1991. The CCL was to be a composite of five reports, sequentially produced. The first document identifies standards for "what students should know and be able to do" that will guide future reports and be coordinated with the state's new portfolio assessments, now being developed by teachers across the state. As originally laid out by the Department, subsequent CCL reports would explore successful learning environments, model instructional programs, effective local action, and successful ways to organize education to reach those core student outcomes. Note that curriculum frameworks were absent from this list. In keeping with its strong tradition of local control, the state wanted to provide a set of common outcomes without describing discipline-based curricular content because the latter were seen as too prescriptive of local practice. Furthermore, discipline-based content, in the eyes of some key VDE staff, would lock in more traditional forms of knowledge and prevent more integrated, interdisciplinary approaches to learning.

Eventually, however, curriculum frameworks were added to the set. The first draft of the CCL report, *Is This Really What Learners Need to Know?* (1992), offered a relatively abstract level of detail on skill-based competencies under the rubric of communication, reasoning and problem solving, citizenship, well-being, and global stewardship. Teachers, the press, the State Board of Education, and others criticized the document's lack of connection to the academic disciplines. They were concerned that standards expressed in a skills-based format would have limited impact on the new portfolio assessments as well as schools, both of which are organized by subject-matter areas. Defenders of the original version counter that the skill-based orientation of the student standards provides a way to break down traditional barriers between academic disciplines and, consequently, promote more integrated learning. The decision was made to organize the vital skills identified in the earlier document under three academic clusters: History and Social Sciences; Arts and Literature; and Science, Mathematics, and Technology. Three curriculum frameworks identifying content and student performance standards will be devised in each of these areas, following a general template developed by the department.

Agenda-Setting is primarily the responsibility of the Vermont Department of Education, which steers the development of the Common Core of Learning. But in many ways, the Department has served as a coordinating center that draws strongly on outside groups. Vermont's approach illustrates a more inductive, populist model of agenda-setting. To develop the report on what students should know and be able to do, the VDE established an ongoing series of town meetings across the state, called "focus forums." Although state department staff initially planned only a limited number of these forums with the business community, they decided to facilitate a forum in any community requesting one. These later forums reached beyond business groups and involved a broader scope of participants. One VDE goal was to engage people not usually active in school affairs. To encourage this more diverse involvement, the Department asked sponsoring communities to select participants at random from voter registration lists.[4] By December 1992, more than forty focus forums had been held, involving 2,000 people.

These forums provided a platform of ideas that, according to VDE staff, strongly guided the work of the writing committee. The reality of who controls the agenda is, of course, more complex; although the focus forums did emphasize skill-based student outcomes, in part that occurred because of the way the meetings were structured. VDE staff directed forum facilitators to organize attendees in small groups, but *not* according to discipline areas (compare this to the South Carolina Curriculum Congress, described in the next section). Furthermore, forum facilitators asked these groups three questions that did not immediately direct attention to subject-matter based discussions. These three questions were:

> 1. What skills, knowledge and attitudes will learners need to be successful in the 21st century?
> 2. What programs exist now that are in harmony with your vision?
> 3. What can schools, communities, and businesses together do today that would make a difference? (Vermont Department of Education 1991, p. 18).

Although determining authority is a complicated matter, it is nevertheless true that the Vermont agenda-setting approach is distinct for its emphasis on the inclusion of a broad cross section of lay citizens and education professionals. The drafting stage of the process also involved lay citizens. The forty-member writing committee (the Common Core Corps) set up by the VDE consisted of parents, students, and business leaders as well as school professionals. The grassroots emphasis of the Vermont strategy also marked its review and feedback process, which has engaged not only the focus forum participants, but also, for the second iteration of the CCL, every teacher in the state. This approach is, of course, more easily managed in a small state with a homogeneous population.

Vermont's populist ideology of authority is expressed in a pamphlet describing the CCL developed by the State Department of Education:

> By working with great numbers of Vermonters and by a thorough examination of the best national and international standards, we hope to build the maximum possible consensus . . . . Schools alone cannot achieve this goal [of excellence and continual learning.] It will clearly take all Vermonters to make this a reality. We feel that it is vital to start this process by going to the people of our state with a blank piece of paper. We want to know their thoughts first, not their reactions to our thoughts (Vermont Department of Education 1991, p. 18).

This inductive approach is important to the legitimacy of state efforts in Vermont, which has a long tradition of direct democracy and citizen involvement in government. It may be particularly important as the state extends its presence into broader spheres of education.

The remaining two states, South Carolina and Kentucky, represent modified, blended versions of the populist and professional elite models. Because many components of their approach to agenda-setting are similar to California's and Vermont's, I will focus primarily on the ways in which these two cases depart from the other models and illustrate interesting alternatives.

South Carolina

Curriculum frameworks have become the fulcrum of recent reform efforts in South Carolina, part of the overall strategy of its new superintendent of education, Barbara Nielson, to shift the focus of the policy system away from its strong emphasis on basic skills and toward more demanding higher-order curriculums. These subject-matter frameworks embody the content standards that will form the foundation for redesigning other state and local policy instruments, with staff development, instructional materials selection, student assessment, and teacher preservice and inservice training among them. In 1992 the Department published its first draft frameworks in mathematics, foreign languages, and fine arts, which are still circulating for review and feedback. Like California's frameworks, they are written in a literary style and discuss each discipline's "big ideas." The frameworks outline student performance standards, examples of different instructional strategies specific to diverse student populations, and criteria for instructional materials selection, among other things.

Agenda-setting in South Carolina is very similar to California's approach, but with some important differences. As in California, members of the framework writing teams are professional elites identified as "one or two standard deviations ahead of the field" who have strong authority over the first draft of the documents and the standards contained therein. The institutional setup resembles California's, although the South Carolina Department of Education (SCDE) has more direct control over appointments to the curriculum teams as well as to a Curriculum Review Panel, which functions like the Curriculum Commission in California.

Perhaps the most unique aspect of South Carolina's agenda-setting process—one that distinguishes it from the professional elite model—is its Curriculum Congress, an advisory body set up by the Department to sustain the involvement of the lay public, as well as grassroots groups of school professionals. Although it was initially a select body, the Congress has now been opened up to all interested parties. Members join a discipline-based subgroup; a work area in curriculum, instruction, assessment, materials, or the professions; and a third team that bridges these two, such as "science assessment." Modelled after a Curriculum Congress held by the Education Commission of the States, relevant Congress teams interact with and advise the framework writing teams on an ongoing basis.

One of the SCDE's primary motivations for creating the Congress was their belief that ongoing involvement in the agenda-setting process would nurture a cadre of teacher leaders involved in and committed to the new curriculum from the beginning. California also has made concerted efforts to create networks of teacher leaders, but these efforts largely follow the agenda-setting process (e.g., through the awareness conferences, summer institutes for teachers, and other staff development activities.)

Another important departure from the California approach occurs at the point of formal review and feedback. Here, South Carolina's process opens dramatically. In 1993, the Department launched a massive campaign to advertise the draft frameworks and generate public involvement. Initially the SCDE distributed more than 4,500 copies of the three draft frameworks, but the number has increased ten-fold since then. Drafts were circulated to beauty salons, barber shops, public libraries, and radio and television media. In an effort to reach the public, the Department even produced a movie trailer about the frameworks. They targeted textbook publishers, educators at all levels of the system (including curriculum supervisors, administrators, teachers, and higher education faculty), the Curriculum Congress, the business community, school improvement councils, a small national group, and others.

Kentucky

Kentucky articulated a long, interlocking sequence of standard-setting activities, with each step an elaboration and refinement of the preceding effort. The state embarked on its first standard-setting initiative in 1989 when the governor formed a temporary Council on School Performance Standards to set the direction on what students should know and be able to do.[5] The Council produced a set of six broad learning goals that are largely skill-based,[6] a strong reflection of the populist component of this agenda-setting approach (see "Agenda-Setting" for Kentucky). In Kentucky, the public emphatically pushed for a greater correspondence between student activities in school and work.

In 1990, the General Assembly passed the Kentucky Education Reform Act (KERA), which among other things charged the Council with specifying the six learning goals in ways that could be assessed. The law set in motion a systemic reform plan by determining that these "valued outcomes" built on the goals would provide the foundation for other reforms in the policy system, specifically, a state curriculum framework and student performance assessments. The Council produced seventy-five valued outcomes that are vocationally oriented. In a table format, the "big ideas" of what students will learn are listed under each of the six goals, with examples of what they should be able to do and how students will benefit. Pedagogy is not specifically discussed. Recently, the KDE began referring to the valued outcomes as "learning outcomes," in response to growing criticism from the religious right who charge the state with imposing politically correct values (see Thomas 1993).

The draft curriculum framework recently approved by the State Board of Education represents a third component of this standards sequence. It further specifies the valued outcomes by providing more examples of what students should be able to do, listed by school level (elementary, middle, and high school); in addition it notes various instructional and assessment strategies, activities across other areas of the curriculum, and ideas for incorporating community resources. Instead of issuing a separate framework for each discipline area, as California and South Carolina do, Kentucky provides a single, comprehensive document of more than 500 pages that attempts to contextualize all its learning goals and valued outcomes within the different subject areas. This is somewhat akin to Vermont's second approach, where skills were organized into the three different disciplinary clusters. Kentucky's framework departs from the literary, narrative style used by California and South Carolina. Rather, following the format of the learning-goals and valued-outcomes documents, the framework lists its points under various headings.

Agenda-setting in Kentucky relies, for the most part, on education professionals throughout each step in the standards sequence. However, an important departure—one that has shaped subsequent efforts—was the Council's decision to go first to the public to help prepare its six learning goals. The Council began its work by holding focus group interviews with business leaders, employers, parents, and educators from around the state; then, based on these responses, the staff developed a telephone survey and interviewed 830 more citizens selected at random. According to the director, the public voiced a clear mandate: make the schools more relevant to work and other after-school life experiences. The specific learning goals were not drafted by lay citizens; this task devolved to drafting committees of educators appointed by the Council. Committee members, however, were reportedly very cognizant of the public mandate. At the end of the process, the Council reconvened the focus groups for feedback on the goals.

When KERA directed the Council to further specify the learning goals, the law designated a similar agenda-setting process by which this was to be accomplished, although it did not require the populist focus group and survey techniques. Again, statewide committees of educators and school administrators were chosen, and again the focus groups were brought together to respond. Once the seventy-five valued outcomes were produced, the Council disbanded. No formal review and feedback process was set up.

The task of developing a curriculum framework based on these valued outcomes went to the Kentucky Department of Education. The Department set up seven writing teams with fifteen professional educators, including an instructional supervisor, teachers, university faculty, and administrators. Like California and South Carolina, Kentucky wanted to make sure that the most competent professionals participated in this task. However, Kentucky has been plagued by a history of nepotism and cronyism (Dove 1991), making it problematic to rely on a reputational, open model of selection. (Indeed, one goal of KERA was to rid the educational system of the persistent problems of nepotism.) Therefore, the KDE used a name-blind application procedure that required individuals to write about various issues pertinent to the educational philosophies undergirding the KERA, such as outcomes-based education. The 450 applications the Department received were scored twice, and the best were then sorted into a representational matrix to ensure geographic and other diversity.

Broad review and feedback on the draft framework was curtailed by budgetary constraints. The KDE distributed 300 copies only to district-level curriculum personnel in regional meetings; they were given priority because the Department views them as the framework's primary audience. However, the Department also set up a curriculum alliance with colleges and universities and professional associations to provide input and feedback on their curricular efforts. Lack of funds for printing has restricted distribution of the final document to one copy per district.

Designing Agenda-Setting Strategies and Standards

States choose agenda-setting strategies for many purposes. Of course, one primary goal is to create well-designed, cutting-edge standards that promote change in the system. For systemic change, the standards must be detailed enough to provide meaningful guidance to the development of other policy instruments, yet flexible enough to allow districts and teachers to pursue alternative pedagogical paths. Another goal of the process is to leverage the legitimacy of the new standards in the eyes of teachers, public interest groups, higher education faculty, and others. Finally, the process has the potential to impact implementation (see Figure 6.2).

The four states described here provide different agenda-setting alternatives. There is, of course, no single set of right answers for how to set up a standard-setting process. Rather, the choices state policymakers make must be responsive to their own array of political interests, policy goals, and linkages. In the next section I will discuss some of the issues that states should consider in developing a strategy for identifying standards. I also will discuss questions about standards design that arise in the course of agenda-setting.

The Populist and Professional Elite Models

Determining who participates and when in the agenda-setting process is a key decision that can effect the balance between two important but often competing goals of the standard-setting process: (1) generating standards that have broad public and professional consensus, and (2) generating cutting-edge standards that can move public education beyond the current status quo. As Deborah Lowenberg Ball wrote of the efforts of the NCTM:

> Twin needs propelled the development of NCTM's standards for schools mathematics: the need to gain consensus and the need to promote change. On the one hand, if these standards were to stand as the banners of the community, then they had to reflect shared values and commitments. On the other hand, if change was desired, then these standards had to do more than reflect current practice. New ideas were needed, ideas that departed from extant assumptions and practices (Ball 1992, pp. 2–3).

Participation is one strategy most relied on for building consensus in public education (Weiler 1981); it builds on our democratic conventional wisdom that direct involvement leads to both better policy outcomes and stronger support. This belief was reflected in the Vermont Department of Education's pamphlet on the Common Core of Learning: "We believe that Vermonters will care about and act on the Common Core of Learning only to the extent that they have had a hand in its design" (Vermont Department of Education 1991). This assumption argues for a more populist and grassroots agenda-setting process.

Another aspect of our conventional wisdom, however, deriving from liberal interest-group politics, is that the broader the participation, the more negotiation and compromise will occur—bargains that in this context may risk diluting decisive leadership that stakes out a position on controversial issues. Certainly this is the tradeoff most clearly perceived by those who attempt to protect the standards process from strong pressure groups and broad public or professional influence during at least the initial stages of standards development. California maximized professional authority over the framework effort until the final stages before the standards were adopted; South Carolina's process is similar save for very broad circulation of its drafts for review and input from the Curriculum Congresses. Kentucky established a mechanism for broad access to the public early on, and then relied on professional groups to elaborate the standards.

The professional elite and populist models both involve a series of benefits and tradeoffs. Various education literature suggests that it is erroneous to assume, as populist approaches often do, that support for reform and implementation will occur *only* with the full participation and early support of everyone impacted (Fullan and Miles 1992; McLaughlin 1991; Fuhrman, Clune, and Elmore 1988). These studies describe how noninvolvement, or even early resistance to reform, was not a barrier to subsequent adoption and support.

Certainly support building does not stop once the standards are adopted. Some stakeholders may not pay full attention until after the standards begin to affect local practices; therefore, support has to be won "foxhole by foxhole," probably even if states pursue the most populist agenda-setting strategy imaginable. In part this is because sustaining grassroots involvement throughout the duration of the developmental process is often difficult; this has been South Carolina's experience with the Curriculum Congress. Most people understand the implications of the standards once they demand change that more directly affects their lives. In California, the history-social science frameworks were adopted by the State Board of Education in 1987, and have won significant backing from state-level interest groups. However, opposition to the materials still emerges in some districts, particularly over the discussion of religion (Massell 1993a).

Although the final products of standard-setting efforts in most instances discussed here are still being reviewed or have not yet been implemented, even the harshest critics would agree that the standards within

California's curriculum frameworks dramatically push beyond the status quo in the different subject-matter areas. Many teachers and curriculum policymakers regard the California frameworks as being at the cutting edge of their respective fields. Further, the structure and composition of these new documents have provided a template for curriculum guidance that others actively promote (see Curry and Temple 1992) and attempt to replicate. In addition, Marsh and Odden's (1991) study of districts and schools that were early, active implementors of the state's new curriculum found that local personnel viewed the frameworks as credible documents, made authoritative and legitimate by the involvement of professional leaders and other subject-matter experts—in short, by the professional elite model of participation.

Of course, restricting involvement in the developmental process risks developing standards that are so far ahead of the field, or so far to one side of professional or public debates, that they are not implemented (Massell 1993b). Again, to use the California history-social science framework as an example, the state has had difficulty convincing many publishers to develop appropriate materials because the framework covers controversial issues like religion. No formal surveys have been done reviewing consensus or awareness of California's frameworks,[7] but other state policymakers looking at the California example have criticized it as exclusionary. Although not a valid statistical sample, a set of well-known studies exploring a small number of teachers' implementation of the mathematics frameworks found that many of them were not aware of the content of the new documents (Darling-Hammond 1990). Even though one cannot generalize from these studies, they did fuel the perception that California teachers were uninformed about the frameworks.

South Carolina's Curriculum Congresses hope to get a head start on developing the kinds of professional networks that have become so vital to building teacher understanding and knowledge for implementation of the California frameworks (see Adams 1992; Lichtenstein, McLaughlin, and Knudsen 1991; and Lieberman and McLaughlin 1992 for research on the efficacy of teacher networks). Together with expanded review and feedback, South Carolina (like Vermont) approaches agenda formation itself as an opportunity for building capacity and understanding.

Indeed, perhaps the strongest argument in favor of a more populist approach in general is that widespread participation can help create an environment more conducive to change. The history of large-scale mathematics, science, and social studies curriculum projects funded by the National Science Foundation forty years ago repeatedly demonstrates the importance of laying the groundwork for change in the wider community.

In these earlier reforms, parents did not understand and school administrators could not defend the curricular reforms they were being asked to make. As a result, these groups placed strong pressure on schools to stay with the older curriculums (Massell 1993c, Carlson 1992). Preparing this environment requires ongoing dialogues and information sharing with diverse communities. It is not an easy task; as Kingdon says: "Getting people to see new problems, or to see old problems in one way rather than another, is a major conceptual and political accomplishment" (Kingdon 1984, p. 121).

Broad professional and public participation, at least at the point of review and feedback, can alert policymakers to where proposed standards will encounter political or practical difficulties. Then policymakers will have to decide whether to resolve the issues by revising the document, or by developing educational or other capacity-building strategies for generating support for different elements once the standards have been adopted. This decision walks the tightrope between consensus and change described by Ball. If controversial elements remain unchanged, policymakers run the risk of the agenda's being ignored (or, worse still, of igniting political battles). Of course, wider reviews open the possibilities for broader criticisms. In any case, reviews may lead to strong pressures to revise the documents in ways that professional leaders or policymakers deem unwise. Thus, the integrity of the process must be protected—states must have the capability of "just saying no" to some of the demands that will be placed on them. Institutional mechanisms that remove agenda-setting from the direct control of politics can help, as can strong leadership. California and Kentucky used participant selection procedures to buffer their frameworks from political bargaining and compromise. In addition, California respondents told of how the active leadership of the superintendent and his staff helped to steer the process through many political battles.

Populist participation at the front end of the process—during standards development—can help bridge the often wide intellectual gap between school and work, one of the major difficulties confronting students' motivations to learn. The traditional curriculum emphasizes abstract rather than applied knowledge (Powell et al. 1985). It is interesting to note that broad lay citizen involvement in both Vermont and Kentucky generated standards with a distinctive and strong vocational orientation, particularly in comparison to California and South Carolina, where professionals had control over the platform of ideas contained in the initial drafts. Determining whether the relationship between process and outcome is a coincidence of my sample, or a more generalizable finding, will require broader research.

These skill-based standards can serve as guideposts for the more technical task of developing curriculum frameworks for the different subject-matter areas, which will require more professional expertise.

Skill and Subject-Matter Focused Standards

A related issue is the question of whether standards should be framed as skills and competencies or as elements identified within the context of particular disciplines. The decision could be consequential for how states address one of the key goals of the new reforms, interdisciplinary learning. Interpretations abound concerning what interdisciplinary knowledge is and how it can best be achieved. Individuals who approach interdisciplinary knowledge as "bridge-building" between relatively firm, independent disciplines often argue that the inquiry skills students learn from traditional academic subjects are a necessary foundation for branching out to other fields. Discipline-based curriculum frameworks with cross-references to other fields of knowledge are appropriate "containers" for this perspective.

Others argue that interdisciplinary efforts should "restructure" knowledge by changing the nature of the disciplines themselves. Some assert that nondisciplinary, skill-based standards provide better opportunities for achieving these new ways of organizing knowledge. Yet without explicit linkage between these skills and academic subjects as they are currently organized, it will be difficult to generate coordinated change in other policy areas. Assessment, teacher certification and training, college-credit requirements, and other policy sectors, as well as school organizations, are traditionally organized by subject-matter areas. Without addressing these constraints in other parts of the system, states that identify only skills and competencies are not likely to see many results. Recognizing this, Kentucky decided to revise its original framework, incorporating all its skill-based learning goals and valued outcomes into subject-matter areas; similar concerns led Vermont to opt for discipline-based curriculum frameworks.

Flexibility in the Agenda-Setting Approach

The efforts to set content guidelines for discipline-based curriculum standards raise many issues unique to the disciplines themselves. Each subject-matter area has a unique topography and history that relates both to the field in general and to its status within particular state contexts. Understanding the internal debates, the interest group politics, the current conditions of practice,[8] and the history of efforts to change the field will help in designing and managing agenda-setting and later capacity-building strategies. States must be prepared to make some modifications in the agenda-setting process to accommodate these differences across fields. For example, California made several addendums to its usual procedures, trying to generate professional consensus in the highly contentious area of history-social science.

In addition, understanding the topography of a field can inform decisions about the sequencing of change. Initiatives should begin with subject-matter areas that already have a high level of national and local consensus. Mathematics provides a logical starting point because of the groundwork already laid by the NCTM. In addition, mathematics does not have the internal divisiveness of many other subject-matter areas with highly competitive subdisciplines, and it does not tend to ignite heated public debates around social issues (Massell 1993c). States should determine where their own professional communities have established a foundation for consensus on standards. One of the first frameworks that South Carolina developed was for performing arts; a long-term project in the state had linked together arts educators for several years. Of course, even in fields where there is relative consensus, debates can and will emerge. But the point is that by beginning where the fields are strongest, the process may move along more smoothly and generate public and professional confidence for subsequent efforts.

Finally, no single format may be appropriate for every field. Although to some extent curriculum documents can and should be shaped by their overall systemic purposes, attempts to formulaically structure documents have led to difficulties. In the early 1980s, California developed an outline that it expected all frameworks to follow. Staff reported that the approach was too constricting for the framework authors, and they eventually abandoned it. Similarly, the National Board of Professional Teaching Standards, which is attempting to establish professional standards in different subject areas, asked each content team to organize around a set of core propositions on "what every teacher should know and be able to do." However, writing committees found these guidelines restrictive and inappropriate to the technical demands of different subject-matter areas, even though they agreed with the core propositions in general terms (Bradley 1992, Pence and Petrosky 1992). States that first set broader, skill-based goals and standards to guide subject-matter frameworks might want to consider these concerns. Formulaic requirements may thwart tailoring the structure, sequence, and design of the document to the unique pedagogical and substantive demands of different discipline areas.

The Rush to Reform

Education reform in the U.S. policy context is remarkable for its attention to new fads and quick fixes. Following this pattern, many states are rushing to develop standards and documents to guide systemic reform. But states err in thinking that consensus and high quality, not to mention implementation, can be so quickly achieved. Finding ways to buffer the endeavor from the short time frames of politics will be important (Fuhrman and Massell 1992, Fuhrman 1993). California takes one to two years to revise each framework, and as we saw, this time period does not include a consensus building process on the front-end of reform. In a more inductive approach, such as the one Vermont has chosen, the agenda-setting process will take even longer. Developing professional consensus takes time (Massell et al. 1993). Furthermore, although California has a relatively long time frame for development and an eight-year cycle of review, implementation at the local level in this time period is difficult; and local district and teacher capacity for change is strained. Even with a staggered review cycle, district curriculum supervisors and elementary teachers must respond to wholesale changes in a different subject area *each* year (Marsh and Odden 1991). Developing the various policy instruments—assessments, staff development, and accountability reviews, among others—can also take time.

As states chart new curriculum reforms, they will confront the ever-present challenges of building consensus for change and constructing meaningful standards. It is clear from this study that agenda-setting strategies and design choices can have significant effects on the quality and shape of the final products, the legitimacy of state leadership, and the translation from policy into practice. Ultimately, states' decisions about how to proceed must take into consideration their own unique political and policy environments, boundary conditions that frame the overall context for change.

Finally, states must recognize that consensus-building is a long-term process that does not end once the agenda has been set. Follow-up strategies must be designed based on the review and feedback received from the various communities. Even when teachers agree with and support the changes, they have not necessarily gained "deep understanding":

> Clearly, deep ownership of something new on the part of large numbers of people is tantamount to real change, but the fact is that ownership is not acquired that easily. And when people are apparently in favor of a particular change, they may not "own it" in the sense of understanding it and being skilled at it, that is, they may not know what they are doing. Ownership in the sense of clarity, skill, and commitment is a progressive process (Fullan, with Stiegelbauer 1991, p. 92).

Although agenda-setting strategies can help leverage consensus, other policy processes and areas are crucial, too. One of the most critical areas, and one that gets short shrift in state policy, is the capacity of local districts and teachers to respond to the high standards. Clearly, professional training and support will be essential to bring these standards reforms to fruition.

Endnotes

[1] The cycle had been seven years, but they recently extended it. Although eight years may seem like a long time frame, it takes between one and a half and two years to revise each document, and then several more years to align the various components of the policy system (textbooks, assessment, etc.) to it. As a result, local educators actually have only a short period when all the pieces are in place before a framework comes up for review again. Further burdens are placed on elementary teachers or district curriculum supervisors who must respond to a new set of standards in a different subject area each year.

[2] On occasion, the state has set up Blue Ribbon task forces prior to convening a framework committee to discuss a particular field, but these have been brief meetings for "brainstorming" purposes. These committees have offered no imperatives that the framework group would be compelled to follow.

[3] Although I do not discuss it here, California is a textbook adoption state; textbooks are selected to match the criteria derived from the frameworks. The adoption of these more detailed standards documents, as it were, provides the public with further say. The State Board of Education and the Curriculum Commission also hold public hearings prior to textbook adoption.

[4] Though this was the department's intent, an observer suggested that at least some focus forum meetings were dominated by local educators. It would take closer empirical analyses to determine how successful the VDE was in their efforts to encourage broad-based involvement.

[5] The Council on School Performance Standards responded to a landmark court ruling that directed the General Assembly to create an "efficient system of common schools." The court defined this as "an organization that provides a free and *adequate* education to all students throughout the state" (*Council for Better Education v. Wilkinson*, No. 85-CI-1759, Franklin Cir. Ct., Oct. 14, 1988; emphasis added). With the phrase "adequate education," the court opened the way for their involvement in the curricular content of schooling.

[6] Although one of the six learning goals makes reference to the academic disciplines, it still strongly emphasizes practicality, (e.g., "Goal 2: Apply core concepts and principles from mathematics, science, social studies, arts and humanities, practical living studies and vocational studies to situations similar to what they will experience in life") (Council on School Performance Standards 1991).

[7] For an example of two studies looking at teachers' awareness of and support for standards, see Weiss (1992) and Zollman and Mason (1992) regarding the NCTM content standards.

[8] For an interesting effort in this regard, see Gehrke, Knapp, and Sirotnik (1992). They review studies on "what schools really teach" in social studies, language arts, mathematics, and science.

References

Adams, J. (1992). "Policy Implementation Through Teacher Professional Networks: The Case of Math A in California." Unpublished doctoral diss., Stanford University.

Ball, D.L. (1992). *Implementing the NCTM Standards: Hopes and Hurdles*. Issue Paper 92-2. East Lansing, Mich.: The National Center for Research on Teacher Learning.

Bradley, A. (June 3, 1992). "Pioneering Board Faces Challenges in Setting Standards for Teachers." *Education Week* 11: 1–16.

California Department of Education. (1988). *Instructional Materials and Framework Adoption: Policies and Procedures*. Sacramento, Calif.: Author.

California Department of Education. (1990). *Science Framework*. Sacramento, Calif.: Author.
Carlson, C.G. (1992). "The Metamorphosis of Mathematics Education." *Focus* 27. Princeton, N.J.: Educational Testing Service.
Cohen, D., and J. Spillane. (1993). "Policy and Practice: The Relations Between Governance and Instruction." In *Designing Coherent Education Policy: Improving the System*, edited by S.H. Fuhrman. San Francisco: Jossey-Bass.
Council on School Performance Standards. (December 1991). *Kentucky's Learning Goals and Valued Outcomes*. Louisville, Ky.: Author.
Curry, B., and T. Temple. (1992). *Using Curriculum Frameworks for Systemic Reform*. Alexandria, Va.: ASCD.
Darling-Hammond, L. (1990). "Instructional Policy into Practice: 'The Power of the Bottom Over the Top.'" *Educational Evaluation and Policy Analysis* 12, 3: 339–347.
Dove, R.G., Jr. (1991). *Acorns in a Mountain Pool: The Role of Litigation, Law, and Lawyers in Kentucky Education Reform*. Lexington, Ky.: The Prichard Committee.
Elmore, R.F., G. Sykes, and J. Spillane. (1992). "Curriculum Policy." In *Handbook of Research on Curriculum*, edited by P. Jackson. New York: Macmillan.
Firestone, W.A., S. Rosenblum, B.D. Bader, and D. Massell. (December 1991). *Education Reform from 1983 to 1990: State Action and District Response*. Research Report Series RR-021. New Brunswick, N.J.: Consortium for Policy Research in Education.
Fuhrman, S.F., ed. (1993) "The Politics of Coherence." In *Designing Coherent Education Policy: Improving the System*, edited by S.H. Fuhrman. San Francisco: Jossey-Bass.
Fuhrman, S.H., W. Clune, and R. Elmore. (1988). "Research on Education Reform: Lessons on the Implementation of Policy." *Teachers College Record* 90, 2: 237–258.
Fuhrman, S.H., D. Massell, and Associates. (June 1992). *Issues and Strategies in Systemic Reform*. New Brunswick, N.J.: Consortium for Policy Research in Education.
Fullan, M.G., with S. Stiegelbauer. (1991). *The New Meaning of Educational Change*. New York: Teachers College Press.
Gehrke, N.J., M.S. Knapp, and K.A. Sirotnik. (1992). "In Search of the School Curriculum." In *Review of Research in Education*, edited by G. Grant. Washington, D.C.: American Educational Research Association.
Hoffmeister, A.M. (in press). "Elitism and Reform in School Mathematics." *Journal of Remedial and Special Education*.
Kingdon, J.W. (1984). *Agendas, Alternatives and Public Policies*. Boston: Little, Brown.
Lichtenstein, G., M.W. McLaughlin, and J. Knudsen. (in press). "Teacher Empowerment and Professional Knowledge." In *The Changing Context of Teaching: 91st NSSE Yearbook, Part II*, edited by A. Lieberman. Chicago: National Society for the Study of Education, University of Chicago Press.
Lieberman, A., and M.W. McLaughlin. (May 1992). "Networks for Educational Change: Powerful and Problematic." *Phi Delta Kappan* 73, 9: 673–677.
Marsh, D.D., and A.R. Odden. (1991). "Implementation of the California Mathematics and Science Curriculum Frameworks." In *Education Policy Implementation*, edited by A.R. Odden. Albany: State University of New York Press.
Massell, D. (1993a) "California and New York History-Social Studies Case Study." In *Formulating Content Standards: Case Studies and Implications for National Content Standards*, edited by D. Massell, M.W. Kirst, C. Kelley, and G. Yee. Washington, D.C.: National Education Goals Panel.
Massell, D. (1993b) "Observations from the Cases and Implications for National Content Standards." In *Formulating Content Standards: Case Studies and*

Implications for National Content Standards, edited by D. Massell, M.W. Kirst, C. Kelley, and G. Yee. Washington, D.C.: National Education Goals Panel.

Massell, D. (1993c). "National Council of Teachers of Mathematics Case Study, with References to the 'New Math.'" In *Formulating Content Standards: Case Studies and Implications for National Content Standards*, edited by D. Massell, M.W. Kirst, C. Kelley, and G. Yee. Washington, D.C.: National Education Goals Panel.

Massell, D., M.W. Kirst, C. Kelley, and G. Yee. (1993). *Formulating Content Standards: Case Studies and Implications for National Content Standards*. Washington, D.C.: National Education Goals Panel.

McLaughlin, M.W. (1991). "The Rand Change Agent Study: Ten Years Later. In *Education Policy Implementation*, edited by A.R. Odden. Albany: State University of New York Press.

Murphy, J. (1990). "The Educational Reform Movement of the 1980s: A Comprehensive Analysis." In *The Educational Reform Movement of the 1980s: Perspectives and Cases*, edited by J. Murphy. Berkeley, Calif.: McCutchan.

National Commission on Excellence in Education. (1983). *A Nation at Risk: The Imperative for Educational Reform*. Washington, D.C.: Author.

National Council on Education Standards and Testing. (January 24, 1992). *Raising Standards for American Education*. Washington, D.C.: Author.

Pechman, E.M., and K.G. Laguarda. (1993). *Status of New State Curriculum Frameworks, Standards, Assessments, and Monitoring Systems*. Prepared for the U.S. Department of Education. Washington, D.C.: Policy Studies Associates.

Pence, P., and A. Petrosky. (1992). "Defining Performance Standards and Developing an Assessment for Accomplished English Language Arts Teaching of Young Adolescents." Paper presented at the annual meeting of The National Council on Measurement in Education, San Francisco.

Powell, A.G., E. Farrar, and D.K. Cohen. (1985). *The Shopping Mall High School: Winners and Losers in the Educational Marketplace*. Boston: Houghton Mifflin.

Smith, M.S., and J. O'Day. (1991). "Systemic School Reform." In *The Politics of Curriculum and Testing*, edited by S.H. Fuhrman and B. Malen. Bristol, Pa.: Falmer Press.

Thomas, J.A. (May 21, 1993). "Eagle Forum Opening Fire Against KERA." *The Mayfield Messenger*, p. 1.

Vermont Department of Education. (1991). *Vermont Common Core of Learning Update*. Burlington, Vt.: Author.

Vermont Department of Education. (March 1992). *Report 1: Is This Really What Learners Need to Know?* Montpelier, Vt.: Author.

Walker, D. (1990). *Fundamentals of Curriculum*. Saddlebrook, N.J.: Harcourt, Brace, Jovanovich.

Weiler, H. (1981). *Compensatory Legitimation in Educational Policy: Legalization, Expertise, and Participation in Comparative Perspective*. Project Report No. 81-A17. Stanford, Calif.: Stanford School of Education (published by the former Institute for Research on Educational Finance and Governance.)

Weiss, I. (1992). *The Road to Reform in Mathematics Education: How far Have We Traveled?* Arlington, Va.: National Council of Teachers of Mathematics.

Zollman, A., and E. Mason. (November 1992). "The Standards Beliefs Instrument (SBI): Teachers' Beliefs about the NCTM Standards." *School Science and Mathematics* 92, 7: 359–363.

7

Systemic School Reform: The Challenges Faced by State Departments of Education

Susan Follett Lusi

Many states across the United States, including California, Kentucky, New York, Texas, and Vermont, are currently engaged in what is termed "systemic school reform." The intent is to increase the coherence and alignment of the state education system to "support school-site efforts to improve classroom instruction and learning" (Smith and O'Day 1991, p. 233). The goal of systemic school reform is that all students be taught and learn ambitious content knowledge and higher-order skills.

State departments of education (SDEs) are key players in these state-level education reforms, responsible for fleshing out and implementing policies passed by legislatures and, in some cases, for shaping the reform agenda. The ability of SDEs to meet the challenges of ensuring policy coherence and implementing policy so as to support school-site efforts to redesign teaching and learning will in large part determine the success or failure of this reform.

I argue that systemic school reform presents SDEs with challenges very different from those of earlier state-level reforms. These new challenges exist because successful systemic school reform requires SDEs to fundamentally alter both their external and internal working relationships. I will illuminate the nature of these new working relationships, particularly the external relationships between the SDE and schools and districts and the internal relationships of the agency, by contrasting them with the working

---

Author's Note: Many thanks to Richard F. Elmore, Michael Barzelay, and Mary Jo Bane for their helpful comments on this chapter. Thanks also to the Innovations in State and Local Government program of the Ford Foundation and the Kennedy School of Government for their generous support of my dissertation research, of which this chapter is a part.

relationships of traditional SDEs. In building this contrast, I have drawn on the literatures of school reform, public management, and innovation, as well as from my preliminary field work in the states of Vermont and Kentucky, and my own experience working with schools engaged in reform.

The Shift in Policy Regimes

The current policy regime, exemplified by the state-level reforms of the 1980s and earlier, has been characterized by a disconnected, piecemeal approach to education reform (Cohen and Spillane 1992, Smith and O'Day 1990). Existing policies in one area of education (what I call component policies) have frequently undermined attempts at improvement in other areas. For example, when numerous states increased graduation requirements in the 1980s with the goal of increasing student achievement, little attention was paid to the fact that a suitable curriculum did not exist for the new courses, nor to the fact that many teachers lacked the prerequisite skills and knowledge to teach such a curriculum if it did exist (Clune with White and Patterson 1989).

Perceived problems in education were addressed with relatively "quick fix" solutions, using existing technologies and administrative arrangements that were available and familiar to SDEs and schools (Firestone, Fuhrman, and Kirst 1989). These solutions, while answering the short-term political need to address the problem, did not necessarily meet the larger stated goal of improving student achievement. For example, student testing increased throughout the 1980s with the intent of making schools more accountable for student achievement, but the tests assessed basic skills and discrete factual knowledge, rather than the complex skills that states, business leaders, and educational reformers said were required of today's students.

In addition, there was no careful examination of the additive effects of the policy regime on schools (Cohen and Spillane 1992). For example, states frequently ranked schools based on student test scores, providing no incentives to teach higher-order thinking skills and ambitious content knowledge because this was not what the tests measured. Nor did teacher testing, which also measures basic skills, give teachers incentives to rethink and redesign their teaching. The additive effects of the policy regime did not support or encourage schools to strive for the teaching and learning of ambitious content knowledge, even though the need for this kind of teaching and learning was commonly espoused.[1]

Overall, the 1980s education reforms, characteristic of the current policy regime, left the nature of teaching and learning unchanged and did not bring about the anticipated dramatic improvements in student achievement (Cohen 1988, Cuban 1990, Firestone et al. 1989). These facts have persuaded some researchers that a new policy regime is needed to bring about the desired level of student achievement (Smith and O'Day 1991).

The Differences

Systemic school reform differs from the reform attempts of the previous policy regime in at least two important ways. First, systemic school reform strives to reform education *as a system*, working for coherence across the component policies, something that the piecemeal reforms of the past did not achieve. When a component policy is designed to promote reform in one area, the component policies in other areas must be aligned with and supportive of this new policy. For example, if the SDE chooses to promote the teaching and learning of ambitious content knowledge and higher-order skills through the development of curriculum frameworks, state assessments must also be redesigned to measure achievement on the knowledge and skills outlined in the frameworks, and teachers must receive the preparation necessary to teach the skills and knowledge in ways that will enable students to learn them.

Second, systemic school reform explicitly strives to support school-site efforts at redesigning teaching and learning with the goal that all students will learn ambitious content knowledge and higher-order skills. Promulgating mandates such as increased graduation requirements from the "top" of the education system (the state) is insufficient. The "bottom" of the system (schools and districts) must be supported and activated to transform teaching and learning. This means that the additive effects of the new policy regime on schools will have to be carefully examined. Policies that do not both require and support schools to fundamentally redesign practice are both counterproductive to the goals of systemic reform.

The Challenges

SDEs will be key players in leading and managing this shift in policy regimes. This kind of far-reaching, intensive change has never before been attempted in the history of education reform. It is not clear how, or indeed if, this kind of reform can be realized. The SDE alone, however, cannot bring about successful implementation. Schools will clearly play a primary role in redesigning teaching and learning, and the SDE will have to work with other external constituencies (e.g., the legislature, business, and universities) to design a coherent policy system that will promote and support these efforts in schools. Successful systemic school reform will require bringing together the collective knowledge and capacity of numerous players in the system.

Bringing about this joint effort and accomplishing this collective work will require the SDE to alter its working relationships both internally and externally. I focus here on two categories—the internal working relationships within the SDE and the external relationships with schools and districts. These working relationships are the most instrumental in changing the core processes of teaching and learning in schools. Changes in other external relationships, such as those between the SDE and the legislature, other agencies in the executive branch, the public, and other constituencies, although equally necessary to the ultimate success of systemic school reform, are less directly instrumental in changing teaching and learning.

The External Working Relationship

The working relationship between SDEs and schools engaged in systemic school reform will need to change along three dimensions: the mission of the SDE, the mechanisms used by the SDE, and the underlying assumptions of the SDE.

The following discussion contrasts the working relationships of traditional SDEs with those engaged in systemic reform to illustrate the differences. In reality, however, it may be that many SDEs are engaged in working relationships that range along a spectrum from purely traditional to purely systemic. Many SDEs may be in the process of changing some aspects of their working relationships, while other aspects remain quite traditional. The description of the traditional working relationship between SDEs and schools relies heavily on a dated (1967) study by Campbell, Sroufe, and Layton. Determining how the SDEs in this 1967 study compare to SDEs today is difficult, since no recent study gives an account of SDE activities in similar detail. An examination of the more recent, albeit limited, sources available leads to the conclusion that while some aspects of SDE activity have changed and are changing, much has also remained the same. Mission statements are one example of such activity.

Mission Statements

The mission of SDEs engaged in systemic school reform will need to shift in focus from regulating compliance in schools to transforming the education system. The mission of traditional SDEs is one of:

> 1. *Advis[ing]* state government on the conditions which government should require and should expect to prevail within the statewide educational system, and on the public policies, priorities, standards, criteria, and actions needed to produce those conditions. . . .

2. *Ascertain[ing]* whether the conditions stipulated by state government actually are being met in each school, school system, or other entity within the state education agency's purview. . . .

3. *Assur[ing]*, by taking suitable actions, that unsatisfactory conditions are corrected wherever and whenever they are found to exist (Friedman 1971, pp. 16–17).

The mission of SDEs engaged in systemic school reform will instead read something like the mission statements of the SDEs in Vermont and Kentucky. The mission statement of the Vermont SDE begins:

> Our mission is to lead and support educational transformation in a continuously improving education system.
>
> We work as a partner with educational leaders and local decision-making teams to ensure that every student becomes a competent, caring, productive, responsible individual and citizen who is committed to continued learning throughout life (Vermont Department of Education 1991).

And the mission statement of the Kentucky SDE reads:

> The mission of the Kentucky Department of Education, as the national catalyst for educational transformation, is to ensure for each child an internationally superior education and a love of learning through visionary leadership, vigorous stewardship, and exemplary services in alliance with schools, school districts, and other partners (Kentucky Department of Education 1991).

Mechanisms

Fulfilling the traditional mission requires establishing a predominantly regulatory relationship with schools—setting regulations for schools to follow, ensuring that schools comply with those regulations, and assisting them in meeting the regulations when needed. The predominate mechanisms used to shape this traditional relationship are consequently regulation and, to a lesser extent, incentives and service.

Traditionally, schools are regulated through the activities of review and supervision (Sroufe 1967). Teachers' credentials—primarily their transcripts and sometimes their test scores—must be reviewed before a teaching license is granted. School reports are also reviewed. These reports include information such as the numbers and kinds of courses offered in the school and the hours devoted to each subject area.

SDEs continue to credential teachers. According to a 1983 Council of Chief State School Officers (CCSSO) report based on a 50-state survey:

> States exercise authority over the certification of teachers by either reviewing the credentials of individual candidates to see that specific certification regulations are met, or by approving collegiate programs of preparation. Most states do both (CCSSO 1983, p. 111).

SDEs also continue to regulate schools' instructional programs and accredit them (Campbell, Cunningham, Nystrand, and Usdan 1985, pp. 65–69; CCSSO 1983, p. 47; Murphy 1974, p. 5).

Supervision is traditionally accomplished through on-site visitation. "Supervisory visits, although often required by law, do provide an opportunity to discuss the appropriateness of procedural regulations or minimum standards and to use methods other than sanctions to secure adequate performance" (Sroufe 1967, p. 20). During these visits, which occur for the enforcement of such regulations as state school accreditation laws, SDE staff examine numerous aspects of school facilities and programs. According to Sroufe, however, the use of supervision is limited because of the small number of SDE staff and the large number of schools. Accreditation, for example, may take place only every three or four years.

There is some evidence, however, that while states via SDEs continue to regulate schools, they are beginning to move away from the traditional regulation of inputs—number of books and minutes of instruction, for example—and processes—teacher certification, for example. Some states are using different types of deregulation, ranging from rule-by-rule waivers to blanket deregulation, and are beginning to focus their regulation on outcomes as opposed to inputs and processes (Consortium for Policy Research in Education 1992). States are also beginning to apply new forms of differential treatment to school districts as part of this movement toward deregulation and a focus on outputs. These newer forms of differential treatment include performance-based accreditation, rewards and sanctions related to performance levels, targeted assistance to low-performing districts, and flexibility to support innovation (Fuhrman and Fry 1989).

SDEs have also used incentives (money and sometimes services) as a mechanism to bring about desired activities in schools. In these instances, incentives are awarded to schools that meet the criteria specified by the SDE (and in some cases, the federal government). Examples of such incentive-based activities are SDE-run programs that award grants and assistance to schools that propose the most innovative plans for school restructuring, such as the Carnegie Schools program in Massachusetts and the Reinventing Vermont Schools program in Vermont.

Traditional SDEs also provide service as a mechanism for encouraging desired behaviors in schools and districts and helping them improve. Examples of SDE service activities include "curriculum consultation, preparation of materials for educational media . . . statistical dissemination, school surveys and related activities, legal reports and advice, and research dissemination activities" (Layton 1967, p. 13). The goal of the majority of service provision is improving instruction, however, and subject matter consultants are the SDEs' "staple" of service (Sroufe 1967, p. 21). Subject matter consultants have discipline-based specialties (e.g., English, math, and science) and generally provide service at the request of an individual or group at a school through on-site visitations (Sroufe 1967). A science teacher may request that the SDE science consultant spend a few hours in her classroom, for example, observing and giving feedback on how she is implementing a new state-recommended science curriculum. Visitations are again limited in their effectiveness:

> It makes little sense for professional personnel to define their role primarily in terms of visitation to the schools, as did most of those we interviewed. There are simply too many schools, too many teachers, and too few qualified personnel. How effective can a two-hour visit once a year by a subject matter consultant be? (Campbell and Sroufe 1967, p. 85).

SDEs continue to provide a variety of services to schools and districts, including "statewide reports, inservice training, planning assistance and curriculum guides and advice" (CCSSO 1983, p. 47). The evidence on the current role of subject matter specialists and how departments approach professional development in general is mixed. Murphy (1974) found that change was coming slowly, if at all, in the use of specialists, in his study of SDE responses to Title V. In Massachusetts, although a variety of new types of SDE positions were called for in the state's Title V proposal, only positions for subject matter specialists were filled. And in South Carolina:

> There are ... some signs of resistance to change. For example, top departmental officials talk[ed] about shifting consultative services away from individual school visitations toward the provision of school district leadership through SEA [State Education Agency] meetings and regional workshops. Undoubtedly there are now fewer school visitations than six years ago, but more continue to take place than the departmental rhetoric implies. Many consultants are reluctant to give up the face-to-face meetings with individual teachers and children, and they persist in maintaining long-established procedures (Murphy 1974, p. 102).

More recent evidence also shows that subject matter specialists continue to visit schools for the purposes of supervision and service, and that these visits have become, if anything, more regulatory in nature. Dowling and Yager (1983), in their national survey of state science consultants, found that "local consul[t]ation was the[ir] primary activity [taking nearly 30 percent of their time] with writing or developing programs second [taking 20 percent of their time]" (p. 774). The written materials developed were probably disseminated during the local consultations, according to the authors. They further found that the job of science consultant had become more regulatory in nature, changing "from a supportive consultant role to a directive supervisory role.... The position of state science supervisor has changed to become not as responsive to local need, not as flexible, not as developmental" (p. 774).

Some SDEs have regionalized their professional development and training activities. California, for example, has fifty-eight county offices of education (Little, Gerritz, Stern, Guthrie, Kirst, and Marsh 1987, p. 47), and Kentucky has recently established eight Regional Service Centers. The state role in professional development is probably changing slowly. Little and others (1987) found that while some California initiatives "exemplif[ied] the state's attempt to develop or support professional development that advances the professionalization of the teaching occupation and of the school as an institution" (p. 62), the majority of "California's staff development resources are spent in ways that . . . reinforce existing patterns of teaching, conventional structures of schools, and long-standing traditions of the teaching occupation" (p. 61, emphasis deleted). Again, SDE approaches to professional development and service provision in general probably range along a spectrum from traditional to systemic.

Assumptions

In addition to the changed mission and mechanisms, the assumptions that underlie the working relationship between SDEs and schools will also change. The traditional working relationship between SDEs and schools is grounded in a number of implicit assumptions. The SDE is positioned as the purveyor of answers. In the 1980s, SDEs (and legislatures) assumed that

- they knew what the problem was in schools—low student achievement;
- they knew how to solve the problem—mandate improved academic inputs; and
- they had the capacity to implement these solutions.

Policies were designed according to these fairly simplistic problem and solution definitions. It was assumed that the answer to improving student achievement was to have schools teach more academic courses and hire more competent teachers. It was further assumed that state-level mandates of increased graduation requirements and teacher testing were the technology necessary to bring these changes about, and that SDEs had the capacity to enforce these mandates. The second and third assumptions were at least partially correct—the state did have the technology and capacity to require increased graduation requirements and teacher testing. It is questionable, however, that increased graduation requirements and teacher testing were the correct solutions to the problem of low student achievement because the desired improvements did not occur.

Systemic school reform calls these simplistic problem-solution definitions into question. Although the broad problem is still low student achievement, the nature of schools and the policy context that creates this problem necessitate closer examination. The solutions to these problems will be achieved through the joint work of SDEs and local schools and districts.

Consequently, the working relationship between SDEs engaged in systemic school reform and schools is predicated on the assumptions that the state cannot precisely identify what schools need to be doing to bring about the desired student achievement, and further, because improving student achievement in the desired ways would seem to require changing the nature of teaching and learning in classrooms, the state does not have the technology and capacity to ensure that schools do what they should be doing. Whereas SDEs may know something about the direction of the desired changes in schools, neither they nor anyone else knows exactly what these changes entail, or how they can be brought about in a systematic fashion. This level of uncertainty about what schools need to be doing and how to bring these activities about leads to the conclusion that schools must take charge in planning and managing their own change.

Promoting and Supporting School Change

The questions for SDEs then become how best to promote and support schools' quest for solutions to the problem of ensuring that *all* students learn ambitious content knowledge and higher-order skills, and also how best to ensure that these learning outcomes are achieved in *all* schools. Reasoning through this problem, and looking at state efforts at improving schools both past and present, it would seem that SDEs could use some combination of at least five different mechanisms to promote and support this work in schools.[2] It should be noted that some states are already using or beginning to use different combinations of these mechanisms. Because many of these state efforts are relatively new, however, the capacity of SDEs to realize these efforts remains to be proven. The five mechanisms are as follows:

1. SDEs could provide incentives such as monetary grants, assistance, and reduction of regulatory burdens to encourage the planning and implementation of reform. For example, grants, assistance, and regulatory waivers might be awarded to schools to help implement school restructuring plans, developed through a schoolwide planning process, that were clearly linked to improving student achievement in the desired ways. The possibility of earning such awards would give schools the incentive to engage in

the planning process and would give them further support during the implementation phase.

2. SDEs could contribute knowledge to the school-change process, in the form of curriculum frameworks, syntheses of current research, and publications distilling learnings from successful and unsuccessful change efforts. Much of this knowledge, although disseminated through the SDE, will probably come from the field or from a combination of field and SDE expertise. Kentucky's curriculum framework and Vermont's Common Core of Learning, for example, are products of the joint work and expertise of practitioners and SDE staff.

3. SDEs could focus schools' attention on the desired learning outcomes and provide them with information on how well they are achieving those outcomes through meaningful state assessment. A meaningful assessment system would measure students' ability to solve problems and perform tasks at the envisioned achievement level, providing useful information to teachers and schools.[3] Having such a system in place becomes of paramount importance if the SDE wishes to hold schools accountable for student outcomes, rather than for credit hours, number of books, number of certified teachers, and so forth. The definition and development of meaningful assessments will again probably be a joint effort of SDE staff and practitioners. The majority of the assessment system used in Vermont, for example, was practitioner designed.

4. SDEs could provide assistance to schools attempting to redesign their programs to improve student learning. Systemic school reform requires dramatic change in schools. The nature of schools' redesign task is uncertain; and schools are trying to achieve outcomes (ambitious teaching and learning) that they have not achieved on any broad scale in the past. For all these reasons, assistance from SDE staff and other outsiders will probably be needed.

An important task for the SDE, then, would be to ensure that the high-quality assistance that is needed is available and accessible to all schools. "Effective assistance is intense, relevant to local needs, varied, and sustained" (Louis and Miles 1990). Any assistance would need to focus on building capacity for assistance provision within schools and districts because SDEs will still be faced with the problem of a limited number of personnel serving a large number of schools. Such assistance might include ongoing professional development specifically directed to a site's questions and issues.

Assistance might also include on-site visitations, but these visits would probably be directed at the particular needs of the school as a whole, because assistance directed at one or two individuals in a school has long been judged ineffective (Campbell and Sroufe 1967). This assistance would also probably differ markedly in both intent and tone from the subject area assistance that is provided by traditional SDEs. Because SDEs cannot know exactly what schools need to do to bring about the desired level of student achievement, SDE staff will not be able to visit schools and tell them how to achieve these goals. Alternative approaches will be needed.

One alternative approach would be for SDE staff or others to support and push schools' work by asking meaningful questions and by helping people in schools to ask those questions themselves and to search for answers. SDE staff would play the role of "critical friend"[4]—a knowledgeable outsider who can ask the crucial questions and help schools find the answers. The critical friend can see potential problems and upcoming challenges, bringing a new perspective and a certain distance to the issues at hand. Examples of questions that a critical friend might ask and help schools search for answers to include: What are we trying to accomplish in this school? What are the student outcomes we care about? How successful are we at helping students achieve these outcomes? What needs to be changed to improve our success in this area? How can we find the answers to these questions? How will we know if the changes we make have been successful?[5]

Working in this way with schools would place SDEs engaged in systemic school reform in the role of askers of questions, as opposed to purveyors of answers. It could also promote joint learning, as SDE staff and school personnel share their expertise and observations.

5. SDEs could regulate schools to some degree.[6] Systemic school reform implies that the regulation of inputs will be substantially reduced and perhaps eliminated, replaced instead by assessment systems that hold *schools* accountable for student achievement. Even with such a system in place however, questions may still exist about programmatic adequacy and equity—Are all students given an equal opportunity to learn ambitious content knowledge and skills? and Are all schools encouraging their students to excel at similar levels?[7]

In considering the changes required in the external working relationship between schools and SDEs engaged in systemic school reform, as outlined here, it is worthwhile to ask how much SDEs can be expected to accomplish by themselves, and how much they should or could rely on other groups or institutions. As stated earlier, it is clear that SDEs cannot successfully implement systemic school reform alone. Instead, success will depend on the collective knowledge and capacity of numerous players in the system.

How SDEs and other players divide that work will doubtless vary from state to state. That SDEs recognize the need and value of dividing the work is demonstrated by the efforts in Vermont and Kentucky. The curriculum and assessment efforts in both states have been shaped through strong practitioner participation. Staff in both states talk about building capacity in schools and districts so that localities are able to do their own training. Both states also rely on outside groups—universities, consortia, and so forth—to provide assistance and training to schools, sometimes by themselves, and sometimes working in conjunction with the SDE.

Other pieces of the work of systemic reform may also be shared with or given to other institutions or agencies. Kentucky's Office of Education Accountability, located in the Legislative Research Commission, for example, monitors the implementation of Kentucky's education reforms. Indeed, other entities may be created to take on some of the new work required of SDEs engaged in systemic reform.

These changes in the mission, mechanisms, and assumptions that underlie the relationship between SDEs and schools have broad implications for how SDE staff think about and conduct their work both with schools and within the agency itself. In the next section, I turn to the implications of systemic school reform for the internal working relationships of SDEs.

Internal Working Relationships of SDEs

The traditional work of SDEs is largely well understood, predictable, and routine. SDE staff know how to license teachers and regulate schools, and they have well-established mechanisms for doing so. As SDEs engage in systemic school reform, however, the nature of their work will change. The work demanded of SDE employees is more akin to innovation—work that is uncertain and knowledge-intensive and for which there is a steep learning curve (Kanter 1988). States have never before succeeded in establishing coherent policy systems that promote and support the redesign of teaching and learning in schools so that all students learn ambitious content knowledge. Neither SDE staff nor anyone else knows how to accomplish this work.

Performing work of an uncertain nature requires continual, collaborative learning. SDE staff will be striving to build what Senge (1990) terms a "learning organization"—an organization in which generative learning occurs—learning that goes beyond what individuals by themselves can create.

For this ongoing learning to occur, the internal working relationships of SDEs will need to change along three dimensions: the structures, mechanisms, and norms that govern the relationships.

As in the preceding discussion of SDE external working relationships, I will contrast the internal working relationships of traditional SDEs to those engaged in systemic reform to illustrate the differences between the two sets of relationships. In reality, SDEs may have changed or be in the process of changing some of these internal working relationships. Because there is no recent literature (and little past literature) on the subject, much of this discussion draws inferences about SDEs from the traditional literature on bureaucracy. These inferences seem to ring largely true from my own work in SDEs, but may or may not accurately characterize individual departments.

Structures and Mechanisms

The "well understood, predictable, routine, and repetitive" work of traditional SDEs is well suited to bureaucratic structures and mechanisms (Perrow 1986, p. 142). The traditional SDE structure is hierarchical, headed by the chief state school officer, and generally includes some combination of deputy commissioners, associate commissioners who head offices, directors who head divisions, professional staff who man each division, and support staff. The number of layers in the hierarchy varies according to the size of the given SDE, but generally follows this, or a similar pattern (CCSSO 1983, Appendix B).

The working relationships of SDEs are further shaped by the mechanisms of clear divisions of labor, rules that govern employee actions, and movement of information up and down, as opposed to across the hierarchy. Roles and responsibilities are clearly assigned to divisions, offices, and individuals in SDEs. For example, in a representative state, the Division of Instruction is responsible for all instruction-related programs and activities; the Office of Curriculum Services, within the Division of Instruction, is responsible for providing curriculum-related services; and Curriculum Specialists, who work in the Office of Curriculum Services, are responsible for visiting and assisting teachers in schools.

Rules govern the actions of SDE employees. The Director of Chapter 1 knows the reporting requirements of the federal government and is obliged to follow them. The director of a grants awarding program knows that certain procedures must be followed before monies can be awarded to schools. An employee in Certification knows that an applicant must properly complete all forms, take and pass all required exams, and fulfill all course requirements before the department can award a teaching license.

The Director of Personnel knows that the rules of the state personnel system must be followed in the hiring of any new employees. Managers see to it that employees follow the appropriate rules and procedures, instead of judging employee performance according to outcomes.[8]

Information in SDEs moves up and down, as opposed to across the hierarchy. The bureaucratic structure of traditional SDEs neither encourages nor requires communication across the various offices. Each office has its specified domain and the authority to act within that domain. Superiors must be apprised of and condone the activities of an office, but there is no parallel responsibility or need to inform other offices in the organization.[9,10]

Traditional SDEs are "segmented" organizations:

> [There are] a large number of compartments walled off from one another ... [and] only the minimum number of exchanges takes place at the boundaries of [the] segments. . . . Segmentalism assumes that problems can be solved when they are carved into pieces and the pieces assigned to specialists who work in isolation (Kanter 1983, p. 28).

Traditional SDE structure and mechanisms do not encourage cross-office initiatives. The work of each office is largely self-contained.

Implementing systemic school reform will require work and learning that spans the boundaries of traditional SDEs. Consequently, the structure and mechanisms of SDEs engaged in systemic school reform will need to change in ways that make SDEs more closely resemble organizations that encourage and support innovative work.

Innovative work is best supported by structures—either formal or informal—that differ substantially from those of a typical bureaucracy:

> Integrative thinking that actively embraces change is more likely in companies whose cultures and structures are also integrative, encouraging the treatment of problems as "wholes," considering the wider implications of actions. Such organizations reduce rancorous conflict and isolation between organizational units; create mechanisms for exchange of information and new ideas across organizational boundaries; ensure that multiple perspectives will be taken into account in decisions; and provide coherence and direction to the whole organization. In these team-oriented cooperative environments, innovation flourishes (Kanter 1983, p. 28).

SDEs engaged in systemic school reform will consequently need to develop structures that are more team-oriented and less hierarchical. Working in teams facilitates the free exchange of information and brings the expertise of numerous individuals to bear on given problems (Kanter 1983). A structure that facilitates teaming may or may not be reflected in the formal organizational chart. In Vermont, for example, the SDE has restructured so that all work is done by three different types of teams. Home teams address certain responsibilities (e.g., Teaching and Learning, Student and Family Support, Core Services) and share a mission and primary customer (Vermont Department of Education 1992). "Initiative teams [drawing members from more than one home team] are focussed on a specific part of the [department's] strategic plan, [such as developing the Common Core of Learning]" (Vermont Department of Education 1992). Project teams focus on short-term tasks that none of the home or initiative teams is equipped to do. Conversely, the revised organizational chart of Kentucky remains hierarchical in structure, but the SDE is developing cross-cutting teams that work on various initiatives. For example, the staffs of the Office of Assessment and the Division of Curriculum Development collaborate as they develop Kentucky's assessment system and curriculum frameworks. Both organizations have the potential for establishing the necessary structures for change-oriented work.

In either case, however, flattening the hierarchy in practice will facilitate the uncertain work of SDEs engaged in systemic school reform:

> The greater the degree of uncertainty regarding the bureau's activities, the flatter its hierarchy is likely to be. When uncertainty prevails, potential relationships among the possible components of a task cannot be foreseen accurately. Hence the task cannot be divided into many parts assigned to specialists unless the specialists are in constant communication with each other and can continually redefine their relationships as they gain more knowledge. This requirement is best served by a flat hierarchy, since it provides greater authority to each official and allows greater emphasis upon direct horizontal relationships. These factors are essential because:
>
> 1. Each official must be free to coordinate directly with a great many others in unpredictable ways, so formal channels cannot be set up in advance.
> 2. The need for dialogues among officials and for constant redefining of tasks makes working through intermediaries inefficient.
> 3. Communications among officials who have about the same status are less likely to be inhibited than those among officials on different levels.
> 4. Coping with highly uncertain tasks requires very talented specialists who can be retained in the organization only if they are given relatively high status and responsible positions incompatible with a many-level hierarchy.
> 5. Talented specialists working under novel conditions often know much more than their supervisors about how to coordinate their activities (Downs 1967, pp. 57–58).

The mechanisms that guide the internal work of SDEs will also change. Because it is uncertain exactly what SDEs need to do to bring about systemic school reform, a high premium will be placed on idea generation and learning.

> Idea generation is . . . aided when jobs are defined broadly rather than narrowly, when people have a range of skills to use and tasks to perform to give them a view of the whole organization, and when assignments focus on results to be achieved rather than rules or procedures to be followed (Kanter 1988, p. 179).

Implementation of systemic school reform must be accomplished through thoughtful "groping along"—making intelligent adjustments along the way as desired actions become clearer.[11]

These approaches to work and implementation imply that SDE staff will need flexibility and autonomy in their work. It will be impossible to predict in advance the actions needed to bring about desired outcomes, and hence to govern their actions and judge their performance based on adherence to rules. The actions of SDE staff will instead have to be governed by a shared set of beliefs, values, and purpose. Whether this set of shared understandings is called *vision* (Senge 1990), *mission* (Wilson 1989), or *culture* (Burns and Stalker 1961), it is clearly important for guiding people's actions in situations where these actions cannot be carefully prescribed. "Shared vision fosters risk taking and experimentation," as well as commitment to the long term (Senge 1990, p. 209). A sense of mission "permits the head of the agency to be more confident that operators will act in particular cases in ways that the head would have acted had he or she been in their shoes" (Wilson 1989, p. 109). And, as in innovative firms in which non-routine decision making is the norm, SDEs in the throes of change

> have to rely on the development of a "common culture," of a dependably constant system of shared beliefs about the common interests of the working community and about the standards and criteria used in it to judge achievement, individual contributions, expertise, and other matters by which a person or a combination of people are evaluated (Burns and Stalker 1961, p. 119).

Shared understandings enable employees to work in concert and to pull and push in the same direction, even if their roles and tasks are ambiguous.

If people's roles and tasks are ambiguous, and they are expected to act on a set of shared beliefs, values, and purpose that permeates the organization, it seems reasonable that they must also be given the power to act. Giving everyone in the organization the power to act implies that information and resources must be widely shared, as opposed to located only in the upper levels of the hierarchy. SDE employees must flexibly respond to needs as they arise. Flexible response is enabled by the wide availability of what Kanter (1983) terms "power tools"—information, resources, and support. According to Kanter (1983), "The degree to which the opportunity to use power effectively is granted to or withheld from individuals is one operative difference between those companies which stagnate and those which innovate" (p. 18, emphasis deleted).

Norms

The norms that determine acceptable work practices in SDEs will also change. The norms of bureaucracy and, by extension, of traditional SDEs promote caution in employees. These norms are promoted in part by the environment: "When any action may have policy implications and thus be subject to political criticism after the fact, people taking those actions will have a natural tendency toward caution" (Wilson 1989, p. 41). These norms are also demanded by the bureaucratic structure itself:

> The bureaucratic structure exerts a constant pressure upon the official to be "methodical, prudent, disciplined." If the bureaucracy is to operate successfully, it must attain a high degree of reliability of behavior, an unusual degree of conformity with prescribed patterns of action (Merton 1980, p. 231).

This emphasis on caution and prudence reinforces the reliance on rules:

> This very emphasis leads to a transference of the sentiments from the *aims* of the organization onto the particular details of behavior required by the rules. Adherence to the rules, originally conceived as a means, becomes transformed into an end-in-itself; there occurs the familiar process of *displacement of goals* whereby "an instrumental value becomes a terminal value" (Merton 1980, p. 231).

That this type of goal displacement has occurred in SDEs is evidenced by Sroufe (1967):

> A central problem confronting SDE's in fulfilling regulatory activities appears to be that the criteria established to determine acceptable performance become too easily and too frequently as important as the actual performance. For a while we asked respondents to indicate what they were trying to accomplish in their particular job, expecting to receive objectives expressed in terms of school system, classroom, or pupil performance. We were disappointed to find that few respondents saw their role in this fashion; most responded in terms of the regulatory criteria which had been set up to monitor performance (p. 20).

When following rules and procedures becomes the goal, it is difficult to violate the norm of caution. Risk-taking is not rewarded in the traditional SDE.

However, risk-taking will be required in SDEs engaged in systemic school reform because no one can ever be sure how best to approach innovative work. Norms that stress caution and the strict following of rules will be dysfunctional in implementing systemic school reform.

Instead, the norms of the SDE must support employees in exercising informed judgment[12] and initiative. Unless the norms of the SDE signal employees that innovation will be well received, creative problem solving will be stifled (Kanter 1988).

Employees must be committed to the SDE and its goals as a whole, as opposed to following only the rules in their narrow area. Burns and Stalker (1961) found that "organic" organizations—those appropriate to changing conditions—were characterized in part by "the shedding of 'responsibility' as a limited field of rights, obligations and methods. . . . [and] the spread of commitment to the concern beyond any technical definition" (p. 121).

Finally, there must be the norm of respect for individuals and their abilities to act in uncertainty in the new SDEs (Kanter 1983). Exercising control over employees through rules springs at least partially from distrust (Gouldner 1980). Unless the norms of SDEs promote trust in individuals, the kind of flexible working environment that I have described will not exist.

These changes in the external and internal working relationships of SDEs, if successfully implemented, will mark a radical departure from the traditional structure and functions of these organizations. Staff members will be asked to conceptualize their jobs differently, starting with the question of how best to promote and support the redesign of teaching and learning in schools, rather than with the question of how best to bring about compliance with state regulations. They will be asked to perform those jobs in different ways, assisting schools and defining and refining implementation as the work progresses, rather than performing a predefined and routine set of tasks. Finally, SDE staff members will be asked to judge their performance by different criteria, using outcomes produced, as opposed to routines followed.

Effecting these changes in SDE working relationships will be extraordinarily difficult. These types of far-reaching changes are not supported by bureaucracy. "All organizations by design are the enemies of change, at least up to a point; government organizations are especially risk averse because they are caught up in a web of constraints so complex that any change is likely to rouse the ire of some important constituency" (Wilson 1989, p. 69).

Changes that are supported by bureaucracy more closely resemble the "more of the same" reforms of the 1980s: "Government agencies change all the time, but the most common changes are add-ons: a new program is added on to existing tasks without changing the core tasks or altering the organizational culture" (Wilson 1989, p. 225).[13] Systemic school reform requires much deeper reforms than bureaucracies typically allow.

In addition, support for this kind of far-reaching change, over the period of time that it is likely to take, will be difficult to sustain in the uncertain environment in which SDEs exist. This uncertain environment includes fiscal instability and programmatic instability—often brought about by frequent changes in leadership of either the chief state school officer, the state board, or the governor (Louis and Corwin 1984). Building a shared vision and shared goals for the system, as proposed by Smith and O'Day (1990), will be of paramount importance if support for systemic reform is to be sustained over the period of time needed to bring about the reforms of the SDE and all other levels.

Adding to the difficulties of this type of change is the evidence that technical assistance and other school improvement strategies judged to be more effective in the long term are harder to garner support for in the short term (Louis and Corwin 1984). Assistance reaches fewer schools in the short term than broader-based strategies such as statewide testing, and the results of assistance, even if successful, take time to become apparent and are "often viewed as . . . difficult to trace to specific student achievement outcomes" (Louis and Corwin 1984, p. 180).

Study of the current and future experiences of states engaged in systemic school reform, such as Vermont and Kentucky, will shed light on the variations in implementation of these reforms, and also on their feasibility. Further study of systemic reform states will also answer the most important question of all: Are these state-level reforms promoting and supporting local efforts to redesign teaching and learning with the result that all students are learning ambitious content knowledge and higher-order skills? The answer to this question—the outcome of systemic reform—will allow us to judge its ultimate success.

Endnotes

[1]To be sure, some state school improvement programs, such as the Carnegie schools program in Massachusetts, encouraged schools to restructure and to redesign teaching and learning. These programs were generally small, however, reaching a limited number of schools, and did not influence the overall impact of the policy regime.

[2]The discussion of mechanisms has been influenced by what I have seen in states attempting systemic reform (particularly Vermont and Kentucky), and also by conversations that took place while I was a staff member of the Coalition of Essential Schools at Brown University.

[3]Vermont is developing such an assessment system. The system is largely performance-based, judging portfolios of student work. Portfolios are judged on numerous criteria that are separately scored. Scores are not reduced to a single composite number and consequently give teachers more detailed information on the strengths and weaknesses of their students' performance.

⁴Rodney L. Reed, Senior Policy Analyst, Education Department of Victoria, Melbourne, Australia, introduced the term *critical friend* to the staff of the Coalition of Essential Schools.

⁵These questions resemble the action research cycle of planning, acting, and evaluating results (see, e.g., Oja and Smulyan 1989).

⁶This discussion of regulation draws heavily on a discussion I had on the topic with Richard F. Elmore on September 30, 1992.

⁷It is possible that state assessment systems can be used to judge program adequacy, as well as measure student achievement. Vermont, for example, is attempting to make judgments about the math and writing programs of its schools through examining the contents of students' portfolios.

⁸This is because SDEs are what Wilson (1989) terms "procedural organizations"—organizations in which "managers can observe what their subordinates are doing but not the outcome (if any) that results from those efforts" (p. 163). According to Wilson, "If the manager cannot justify on the grounds of results leaving operators alone to run things as they see fit, the manager will have to convince political superiors that the rules governing government work are being faithfully followed . . . . . Management becomes means-oriented in procedural organizations" (p. 164).

⁹This description is probably a somewhat extreme caricature of communication in traditional SDEs, since SDEs—like other organizations—do have informal as well as formal communications networks. The point is that there is no formal obligation, in most cases, for offices to keep their counterparts in the organization informed of their activities.

¹⁰This description of the internal mechanisms of SDEs—clear assignment of roles and responsibilities, rules governing employee action, and information passed only up the hierarchy—is similar to Kanter's (1983) description of the behavior of segmentalist organizations—those that tend to stifle innovation and creativity.

¹¹There is some evidence that implementation occurs in this way in other innovative human service programs as well. See Golden (1990).

¹²For a discussion of this type of change in norms in another bureaucratic organization, see Barzelay's (1992) Chapter 4, "Reworking the Culture and Producing Results," pp. 58–78, especially pp. 60–61.

¹³Downs (1967) also makes this point when he says: "Organizations, like individuals, are reluctant to accept any change in their environment . . . if such acceptance would require them to make a significant alteration in their customary behavior patterns" (p. 174).

References

Barzelay, M., with the collaboration of B.J. Armajani. (1992). *Breaking Through Bureaucracy: A New Vision for Managing in Government*. Berkeley: University of California Press.

Burns, T., and G.M. Stalker. (1961). *The Management of Innovation*. London: Tavistock Publications, Ltd. (Distributed in the United States by Barnes & Noble Inc.)

Campbell, R.F., L.L. Cunningham, R.O. Nystrand, and M.D. Usdan. (1985). *The Organization and Control of American Schools*. 5th ed. Columbus, OH: Charles E. Merrill.

Campbell, R.F., and G.E. Sroufe. (1967). "The Emerging Role of State Departments of Education." In *Strengthening State Departments of Education*, edited by R.F. Campbell, G.E. Sroufe, and D.H. Layton. Chicago: Midwestern Administration Center, The University of Chicago.

Campbell, R.F., G.E. Sroufe, and D.H. Layton, eds. (1967). *Strengthening State Departments of Education*. Chicago: Midwestern Administration Center, The University of Chicago.

Clune, W.H., with P. White and J. Patterson. (1989). *The Implementation and Effects of High School Graduation Requirements: First Steps Toward Curricular Reform*. New Brunswick, N.J.: Center for Policy Research in Education.

Cohen, D.K. (1988). "Teaching Practice: Plus Que Ca Change . . . ." In *Contributing to Educational Change: Perspectives on Research and Practice*, edited by P.W. Jackson. Berkeley, Calif.: McCutchan.

Cohen, D.K., and J.P. Spillane. (1992). "Policy and Practice: The Relations Between Governance and Instruction." In *The Review of Research in Education*, Vol. 18 (pp. 3–49), edited by G. Grant. Washington, D.C.: American Educational Research Association.

Consortium for Policy Research in Education. (1992). "Ten Lessons about Regulation and Schooling." *CPRE Policy Briefs*. New Brunswick, N.J.: Author.

Council of Chief State School Officers. (1983). *Educational Governance in the States: A Status Report on State Boards of Education, Chief State School Officers, and State Education Agencies*. Washington, D.C.: U.S. Department of Education.

Cuban, L. (1990). "Reforming Again, Again, and Again." *Educational Researcher* 19, 1: 3–13.

Downs, A. (1967). *Inside Bureaucracy*. Boston: Little, Brown.

Firestone, W.A., S.H. Fuhrman, and M.W. Kirst. (1989). *The Progress of Reform: An Appraisal of State Education Initiatives*. New Brunswick, N.J.: Rutgers University, Center for Policy Research in Education.

Friedman, B.D. (1971). *State Government and Education: Management in the State Education Agency*. Chicago: Public Administration Service.

Fuhrman, S.H., and P. Fry. (1989). *Diversity Amidst Standardization: State Differential Treatment of Districts*. New Brunswick, N.J.: Center for Policy Research in Education.

Golden, O. (1990). "Innovation in Public Sector Human Services Programs: The Implications of Innovation by 'Groping Along.'" *Journal of Policy Analysis and Management* 9, 2: 219–248.

Gouldner, A.W. (1980). "About the Functions of Bureaucratic Rules." In *Organizations: Structure and Behavior*. 3rd ed., edited by J.A. Litterer. New York: John Wiley & Sons.

Kanter, R.M. (1983). *The Change Masters: Innovation for Productivity in the American Corporation*. New York: Simon and Schuster.

Kanter, R.M. (1988). "When a Thousand Flowers Bloom: Structural, Collective, and Social Conditions for Innovation in Organizations." *Research in Organizational Behavior* 10: 169–211.

Kentucky Department of Education. (1991). *Kentucky Department of Education: National Catalyst for Educational Transformation: Mission, Beliefs, Parameters, Goals, Strategies*. Frankfort, Ky.: Author.

Layton, D.H. (1967). "Historical Development and Current Status of State Departments of Education." In *Strengthening State Departments of Education*, edited by R.F. Campbell, G.E. Sroufe, and D.H. Layton. Chicago: Midwestern Administration Center, The University of Chicago.

Little, J.W., W.H. Gerritz, D.S. Stern, J.W. Guthrie, M.W. Kirst, and D.D. Marsh. (1987). *Staff Development in California: Public and Personal Investments, Program Patterns, and Policy Choices*. Executive Summary. Palo Alto, Calif.: Far West Laboratory for Educational Research and Development and PACE.

Louis, K.S., and R.G. Corwin. (1984). "Organizational Decline: How State Agencies Adapt." *Education and Urban Society* 16, 2: 165–188.

Louis, K.S., and M.B. Miles. (1990). *Improving the Urban High School: What Works and Why*. New York: Teachers College Press.

Merton, R.K. (1980). "Bureaucratic Structure and Personality." In *Organizations: Structure and Behavior*. 3rd ed., edited by J.A. Litterer. New York: John Wiley & Sons.

Murphy, J.T. (1974). *State Education Agencies and Discretionary Funds: Grease the Squeaky Wheel*. Lexington, Mass.: Lexington Books, D.C. Heath and Company.

Perrow, C. (1986). *Complex Organizations: A Critical Essay*. 3rd ed. New York: McGraw-Hill.

Senge, P.M. (1990). *The Fifth Discipline: The Art and Practice of the Learning Organization*. New York: Doubleday Currency.

Smith, M.S., and J. O'Day. (1991). "Systemic School Reform." In *The Politics of Curriculum and Testing: The 1990 Yearbook of the Politics of Education Association*, edited by S.H. Fuhrman and B. Malen. New York: Falmer Press.

Sroufe, G.E. (1967). "Selected Characteristics of State Departments of Education." In *Strengthening State Departments of Education*, edited by R.R. Campbell, G.E. Sroufe, and D.H. Layton. Chicago: Midwestern Administration Center, The University of Chicago.

Vermont Department of Education. (1991). *Restructuring the Department of Education: Presentation to Commissioner Mills*. Montpelier, Vt.: Author.

Vermont Department of Education. (1992). *Department of Education Restructuring: Home Team Proposal*. Montpelier, Vt.: Author.

Wilson, J.Q. (1989). *Bureaucracy: What Government Agencies Do and Why They Do It*. New York: Basic Books.

8

"Will This Be on the Test?" Reflections on State Curriculum Leadership

Richard P. Mills

"**W**ill this be on the test?" Every high school teacher hears that question and is dismayed. It signals adolescent skepticism that what you are teaching is really something they need to know. How to answer it? I always wanted to say, "Yes, this *is* important." But they knew that not everything would be on the test. Teachers are on their own when that question arises. Besides being the wrong question, it always seems to come up at the wrong time.

Teachers shouldn't have to stand alone in answering this question—and, increasingly, they do not. The states individually and the nation as a whole are trying to answer the *right* question by turning with new rigor to the design of curriculum frameworks and guidelines. In a world engaged in rapid creation and sharing of knowledge, we are turning to a fundamental human question: "What is worth knowing?" And then we must answer its corollary: "How do we learn that?"

The Quest for Answers

Chapters 6 and 7 of this yearbook examine the progress of that quest in several bellwether states. In thinking about these chapters, I have reached three conclusions that seem inescapable:

• *How states develop curriculum guidelines matters.* Should states pick an expert elite or go to the grassroots when crafting curriculum guidelines? They need both, but a distinct bias toward the grassroots is more likely to change teaching and learning. Although the formula is simple—involve everyone repeatedly, and drive standards upward relentlessly—it is complex in practice.

- *Context matters*. Curriculum guidelines work only when a whole set of education policies work in concert. Statewide education goals, curriculum frameworks, assessment, professional education, instructional practice, finance, and accountability have to point in the same direction: very high skills for every student—no excuses and no exceptions.
- *Old-style state education bureaucracies can't do this job*. A traditional education department approaches curriculum guidelines as a set of rules, and regulates schools for compliance. It will not have built the partnerships needed to craft modern curriculum guidelines in the first place, or to secure their widespread use. A state contemplating large-scale design of curriculum guidelines had better also be deep into a restructuring of the state education department.

Role of State Education Agencies

What should state agencies do as they join state governments in revamping curriculum frameworks? In Chapter 6, "Achieving Consensus," Diane Massell distinguishes two strategies that states have used to set the agenda for curriculum reform.

- A *professional elite* approach assigns curriculum guideline design to a small group distinguished by its expertise. California is a leading example of a professional elite strategy.
- A *populist* strategy is a grassroots effort, involving as many people as possible. Massell views Vermont as having a populist strategy.

I suggest another category: a *mixed* strategy. I would put Vermont in the mixed-strategy category. Massell thinks Kentucky and South Carolina also represent a mixed strategy.

Which approach to choose? Because states have to achieve both high quality and widespread acceptance, both approaches have advantages—and disadvantages. In the end, Massell opts for a populist approach because it creates an environment more accepting of change. But she warns states not to expect rapid design and implementation—especially if they adopt a more populist approach. Consensus building never really ends. It is one thing to get people to agree to the draft, and quite another to lead them to a "deep understanding" that has them promoting change where it really counts.

Role of Systemic Reform

In Chapter 7, "Systemic School Reform," Susan Follett Lusi shows that systemic reform, including reform of the curriculum, imposes fundamental changes in state education agencies—changes in the internal and external structure, norms, and working relationships. The new systemic approach to education reform demands a very different kind of education department.

Systemic reform, she reminds us, is unlike earlier reform efforts in that it seeks coherent change across the whole system of education and strives to support the transformation of teaching and learning in schools so that all students achieve high skills. This task is massive, complex, and uncertain. It cannot be achieved by the education department acting alone.

What can the state agency do? Lusi produced a useful list from her observations in Vermont and Kentucky:

- Provide incentives—such as grants and deregulation;
- Contribute knowledge—for example, through curriculum frameworks, or a Common Core of Learning;
- Focus attention on desired outcomes—assessments that are "meaningful" do this;
- Provide assistance to schools that are restructuring—state agencies do this when they act in the role of critical friend and provider of continuous, intense training; and
- Retain some degree of regulation—but it is regulation of results more than process.

Lusi finds that internal relationships in the agency must also change dramatically. The organization must reflect a mission and a shared culture. It must share information across lines and knit together what had been disconnected segments in the traditional organization. People must learn to work in teams. The education department must reward idea generation, continuous learning, and "thoughtful groping along."

What lessons do these chapters suggest about developing state curriculum frameworks? Involve everyone, make sure the pieces fit, and don't try to make do with a traditional state education department. I will have most to offer on the first point, because it seems to me the most perplexing, and the most neglected.

Involve Everyone

A mixed strategy seems best. A state adopting an elitist strategy can control for high standards but will be forever behind the curve on implementation. If a state relies solely on what the grassroots say, it will replicate the status quo. Resolve to do contradictory things: insist on involving everybody, and insist on higher quality. And keep going back to the people with new drafts, as well as new evidence of what other people are thinking about the same problem.

This may be a good point to add something about my experience in Vermont. Massell's view of the Vermont approach is incomplete—a criticism she anticipates when she notes that the process is evolving rapidly in each state and may already have moved beyond what she saw. Vermont has a fundamentally grassroots approach, but I would put it in the mixed category.

A key feature of Vermont's approach was the interactive nature of its construction of the Common Core of Learning. It began with the education goals—250 people helped write them—and Goal 1 led to discussion of what we meant by competence and mastery of a challenging curriculum.

We invited 400 educators to think about the nature of a challenging curriculum—"what we teach, how we teach it, and what students learn." A continuously expanding set of focus forums evolved into a broad-based commitment to create a Common Core of Learning. More than 4,000 people contributed their ideas to the writing of the common core. We sent thousands of copies of the first draft to the people of Vermont and urged that they comment. The design team asked me to scrawl my comments in the margins, and they printed it that way to drive home the point that everyone was expected to take pen in hand and mark up the draft. As the comments poured in, we picked an elite group of teachers to study them, concentrate on the most demanding of the suggestions for change, and help prepare another draft. We also asked the design committee to react to the views of those in other states on the same matter. We did all of that because the initial version seemed not challenging enough. Then we distributed 14,000 copies of the second draft, again with insistent calls for comments. The state board of education and I pressed for ever larger numbers of participants and exerted continuous pressure to make the standards more challenging.

For Vermont, the process has entered yet another phase with state board adoption of the Common Core of Learning; and we have begun to develop a more detailed curriculum framework to match. The framework will be the work of about 100 people chosen for their expertise. Without a doubt, their work will go back to the public with the same insistence that everyone pay attention and comment. The need to involve everyone cannot be stressed too much:

- *Involve the teachers because the curriculum is in their hands*. Think about how teachers are going to actually use this information. The best way to keep this perspective in the foreground is to make sure that several thousand teachers are part of the work from the start.

- *Involve the students because they can be the most powerful forces for change.* None of the authors mentioned students in the design work. When I visit schools for a day every two weeks, I have one question for students, which I ask in endless variations: "Is the work you do challenging?" For months on end, the answer is often "No!" After each such visit, I talk to the parents, boards, teachers, press—anyone who will listen. We used interactive television to review the draft of the common core with students and held a press conference for all student editors to talk about it. The students seem to think that a curriculum based on the common core would make their work in school more challenging, more interesting. But they are doubtful that we will follow through. And so I told the public about that, too.

- *Involve the business community because they have a lot of useful things to say about curriculum.* People in the business community control the ultimate incentive—a job. And they also conduct assessments of the school system every time they interview a graduate. They were there at the start in Vermont, and they got repeated drafts along the way. A great many responded with detailed suggestions.

Make Sure All the Pieces Fit

Much useful literature is available on the meaning of systemic change and the importance of doing a few significant things in concert. That is advice to be heeded by curriculum guideline writers. The matter has become so obvious now that a few reminders should suffice. For example, the curriculum guidelines will take hold when we see correspondences among assessment practices, professional development, and teacher education. School approval processes should put aside the checklists, take up the curriculum standards, and look at the student work that results.

The same message also comes in plain words from practitioners. The most common question I hear from educators in response to any proposal is: "How does this all fit?" They won't be put off by rhetoric. They insist on seeing an explicit conceptual model of how all elements of the reform interact. Designers of curriculum guidelines should see to it that their work springs from such a framework; and if one has not emerged already from the state policy process, they should fill the gaps themselves.

Fit is important in at least one other way. As the good work of curriculum standard setting goes forward, we need to pause and think about how students will experience it. As each discipline comes forward with its issues and essential concepts, the implied time demands mount, and I wonder what a school year would feel like to a student. Do we really think students should know and be able to do all that we propose? Do we think it possible?

Don't Try to Make Do with a Traditional State Education Department

A traditional department of education would probably not be able to support, let alone create the kind of curriculum guidelines that schools need now. No state department can possess all the expertise and experience needed for the task. And modern curriculum guidelines won't work if viewed as subjects for compliance monitoring.

Guideline developers should think before they replicate. States are at very different stages in the evolution toward systemic approaches. Curriculum guidelines are the products of different kinds of state education agencies, at different stages of their own transformation.

Curriculum reform can't be put off until the state education department restructures. But curriculum reform and transformation of the state agency should be done at the same time. Both are long-term works in progress. This concurrent development can make the design of the guidelines problematic. The field greets each draft of the guideline as if it were a product of the old organization: "Is this a mandate?" The answer is "No—in the traditional sense." But if 4,000 people help write it, and the employers endorse it and say that they will ask graduates to demonstrate competence in it when they come to an interview, the Common Core of Learning is mandated in a far more powerful way than the traditional state agency ever could.

Editors' Note: The September 1993 issue of the ASCD journal, *Educational Leadership*, has the theme "Inventing New Systems." It includes an interview with Marshall Smith, co-author of Chapter 2 of this yearbook [O'Neil, J. (September 1993). "On Systemic Reform: A Conversation with Marshall Smith." *Educational Leadership* 51, 1: 12–13].

III

District and School Roles in Curriculum Reform

9

Standard Setting as a Strategy for Upgrading High School Mathematics and Science

Andrew C. Porter, John Smithson, and Eric Osthoff

The 1983 report, *A Nation at Risk: The Imperative for Educational Reform*, published by the National Commission on Excellence in Education, found that "secondary school curricula had been homogenized, diluted, and diffused to the point that they no longer have a central purpose. ... This curricular smorgasbord, combined with extensive student choice, explains a great deal about where we find ourselves today" (p. 18).

The hard-hitting report concluded that too small a percentage of high school students were taking serious academic coursework. The report recommended that state and local high school graduation requirements be strengthened to require at least three years of science and three years of mathematics. The report also indicated, in general terms, some of the characteristics that the required coursework was to reflect. A focus on understanding and applications was to characterize instruction in all academic subjects and for all students.

Three to four years later, many states had acted on *A Nation at Risk*'s recommendations by increasing the coursework required for graduation. Professional societies also responded to the report's call for curriculum reform. In 1989, three reports on mathematics and science curriculum reform were published:

Authors' Note: The research reported in this chapter was supported by the Center for Policy Research in Education through a grant from the National Science Foundation (Grant No. SPA-8953446) and by the Wisconsin Center for Education Research, School of Education, University of Wisconsin-Madison. We thank especially Mike Kirst and Steve Schneider, who were a part of the data collection team and were primarily responsible for data collection in Arizona, California, and Pennsylvania. The opinions expressed here are those of the authors and do not necessarily reflect the views of the National Science Foundation, the institutional partners of the Center for Policy Research in Education, or the Wisconsin Center for Education Research.

- *Everybody Counts: A Report to the Nation on the Future of Mathematics Education*, published by the National Research Council;
- *Science for All Americans*, published by the American Association for the Advancement of Science; and
- *Curriculum and Evaluation Standards for School Mathematics*, published by the National Council of Teachers of Mathematics.

The three 1989 reports placed much less emphasis on rote memorization of facts and acquisition of routine skills and much greater emphasis on conceptual understanding, reasoning, and application. Characterized as "hard content for all students" (Porter, Archbald, and Tyree 1991), the shift in content and how it was presented was not for the academically elite alone, but for all students.

The following discussion is based on a study of curriculum upgrading by states, districts, and schools in response to these calls for reform. It focuses particularly on policy and its effects on high school mathematics and science. Policy includes increasing course requirements in academic subjects for high school graduation, developing curriculum frameworks and guides, initiating various types of student assessment, and providing staff development. Can policies significantly upgrade instruction? What are the effects of various curriculum policies on what happens in the classroom? How do policies interact with one another and with other factors that shape classroom practice? Our analyses suggest that policy effectiveness is increased as elements of clarity, coherence, authority, and power increase in the formulation of policy initiatives.

We have studied a relatively specific school output: the nature and quality of the mathematics and science curriculum as offered by teachers and experienced by students. We consider initiatives from professional organizations, such as the National Council of Teachers of Mathematics (NCTM) *Curriculum Standards* (1989), and initiatives of the federal government, such as the Eisenhower Mathematics and Science Education Program; but our focus is primarily on state, district, and school initiatives as they interact and intersect across levels of the formal school hierarchy and ultimately bear on the deliberations and practices of teachers and students.

We recognize that much education policymaking occurs piecemeal over time, with each piece motivated by a different purpose. From the perspective of the classroom, the pieces often appear disjointed and fragmented, with no coherent message. Thus, despite our somewhat rational and linear approach to describing and analyzing policy initiatives and their effects, we recognize that, at least to date, education policymaking has been far from rational and linear (though the calls for systemic reform may change this in the future; see Smith and O'Day 1991).

The brief chronology of policy initiatives described earlier focuses on what some have referred to as the first- and third-wave reforms (Firestone et al. 1991, Murphy 1990). These two waves of reform directly address the nature of teaching and learning in classrooms. The so-called second-wave reform had less direct bearing on curriculum, focusing instead on restructuring classrooms and schools and the nature of teachers' work (Firestone, Fuhrman, and Kirst 1989). Essentially, second-wave reforms challenged the top-down, curriculum-control strategies of the 1970s, arguing that they be replaced with empowerment strategies (Rowan 1990). Despite the second-wave reform's lack of direct relevance to the work reported here, all three waves coexisted at the time of our study; and this second wave represents an additional backdrop for interpreting results.

The timing and character of the first- and third-wave reforms are important for interpreting the school and classroom results reported here. Our study was conducted during the 1989–90 and 1990–91 school years. Thus, first-wave reform effects should be observable, but third-wave reform efforts may not have had sufficient time to show effects, even though the third-wave reforms were foreshadowed not only in *A Nation at Risk* in 1983, but also in some state curriculum frameworks, most notably the *Mathematics Framework for California Public Schools, Kindergarten Through Grade Twelve* (1985).

Policy Instruments of Curriculum Control

The policy instruments of curriculum control are, at this point, fairly well known (McDonnell and Elmore 1987). They include state and district requirements concerning curriculum, instructional materials, and student testing. The requirements are intended to prescribe desired practice, using a variety of policy instruments that are consistent among themselves in the practices they prescribe. Policy instruments influence practice through rewarding and sanctioning compliance and through the authority to persuade based on legal status, consistency with norms, a basis in expertise, and charismatic advocacy (Porter, Floden, Freeman, Schmidt, and Schwille 1988). Clearly, state high school graduation requirements fit the curriculum-control strategy.

In contrast, the policy instruments of empowerment are much less well defined. Generally, however, the intention is to move control out of the hands of the education hierarchy and into the hands of teachers. The policy instruments for this approach are site-based management and deregulation. From an accountability perspective, second-wave reforms replace school process requirements with school output requirements, especially the output of student achievement (Porter et al. 1991).

Our approach to policy analysis is somewhat atypical. Most policy analyses focus on activity at one level or another of the education hierarchy, taking a broad view of initiatives at that level. Some policy analyses focus on a particular policy instrument, such as curriculum frameworks. These analyses have been enormously useful in clarifying such matters as policy formulation and policy implementation. In contrast, by focusing on a particular school output, the nature and quality of the enacted mathematics and science curriculums in high school, our analyses slice the policy layers vertically. We look through the layers of the education hierarchy and into the classroom to determine coherence across levels as seen from the perspective of teachers, and to identify the relative influence of various policy instruments. In conducting these analyses, we draw on a large and rich empirical data base consisting of both quantitative and qualitative data characterizing policy, classroom practice, and their connections. This attempt to connect classroom practice to policy has been identified as lacking and much needed (Stecher 1992; McDonnell, Burstein, Ormseth, Catterall, and Moody 1990).

Description of the Study

The study involved math and science teachers in eighteen high schools (grades 9–12) in twelve districts in six states. In each state, one large urban district was contrasted with one smaller suburban or rural district. In each large district, we selected two high schools to give a sense of within-district variability. In the smaller district, we studied a single high school. In each school, four course sections—two for mathematics and two for science—were studied intensively. Data collection began in the middle of the 1989–90 school year and continued through the 1990–91 school year. Because of funding timelines, the academic year as described in the study consisted of the spring semester of 1990 coupled with the subsequent fall semester of 1990 for California, Florida, Missouri, and Pennsylvania. For Arizona and South Carolina, the academic year consisted of the fall semester of 1990 followed by the spring semester of 1991.

At the state level, we interviewed key individuals at the department of public instruction to learn of state policy relative to standard setting in high school mathematics and science. At the district level, interviews determined administrators' understanding of state policy and how it is passed on to schools, as well as identifying district policy aimed at upgrading math and science curriculums. The school-level data came in two forms: interviews of school administrators to learn of math and science practices in the school, and a questionnaire survey of all mathematics and science teachers in each participating high school. We obtained data on classroom practices from the target sample of courses. We collected classroom practice data through teacher interviews, daily logs describing the content and pedagogy of instruction, and weekly questionnaires describing special instructional and professional activities in which teachers participated. We used a prelog survey to obtain basic demographic information. In addition, we observed all target sample teachers at least once (and usually twice) as they taught the target classes.

The data set is large, rich, and complex, consisting of the following:

- daily records of instructional practices for 62 teachers,
- 116 observations of 75 target teachers,
- 81 target teacher interviews,
- 312 mathematics and science teacher questionnaires,
- 76 school administrator interviews,
- 44 district administrator interviews, and
- 18 interviews of state department of education administrators.

States were selected for contrasts in both the nature and the focus of state curriculum upgrading and standard setting. At the time of this study, Florida and South Carolina represented good examples of states using curriculum-control strategies to achieve basic skills goals. In contrast, California and Arizona had already adopted the goal of hard content for all students; using a variety of strategies for pursuing that goal, they were less heavily committed to control strategies alone. Missouri and Pennsylvania stood between these two extremes in the sense that they had relatively few state curriculum-upgrading initiatives of any kind. Our design also contrasted large urban districts with smaller suburban/rural districts to clarify the possible differing roles districts might play in interpreting or adding to state initiatives. Throughout, our focus was on schools serving high concentrations of relatively low-achieving students because these schools and students were the primary focus of the curriculum-upgrading initiatives. The contrast between mathematics and science allowed us to explore limits on generalizability across subject areas of our policy analyses. In selecting target teachers and target classes, we used the criterion of enrollment gains since initiation of increased state graduation requirements in mathematics and science. This selection resulted in a sample dominated by basic courses and beginning college preparatory courses in both subjects. The difference between our target sample of seventy-two courses and our achieved sample of sixty-two reflects sample attrition.

Mathematics and Science Standard Setting

In some ways, it is difficult to know what the full list of policies and practices relevant to standard setting and curriculum upgrading might be. Some policies have unintended effects, usually negative; others (teacher salaries, for example) may have effects but are so remote from high school math and science classroom practices that those effects are difficult to trace. The focus here is on policies and practices designed to have a direct influence on high school mathematics and science instruction.

Increasing High School Graduation Requirements

Figure 9.1 summarizes credit requirements for graduation in the six states. Several points can be made from the information contained in this figure. First, increases in math and science graduation requirements occurred in each of the six states during the period from 1987 to 1989. Of the six states, only Florida and Pennsylvania set their requirements at the level recommended by *A Nation at Risk* (i.e., three credits of mathematics and three credits of science). Florida enacted the largest increase, with three credits in each subject. According to Meyer (1990), only three states require three science credits (these three states also require three credits of math), and only ten states require three mathematics credits.

Although not shown in Figure 9.1, Florida provides financial incentives to schools certifying that their lab science courses include 40 percent lab work. South Carolina requires lab science, but only 20 percent of a lab course must be spent in lab work. South Carolina also allows one of the math credits to be satisfied with computer science. Florida, South Carolina, and Missouri grant an academic diploma, as distinguished from a regular diploma. For example, Florida's academic diploma requires four years of mathematics (to include algebra, geometry and trigonometry) and four years of science.

In each state, university entrance requirements frequently exceed the state high school graduation requirements. Arizona universities require three credits of mathematics and three credits of science, including two credits in lab science. California universities require three credits of mathematics and two credits of science, including one credit in lab science. Missouri university requirements match state graduation requirements in quantity, but the two math credits must be algebra or higher, and the two

Figure 9.1
High School Graduation Requirements in Six States

State and Prior Req.	New Req.	Date	Change	Requirements[a] in Core Subjects				Graduation Rate	
				Subject[b]	Prior	New	Change	Rate	Rank[c]
Calif.				English	Local	3	3		
				Math		2	2		
				Science		2	2		
Local	13	1987	13	Social Studies		3	3	66.7	41
				Core		10	10		
				Other		3			
				Total		13			
Fla.				English	Local	4	4		
				Math		3	3		
				Science		3	3		
Local	24	1987	24	Social Studies		3	3	62.0	50
				Core		13	13		
				Other		11			
				Total		24			
Mo.				English	1	3	2		
				Math	1	2	1		
				Science	1	2	1		
20	22	1988	2	Social Studies	1	2	1	75.6	22
				Core	4[d]	9	5		
				Other	16	13			
				Total	20	22			
Pa.				English	3	4	1		
				Math	1	3	2		
				Science	1	3	2		
13[e]	21[e]	1989	8	Social Studies	2	3	1	78.5	14
				Core	7	13	6		
				Other	6	8			
				Total	13	21			
Ariz.				English	3	4	1		
				Math	1	2	1		
				Science	1	2	1		
18	20	1987	2	Social Studies	2.5	2.5	0	63.0	47
				Core	7.5	10.5			
				Other	10.5	9.5			
				Total	18	20			
S.C.				English	4	4			
				Math	2	3[f]	1		
				Science	1	2	1		
18	20	1987	2	Social Studies	3	3		64.5	43
				Core	10	12	2		
				Other	8	8~			
				Total	18	20			

Figure 9.1—continued

Note: Prior req. means total number of required credits prior to 1987 for each state.
New req. means total number of required credits since 1987.
Date refers to the effective date of the new requirements.
Change refers to the change in total number of required credits.
Local in the California and Florida columns refers to the local options that prevailed prior to the new requirements.

^aRequirements are defined as the necessary prerequisites for a standard high school diploma.
^bSocial studies includes courses such as American History, Civics, Economics, state history, etc. English includes language arts, communication skills, etc.
^cRank includes District of Columbia in 51st place.
^dMissouri requires 2 additional years from among core subjects.
^eIn 1989, Pennsylvania students must complete 13 credits in the last 3 years of high school; in 1989, they must complete 21 credits in 4 years.
^fSouth Carolina's requirement of 3 credits in math may include 1 credit of computer science.

Sources:
Data in columns 1–8 are from:

Belsches-Simmons, G., P. Flakus-Mosqueda, B. Lindner, and K. Mayer. (March 1987). *Recent State Educational Reform: Initial Teacher Certification, Teacher Compensation and High School Graduation Requirements.* Denver, Colo.: Education Commission of the States.
Education Commission of the States. (August 1987). *Minimum High School Graduation Course Requirements.* Denver, Colo.: Author.
Goertz, M.E. (1988). *State Educational Standards: A 50-State Survey.* Princeton, N.J.: Educational Testing Service.
National Center for Education Statistics. (1988). *The Condition of Education: Elementary and Secondary Education.* Washington, D.C.: U.S. Department of Education.

Data in columns 9 and 10 are from:

U.S. Department of Education. (February 1988). *State Education Statistics.* Washington, D.C.: Author, Office of Planning, Budget and Evaluation.

science credits must include lab work. Similarly, in South Carolina and Florida, the state universities match the state high school graduation requirements in quantity, but stipulate that the three mathematics credits must be algebra or higher, and that one or two of the science credits (depending on the university) be in a lab science. (See the section "Effects of State and District Standard Setting" for the effects of state and district standards on course enrollments and offerings.)

In addition to credit requirements for graduation, two of the six states require exit exams of one form or another. In Florida, students must pass a minimum competency exam in language and mathematics, but not science. Similarly, South Carolina has a 10th grade exam that covers reading, writing, and mathematics, but not science. In both states these exams assess basic skills and minimum competencies, and students must pass them in order to graduate.

Curriculum Frameworks

Of the six states, two use curriculum frameworks as their lead policy instrument in efforts to influence and support the quality of instruction in schools. California's 1985 mathematics framework influenced the development of the NCTM *Curriculum and Evaluation Standards for School Mathematics;* now, California is revising its mathematics framework to bring it into alignment with the NCTM *Standards*. California's 1985 science curriculum framework, which was revised in 1990, about the same time as our study, had been influenced by the *Science for All Americans* report.

California's approach to curriculum frameworks makes more use of leadership and persuasion than it does of prescription and requirements. These frameworks focus on a rationale for curriculum reform and "big ideas" rather than on the specification of particular mathematics or science topics that should be taught. The science framework has forty major ideas, and the mathematics framework has seven "strands." In both mathematics and science, the California frameworks reflect the 1989 curriculum reform movement toward an emphasis on higher-order thinking and problem solving and away from an emphasis on facts and low-level skills. The curriculums described by the frameworks are not required, though they are advised.

Arizona also uses curriculum frameworks as a lead policy instrument, though their framework is called "essential skills." Initiated in 1972, mathematics essential skills were revised in 1988; science essential skills were being revised at the time of our study, based on the *Science for All Americans* report. Both revised frameworks reflect a focus on higher-order thinking and problem solving. Nevertheless, the revisions were occurring too close to the time of our study to have had any noticeable influence on classroom data.

The other two states that provided curriculum leadership, South Carolina and Florida, both had curriculum frameworks that focused on basic skills. The South Carolina framework, *Teaching and Testing our Basic Skills Objectives* (1982), presents objectives and related activities at the course level. The science basic skills were revised in 1985 to specify 20 percent lab time. Florida's *Student Performance Standards of Excellence for Florida Schools* (1984) state expected learner outcomes for grades 3, 5, 8, and 12 in both math and science. Florida also has a curriculum framework for grades 9–12 that lists courses with twenty to forty objectives per course. These curriculum frameworks are clearly not the lead policy instrument in either state; tests are. Both focus on basic skills; however, at the time of our study, both states were considering revising their curriculum focus to reflect the 1989 curriculum reform.

Missouri's *Core Competencies and Key Skills for Missouri Schools* (1986, revised 1990) covers math and science objectives for 4th through 10th grades. However, the state does little to promote these competencies, which, at the time of our study, predated the 1989 curriculum reform. During the study, Pennsylvania had no curriculum framework at all, though *A Recommended Science Competency Continuum for Pennsylvania Schools* (1987, reprinted 1991), and a set of *Mathematics Content Lists* (1987) provided suggestions for math and science curriculums. At the time of this writing, Pennsylvania had begun considering an outcome-based curricular strategy aligned with NCTM *Standards,* but was still in the process of determining the level of specificity at which frameworks (and outcomes) would be aimed. (See the section "Effects of State and District Standard Setting" for effects of standards on the nature of instruction.)

State Testing

Although testing is the lead curriculum-control policy instrument in South Carolina and Florida, it occurs much more frequently in the early grades than it does in high school. Both states test only in 10th grade at the high school level and only in reading, writing, and mathematics. Both states' testing programs are aligned to their frameworks, which focus on basic skills and minimum competencies. Florida began its testing program in 1986, South Carolina in 1985.

In Florida, students who fail state tests in any of the grades tested (3, 5, 8, and 10) must be provided remedial instruction. In South Carolina, a School Incentive Reward Program (begun in 1985) gives cash awards to schools based on gains made in student achievement scores.[1] In both South

Carolina and Florida, students are required to pass the 10th grade test to graduate from high school. In Florida, students can take the test as many times as they wish; students in South Carolina are limited to five tries.

In the two states whose curriculum goals reflected the 1989 curriculum reform, testing programs were being revised. Arizona was in the process of replacing its 12th grade test (TAP) and its Iowa Test of Basic Skills (ITBS) in grades 2 through 12 with a new Arizona State Assessment Program (ASAP). The TAP and ITBS tests are not well aligned to state essential skills; however, the new ASAP will reflect the state essential skills, including higher-order thinking and problem solving. ASAP will be given in grades 3, 8, and 12; begin in 1992–93; involve performance assessment; and include mathematics and science. Similarly, the California Assessment Program (CAP) was being revised at the time of the study to emphasize performance assessment and alignment with the state frameworks. At the time of our study, testing was done in grades 5 and 11 in mathematics but not science. Testing was done on a matrix sampling basis for students but reported at the school level, with high-performing schools receiving noncash recognition awards. In 1991–92 California suspended its testing program.

Both Missouri and Pennsylvania have basic skills-oriented testing programs. In Missouri's testing program, Missouri Mastery and Achievement Tests (MMAT), begun in 1985, districts are required to test students four times between grades 2 and 10, but they are not required to report the results. The MMAT is aligned to the state "core competencies" and "key skills," and both mathematics and science are tested. In Pennsylvania, a program called Testing for Essential Learning and Literacy Skills (TELLS) tests basic skills in reading and mathematics each year in grades 3, 5, and 8. There is no science testing and no testing at the high school level. Since our study, the Pennsylvania testing program has been renamed the Pennsylvania State Assessment Program (PSAP), and is to be expanded to include grade 11. It will be administered each year to one third of the schools in the state.[2] At the time of our study, the focus of state testing was to remain on basic skills and minimum competencies.

Several facts are apparent from these state approaches to testing. First, testing is a much more common policy instrument at the elementary school level than at the high school level. Testing is also much more prevalent in mathematics than in science. While testing is the lead policy instrument in states with an emphasis on basic skills, it was not, at the time of our study, the lead policy instrument for either of the states emphasizing a curriculum oriented toward higher-order thinking and problem solving. At that time, states with a curriculum reform agenda had testing programs that were not aligned with that agenda. Efforts were underway to revise or replace old basic skills testing programs with testing programs aligned to the new state curriculum frameworks.

Although all six states used testing as a policy instrument, four did little to add power to their testing programs. California provided weak incentives to high-performing schools; Arizona and Pennsylvania reported results by school, but did nothing else; Missouri did not collect the results. In sharp contrast, South Carolina and Florida gave considerable power to their testing programs.

Staff Development and Textbook Adoption

Somewhat surprisingly, neither of the two states aggressively adopting the 1989 curriculum reforms had a well-funded, coherent program of staff development to support the desired (substantial) changes in teacher practices. Like all states at the time of our study, Arizona and California received federal Eisenhower Mathematics and Science Education Program funds, approximately two thirds of which were to be passed on to districts for staff development. Neither state targeted these flow-through funds in ways that might have given them more leverage in accomplishing state curriculum reforms. California did, however, ask for district plans and required that the funds be used in ways consistent with state frameworks.[3] Generally, these Eisenhower funds are spent on teachers who volunteer for short-term training efforts (Knapp, Zucker, Adelman, and St. John 1990).

One important exception to the nonprogrammatic and limited nature of state staff development efforts is California's Math A program, a teacher-designed (but state-promoted) course for students who might otherwise take 9th grade general mathematics (for a more detailed description of this program and its effects, see the section "Effects of State and District Standard Setting"). The intention is to give these students mathematics instruction consistent with the state framework that might potentially bridge students into more advanced courses in subsequent years. The state provides a required five-day summer inservice for all new Math A teachers. Several local sites have extended the state's staff development requirement by increasing the summer program to four weeks and adding inservice programs during the academic year.

The only state funding a significant investment in staff development was Florida, which spent approximately $10 million during the year of our study to support sixty-hour summer institutes focused on mathematics and science. A legislative initiative, the program dealt with the demand for more certified math and science teachers as a result of increased graduation requirements in those subjects. The summer institutes were also used to keep teachers current on math and science related issues. Although the state provided the funds, decisions regarding the structure and content of the institutes were left to local discretion.

State textbook adoption was a relatively unused, weak curriculum guidance strategy in the six states. At the time of the study, Pennsylvania and Missouri had no textbook adoption policies. Arizona and California had adoption policies, but only for grades K–8. South Carolina and Florida had textbook adoption policies that affected high schools. For example, Florida adopted three to five texts per subject on a four-year cycle. However, neither of these states used its adoption policies as leverage over publishers. Because adoption lists in both states included options, and because textbooks are not prescriptive of classroom practice, the potential for state textbook adoption policies to influence instruction was limited.

As indicated by this description of state curriculum policies, in 1989–90 and 1990–91, state approaches to curriculum upgrading were piecemeal; not all of the policies fit together in consistent ways. In particular, states attempting to reform curriculums consistent with recommendations of professional societies used tests that were not consistent with their curricular goals. Also, the study occurred during a time of transition; four of the six states were attempting to move away from basic skills and toward higher-order thinking and problem solving.

As a way to preclude piecemeal approaches to reforms in curriculum, instruction, and testing, Smith and O'Day (1991) have called for systemic school reform. This approach begins with clear and challenging standards for student learning. Policy instruments are to be tied to these standards for student learning and are to be consistent with each other, so that there is coherent instructional guidance to schools and teachers. Within this environment of clear goals and consistent policies, schools are to be given flexibility to develop strategies as needed.

In the six states included in this study, we found no good examples of systemic school reform directed toward the 1989 goal of hard content for all students. Both California and Arizona appeared to be moving in that direction, with California in the lead; but at the time of our study, both efforts remained seriously incomplete. The California frameworks are an excellent starting point for systemic reform toward hard content for all students. California tests, however, were still in the process of being revised. California did not coordinate its staff development efforts with its curriculum guides, and generally had an insufficient staff development program to support the kind of teacher change envisioned by its frameworks. Similarly, Arizona was moving to revise its testing program, but at the time of our study state tests stood in sharp contrast to what state essential skills sought to promote.

Reactions to State Initiatives

In our study, we found that people at the district and school levels have different perceptions of what is intended by state initiatives. In addition, teachers also vary in the extent to which they believe state initiatives should or must influence their practices. The general tendency is thus toward uniqueness of response, not standardization of practice. There were, however, some important general tendencies.

District Responses

State initiatives in curriculum upgrading and standard setting tend to stimulate additional initiatives by districts. Even state initiatives with little power and modest prescriptiveness receive some attention by districts. Often districts go well beyond what is required, adding their own extensions and enhancements.

State and district curriculum frameworks are a good illustration of this point. The urban district in Arizona used state essential skills as the basis for developing curriculum guides in each subject area; the district subject guides were far more detailed and elaborate than the state skills. In California, both the urban and rural districts developed curriculum guides based on state frameworks. The urban district went even further, adding Math A as a new offering consistent with the state mathematics framework, and revising science guides to reflect the integration across science disciplines found in the state framework. In Missouri, with its briefly defined set of core competencies and key skills, both the urban and the rural districts had developed their own curriculum guides to reflect and elaborate on the state's guidelines. South Carolina and Florida urban districts offer even better examples of districts taking state curriculum guides with relatively little information and expanding them into detailed and prescriptive documents including student objectives and teacher activities.

Districts also used state tests in ways that went well beyond the states' suggestions. The Florida urban district used the state test to evaluate schools. The Missouri rural district administered the state test at every grade level, from grades 2 through 10, despite the state's requiring testing at only four grade levels. In the Missouri urban district, the state test was used as an indicator of school success; principals believed that their jobs were on the line if student performance did not improve. The state of Missouri, however, did not require that the test results be reported.

In Florida and South Carolina, with their test requirements for high school graduation, both urban and rural districts developed remedial courses so that students who initially failed could receive the preparation necessary to ultimately pass the test.

Generally, the more curriculum-upgrading and standard-setting activities at the state level, the more additional curriculum-upgrading and standard-setting activities at the district level. Florida and South Carolina districts had the most comprehensive sets of district initiatives, while district initiatives in Missouri and Pennsylvania were fewest in number and strength. California and Arizona districts fell between these two extremes. At least in curriculum matters, districts appear less inclined to fill voids left by their state than they are inclined to be stimulated into action by state leadership.

Large urban districts are more active in standard setting and curriculum upgrading than small suburban and rural districts. The South Carolina urban district had developed detailed curriculum guides for each subject. In addition to the state test in grades 1, 2, 3, 6, 8, and 10, they required Stanford achievement testing in every grade, and district-developed final exams in Algebra 1 and General Math. Similar district required final exams were planned for Physical Science. In contrast, in the South Carolina rural district, which had a policy of principal leadership, state testing requirements were met; but district initiated testing was modest and being reduced. In Arizona, the urban district had developed curriculum guides that went well beyond the state essential skills. They had created their own criterion-referenced tests for twenty-three math courses and nine science courses. The district was attempting to eliminate tracking and had already targeted 9th grade general math for elimination. A districtwide effective schools initiative required school improvement teams at each school. In contrast, the rural district in Arizona used high school personnel to serve in dual roles as district personnel; for example, high school math and science department chairs served as district curriculum specialists. The rural district had no special initiatives of its own in the areas of frameworks, testing, or staff development.

There are several possible explanations for why urban districts are more active in curriculum upgrading and standard setting than rural districts. First, the urban districts have larger bureaucracies for implementing state initiatives and for adding to state initiatives in ways unique to the district. Second, urban district personnel usually are more convinced that change is necessary; they are often more highly motivated toward change than are rural district personnel. Third, there appears to be a much greater commitment to controlling classroom practice in urban districts than in rural districts. This may in turn be explained by urban schools' typically receiving less direction from parents than do rural schools.

School Responses

The most substantial standard setting and curriculum upgrading we encountered occurred at the school level. One school had eliminated all remedial courses and required that all freshmen take college prep coursework. Slightly less dramatic, but still substantial, were school efforts to counsel students into the college prep track in greater numbers than had been done historically.

The impetus for increasing enrollments in challenging academic content cannot be found in any straightforward sense in state initiatives. State increases in credit requirements for high school graduation did not specify that credits be in demanding academic content. As was noted, the Arizona urban district was eliminating general mathematics, but one high school in the district had gone well beyond the district's vague initiative, eliminating all general math and general science classes and requiring all freshmen to take algebra and chemistry/physics. The school hopes this will eventually lead to increased enrollment in upper division mathematics and science classes. Another high school in the same district had taken a softer approach, eliminating many, but not all, sections of lower level science and mathematics courses, while adding an advanced placement curriculum. A summer school program was instituted to assist students in advancing more quickly through the curriculum so that they could take higher level courses. In the suburban Pennsylvania district, basic science and mathematics courses were eliminated. In one school, all students were required to take basic algebra followed by basic geometry. "Math 9A" was developed to serve remedial students, and honors algebra was made available for advanced students. Still, of the eight freshman math classes, six were basic algebra.

Motivated primarily by desegregation, urban districts also created magnet schools. In the Arizona and Missouri urban districts, desegregation funds supported the magnet school initiatives. In the Pennsylvania urban district, a science magnet at one school had the unfortunate effect of attracting the best students away from other schools. As a result, honors programs in the nonmagnet schools had been eliminated; teachers reported that students no longer had the background to complete advanced coursework in science and math. This complaint was echoed by teachers and administrators in the Missouri urban district, primarily because of the "siphoning" effect of magnets.

Even in districts with substantial curriculum control, we found many instances of important differences among schools. At one high school in the Florida urban district, site-based management was a high-profile issue, with teachers organized into a body politic that voted on a variety of issues related to the school. The administration placed a high priority on school esprit de corps and academic excellence. In that same district, another school was characterized by antagonisms among administrators, teachers, and students. This antagonism apparently originated with the creation of a "school within a school," with two teacher cadres and two administrative units. In the South Carolina urban district, the two high schools differed in the extent to which students were pushed toward more demanding curriculums. In one school, teachers favored higher-ability groups and excluded at-risk students from advanced courses. Another school was committed to enrolling as many students as possible into college prep courses, nurturing different ability levels while challenging all students to try harder.

Many urban and rural schools serving high concentrations of low-achieving students are impoverished, making it difficult for them to accommodate state and district policy, such as the requirements for more course offerings, and consequently, more qualified teachers. The 1989 curriculum reform emphasis on active learning and real-world applications left teachers struggling to find the funds to purchase manipulatives and to take students on field trips. In the Pennsylvania and Florida urban schools, obtaining such basic supplies as textbooks was a problem. Some urban schools, however, have been more fortunate. One of the high schools in the Arizona urban district received approximately $2 million per year in additional funds from a court-ordered special property tax levied to support a desegregation order. Similarly, in the Missouri urban district, each department received state funds each year for complying with the desegregation order. Unlike the Arizona urban high school, which expects to receive its property tax funds indefinitely, the Missouri school expected desegregation monies to be discontinued in 1992. (A follow-up call in August 1993 revealed that in 1992 the court gave a two-year extension to the desegregation plan and funding.)

Teachers' Reactions

Contrary to findings by Rosenholtz (1987) and McNeil (1988a, 1988b, 1988c), we saw surprisingly little evidence that teachers were unhappy about or resistant to state and district curriculum standard setting. Several reports from teachers indicated that state and district controls were appropriate and were having positive effects. For example, one of the most powerful and prescriptive policies, the South Carolina urban district area exams, were seen by teachers as a necessary evil to help them hold to standards. Where complaints were registered, they tended to be the following types:

- State/district requirements were too hard for some students;
- The bureaucracy supporting state and district controls required too much paperwork from teachers; and
- State and district initiatives failed to provide necessary resources for implementation (e.g., materials, laboratory space, staff development).

Perhaps teachers did not resist state and district standard setting and curriculum upgrading because they helped formulate the initiatives. If teachers perceived their viewpoints and expertise reflected in policy initiatives, they appeared more likely to support those policies.

Typically, teachers were involved in curriculum framework development, as well as textbook selection, at both the state and district levels. They have also been included in curriculum guide revisions at the district level and in the development of new testing programs, such as those in Arizona and California. To some extent, this increase in teacher involvement may reflect second-wave reforms of restructuring classrooms and schools. Clearly, shared decision making and site-based management at the school level are consistent with teacher participation at other levels of the school hierarchy.

Despite this increase in teacher involvement, a tension existed between state and district standards and teachers' expectations about what students can accomplish in those schools and districts most involved in standard setting and curriculum upgrading. All too often, teachers complained about students in college prep classes who didn't belong. A South Carolina teacher stated: "We have five college prep biologies, I think, and three general biologies, and it should be the opposite."

Teachers' expectations sometimes lead them to discourage students from taking demanding academic work. Many teachers who find their classrooms filled with low-achieving, disaffected students believe they must resort to highly controlling methods of instruction. Student collaborative work, student discussion, and independent projects, all of which are called for in the 1989 curriculum reform, are seen as possibilities for losing control of students.

There are at least three plausible explanations for why, despite teacher participation in standard setting, some teachers feel that at least some of their students cannot meet the standards:

- Because K–12 schooling is organizationally flat (especially from the perspective of implementation, which rests largely with individual teachers), not all teachers will necessarily feel represented in the standard-setting process.

- Teachers may not agree with the standards that are established (regardless of their views on representation).
- Even if they consider the standards appropriate, teachers may still feel that some students fail to get the support (whether from home or previous school experiences) or motivation necessary to meet those standards.

No state or district initiative that we saw had an adequate response for addressing these teacher concerns. To the contrary, much of the staff development, instructional materials, and assessment procedures reinforce their concerns and serve as a deterrent to desired change.

Effects of State and District Standard Setting

Characterizing policy effects on practice is not easy. Changes in policies, as well as changes in practice, must be documented. Changes in practice must be preceded by and correlated with policy shifts. Policy shifts occur simultaneously with each other and with other changes. What is causing what? To some extent, documenting intermediate changes helps to build links between policy and practice. Attributions by teachers and administrators can be helpful, but they can also be deceiving. Occasionally policy initiatives are attributed effects that they do not have (e.g., when teachers say they emphasize basic skills in their instruction because basic skills are emphasized on tests, but really they emphasize basic skills because they believe basic skills are most important and what they feel most comfortable teaching). The policy "effects" noted here are not without caveat and ambiguity. Still, based on our analyses, we are convinced of their validity.

Effects of State and District Standard Setting on Course Enrollments

Increasing the number of credits required for graduation has resulted in more students' taking more mathematics and science, particularly the beginning academic courses. In states with high school graduation tests (Florida and South Carolina), enrollments increased in remedial courses for the tested subject, mathematics. In states without high school graduation tests, enrollments increased in college prep courses in both mathematics and science. Our findings are as follows:

- Based on transcript analyses in four of the six states studied (California, Florida, Missouri, and Pennsylvania), increases in the number of students taking science courses was substantial, with beginning academic courses the biggest enrollment gainers. The numbers taking mathematics courses also increased, again with beginning academic courses the leading gainers. On average, increases were one year or more in science and one-third of a year in mathematics. There was no evidence of increases in dropout rates or decreases in high school graduation rates.

- In states with high school graduation tests (Florida and South Carolina), enrollments increased in remedial courses designed to help students pass the tested subjects. Low-achieving students met their entire mathematics requirement through remedial work. This was not true in science, which was not tested. Thus, although low-achieving students in Florida and South Carolina took more credits of mathematics, the nature of the mathematics that they studied was sharply limited. They did not take high school college prep mathematics, such as algebra, geometry, and calculus.

- In the absence of high school graduation tests (and for students who easily meet the test requirements), there was an enrollment increase in college prep courses in both mathematics and science. As one mathematics teacher stated, "When you require more mathematics from students who are average or bright, then they will take classes where they will learn something." This practice was reinforced by college requirements, which universally stipulated not only the *amount* of mathematics and science they required for admission, but also the *nature* of that mathematics and science.

Effects of State and District Standard Setting on Course Offerings

In addition to states and universities' mandating the number and nature of science and mathematics courses, districts and schools took further steps in determining course requirements and designing course content, as follows:

- In addition to state and university initiatives to increase the amount and quality of mathematics and science students take, some districts and schools took additional steps. Remedial classes in mathematics and science were eliminated, or all freshmen were required to take a particular math or science course (e.g., algebra and chemistry/physics). Obviously, these initiatives changed the course-taking patterns of students; they did not necessarily guarantee the nature of instruction students received in those courses.

- As mentioned earlier, an especially promising strategy for curriculum upgrading was the development of "bridge" courses in mathematics, such as Math A in California. Originally conceptualized in the 1985 California

Math Framework, Math A was designed as an intermediate step for students who might otherwise have taken 9th grade general mathematics but who might not be ready for Algebra 1. Math A emphasizes group work, use of manipulatives, less emphasis on lecturing and more emphasis on student participation, less emphasis on specific answers and more emphasis on open-ended questions, and more emphasis on written responses and student portfolios. Developed by teachers but with state support, there are 13 Math A units. Each unit generally takes three to four weeks to cover. Math A is not a state requirement, but an option that some districts, some schools, and some individual teachers have chosen to adopt. Before a teacher can teach Math A, a five-day inservice program is required. Some districts and schools have added to this minimum inservice requirement, sometimes substantially.

• In the three instances in which we had detailed descriptions of the enacted curriculum for courses required of all freshmen, the content of these required courses looked much like that of courses with the same title that were not required of all students.[4] Algebra 1, which was required in the Pennsylvania suburban high school, looked very much like Algebra 1 in sites where it was not required. Eighty-seven percent of instruction was on algebra, as opposed to other content areas in mathematics, such as arithmetic, measurement, and geometry. The average amount of time spent on algebra across all algebra courses was 82 percent, with a standard deviation of .11. In the Arizona high school, which required algebra for all freshmen, 61 percent of the time was spent on algebra. An additional 38 percent of time was spent on arithmetic and number concepts. This required Algebra 1 course looked more like a typical algebra course than a typical prealgebra course (prealgebra courses had a mean time on algebra of 43 percent, with a standard deviation of .17). In the one example of a science class required of all students, the Arizona urban high school, teachers of freshman chemistry/physics spent 74 percent of instructional time on chemistry and physics. Unfortunately, there were no other chemistry/physics courses in the sample with which to compare these courses. These data are largely reassuring that when college prep courses are required of all students, the content of instruction is not necessarily compromised.

• Despite 1989 curriculum reforms calling for hard content for *all* students and reinforced in the California frameworks, some form of tracking occurred in every high school studied. Many administrators and teachers reported that they intended to eliminate tracking in the near future; some schools had initiatives in that direction already, but the results were discouraging. The Pennsylvania suburban school that sought to require algebra of all students had compromised by offering one honors section and one prealgebra section. In an urban high school in Arizona, all students took algebra and chemistry/physics in their freshman year; but in subsequent years, traditional tracks emerged.

Effects of State and District Standard Setting on the Nature of Instruction

Although the curriculum-upgrading initiatives had an effect on the numbers and kinds of courses students took, the instruction students received did not necessarily reflect much of the 1989 curriculum reform, with its emphasis on instruction that places a premium on student understanding and problem solving and that places students increasingly in control of their own learning.

Unfortunately, with one possible exception, none of the mathematics and science courses reflected much of the 1989 curriculum reform, not even courses in California, with that state's highly visible frameworks. As Figure 9.2 shows, over half of the instructional time was spent in lecturing

Figure 9.2
Average Percentages of Time Spent on Instructional Strategies and Expected Student Outcomes

Strategies and Outcomes	Math	Science
Instructional Strategies		
Exposition	.562	.644
Pictoral Models	.079	.146
Concrete Models	.065	.048
Equations/Formulas	.237	.046
Graphs	.038	.014
Lab Work	.016	.095
Field Work	.000	.006
Expected Student Outcomes		
Memorizing Facts	.086	.310
Understanding	.295	.428
Collecting Data	.015	.078
Order/Estimation	.011	.050
Routine Procedures	.392	.022
Routine Problems	.148	.049
Interpreting Data	.023	.040
Novel Problems	.020	.017
Theory/Proof	.003	.003

Note: Entries are proportions of instructional time for a full school year and averaged over courses studied.

and reading (exposition) in both mathematics and science. Despite state and university requirements for lab work in science, only 10 percent of science instructional time was spent in lab work and field work combined. As for expected student outcomes, heavy emphasis was placed on memorizing facts, understanding concepts, and completing routine procedures such as computation. Virtually no time was spent involving mathematics students in data collection and data interpretation, and only 2 percent of time was spent involving them in solving novel problems. Even in science, only 10 percent of instructional time was spent on data collection and interpretation.

The one exception to these findings is California's Math A. In the class studied, over 25 percent of the time was spent on instruction using concrete models, including manipulatives. Similarly, in the area of expected student outcomes, 60 percent of time in the Math A class was devoted to promoting student understanding, twice the average for other math courses. Fourteen percent of instructional time was spent collecting data, whereas in other math classes the average was less than 2 percent. Even so, less than 5 percent of instructional time was spent on the much emphasized goal of solving novel problems. And even in Math A, over half the time was spent in exposition (lecture).

The Most Influential Policy Initiatives

Based on our analyses of math and science instruction in eighteen high schools across twelve districts in six states, a pattern emerges as to the nature of curriculum standard-setting and upgrading policies that are most influential on practice. Simply put, the most influential policy initiatives are the ones backed with authority and power that clearly describe the goal and specify how it is to be obtained. This confirms and extends previous findings on policy implementation, whether initiated at the federal level (Elmore and McLaughlin 1982, Sabatier and Mazmanian 1980) or focused on elementary school mathematics (Porter et al. 1988). As the clarity, focus, and power of policy initiatives decrease, influence becomes more variable.

High school course requirements for graduation are an excellent example. Requirements, and consequences for not meeting those requirements, are clearly specified, easy to communicate, and simple to understand. What schools must do is less clearly specified; as a result, we saw considerable variance in school response. Some schools attempted to push students into demanding content in higher level courses while others did not. In some cases, schools did receive direction as to the nature of changes they were to make. For example, Florida and South Carolina emphasize lab work in science courses. However, this lab work requirement is much more difficult to monitor than student course completion. In Florida, schools needed merely to assure the state that they were meeting the 40 percent lab requirement. In South Carolina, there was no monitoring at all. These state requirements for lab work in science had much smaller and more variable effects on practice.

Requiring students to pass tests for high school graduation had predictable effects as well: more remedial work for low-achieving students in tested subjects. Again, the policy is clear and so are the consequences for lack of compliance. Students know what they must do. As in the case of high school graduation course requirements, what schools must do is less clear. Schools must determine for themselves how best to serve students. Because the requirement is a minimal standard, schools serving high concentrations of high-achieving students—and high-achieving students in other schools—meet the requirements without even trying. In short, minimum test performance is prescriptive only to a subset of students and only in the subjects tested.

Assessing the Third Wave of Curriculum Reform

Although increased graduation requirements and test performance have had the intended effect, the curriculum reform of 1989, calling for hard content for all students and emphasizing conceptual understanding, problem solving, and higher-order thinking, is a long way from being reflected in high school math and science. Tracking is alive and well; and although some states have intensified basic skills instruction, no state has attempted to systemically coordinate policy to emphasize the goals of curriculum reform. Whether the policy instruments used to intensify basic skills can be turned to these newer goals remains an open question. Clearly, it would be premature to declare the curriculum reform a failure (our study was conducted within a year of the reform's beginning); nevertheless, new and much more powerful policy initiatives will be required.

Curriculum frameworks are neither very prescriptive, nor, by themselves, a strong influence on practice. The highly visible California frameworks present a curriculum philosophy and general directions for change, but leave a great deal of discretion to individual interpretation. Not surprisingly, many teachers interpret the frameworks as justification for their current practice. Many other teachers are unsure of how to change their instruction to make it consistent with the framework (Cohen and Ball 1990).

Where frameworks are translated into clearer statements of what is desired (for example, Math A in California), the effects are much more pronounced and much more predictable. But even Math A appears to fall short of providing all of the clarity and support necessary to produce widespread, lasting change.

The 1989 curriculum reform, unlike the mid-'80s standard-setting initiatives, requires substantial changes in teacher practice and curriculum. We found plenty of evidence that there was a serious lack of teacher capacity for achieving the 1989 curriculum reforms, at least among schools serving high concentrations of low-achieving students.

First, teachers, counselors, and administrators did not know how to deal with the student diversity resulting from the elimination of tracking. This is perhaps the single greatest tension created by curriculum upgrading. As more students are pushed into more demanding academic work at the high school level, teachers are confronted with new and more pressing problems: how to communicate with students, how to motivate students, and how to conduct classes in which students' prior achievements, aptitudes, and interests differ dramatically.

Compounding this problem of how to deal with student diversity is a lack of clarity as to exactly what is meant by frameworks and professional standards calling for hard content for all students. Does this mean that all students are to study exactly the same curriculum across the entire K–12 experience? Or does this mean that all students should be exposed to and master a core curriculum containing a balance between facts and skills, on the one hand, and higher-order thinking, problem solving, and reasoning on the other? If there is to be a common core of content for all students, what is the definition of that core, and how should schools and teachers be best organized to deliver that core to students in a way that benefits them regardless of their backgrounds and aspirations? Amidst this confusion caused by lack of a clear goal, schools and teachers are trying a variety of approaches, but without total commitment.

Teachers' qualifications present yet another problem in mathematics and especially in science, where graduation requirement increases were most dramatic. Nationally, only two thirds of the high school science teachers have a major in science or science education (Blank and Dalkilic 1991). In our sample of all math and science teachers in three high schools per state, 32 percent of the California science teachers and 38 percent of the South Carolina science teachers had majors in science. Similarly, only two-thirds of the high school mathematics teachers in the United States have a major in math or mathematics education (Blank and Dalkilic 1991).

In our sample, state percentages averaged 70 percent, with all above 60 percent.

What these figures cannot show is how much high school math and science teachers are prepared to change their instruction to fit the vision of the NCTM *Standards* and the new state frameworks in California and Arizona. Such a change depends on teachers who feel comfortable with their subject matter in a way that allows them to be flexible and responsive. We saw considerable evidence that teachers lack the knowledge and energy to deliver a curriculum that places a premium on deep conceptual understanding and that facilitates problem solving and reasoning. There are many probable explanations for such deficits:

• Instructional materials consistent with the goal of hard content for all students are not always available.

• Testing practices at the state, district, and classroom level often are not consistent with the new reforms.

• Access to good, concrete models of the desired instructional practices is limited.

• Instruction consistent with the curriculum reform is simply more work.

We saw painfully little indication that states and districts are prepared to spend the time and money necessary to support the types of changes required to address these deficiencies. Money was a serious problem in all urban sites except those enjoying special benefits from desegregation rulings. Even basic instructional materials, such as textbooks, were in short supply. Lab space was inadequate—in amount, conception, and maintenance. Although we saw some serious efforts to address the assessment problem at the state level, most notably in Arizona and California, we saw no serious efforts to address the shortage of appropriate instructional materials.

Most disappointing was the quantity and quality of staff development. Although a great deal of money is spent on staff development in the United States—millions per year—only a few dollars per year is spent on each teacher. Not surprisingly, this has resulted in fragmented and episodic approaches to staff development. Often, someone far removed from the classroom decides what teachers need and arranges to have it delivered in the form of a half-day workshop to those who volunteer. We saw no evidence of states' using the Eisenhower money in a programmatic approach to supporting teachers in curriculum upgrading. We are convinced that staff development needs to be completely rethought so that schools and teachers are the initiators and main providers of their own professional development. Experts from beyond the school should be called on only as needed and only as they can serve a school-based strategy for improvement. Developing such a strategy, of course, would require schools to see their responsibilities in a new light. It would also require additional funds, first and foremost, to provide teacher release time. Unfortunately, the 1989 curriculum reform coincided with the 1989 recession, making traditionally tight funds for educational improvement nonexistent.

We did see a few exciting projects for curriculum upgrading, but invariably these were add-ons—not part of a main program—with questionable futures. Math A in California appears promising and has been embellished in some sites to include serious staff development. The urban high school in Arizona has used its substantial increase in funding to accomplish exciting curriculum upgrading and to support staff development. We saw little sign, however, that empowerment strategies were replacing curriculum-control strategies as the primary mechanism for curriculum upgrading (Porter et al. 1991), or that serious policy and structural changes were being addressed to bring high school mathematics and science into alignment with the vision of the NCTM *Standards* and the *Science for All Americans* report.

Endnotes

[1] Student gains are determined by first placing schools in quintiles according to student socioeconomic status and teachers' years of education, and then within each quintile deviating actual gains from predicted gains.

[2] Rotated, so that once every three years each school will be tested.

[3] In 1988–89, the Eisenhower program was funded for $124 million nationally, which translated into an average of $30 per teacher (approximately $1.5 million in Arizona and $13.5 million in California).

[4] Teacher logs were the source of information for describing the enacted curriculum; logs were kept daily, reported weekly, and aggregated to a full year.

References

American Association for the Advancement of Science. (1989). *Science for All Americans*. A Project 2061 report on Literacy Goals in Science, Mathematics, and Technology. Washington, D.C.: Author.

Belsches-Simmons, G., P. Flakus-Mosqueda, B. Lindner, and K. Mayer. (March 1987). *Recent State Educational Reform: Initial Teacher Certification, Teacher Compensation and High School Graduation Requirements*. Denver, Colo.: Education Commission of the States.

Blank, R.K., and M. Dalkilic. (1991). *State Indicators of Science and Mathematics Education 1990*. Washington, D.C.: Council of Chief State School Officers.

California State Board of Education. (1985). *Mathematics Framework for California Public Schools, Kindergarten Through Grade Twelve*. Sacramento, Calif.: Author.

Clune, W.H., P.A. White, S. Sun, and J.H. Patterson. (1991). *Changes in High School Course-Taking, 1982–88: A Study of Transcript Data from Selected Schools and States* (CPRE Research Report Series RR-022). New Brunswick, N.J.: Rutgers University, Center for Policy Research in Education.

Cohen, D.K., and D. Ball. (1990). "Policy and Practice: An Overview." *Educational Evaluation and Policy Analysis* 12, 3: 347–53.

Education Commission of the States. (August 1987). *Minimum High School Graduation Course Requirements*. Denver, Colo.: Author.

Elmore, R.F., and M.W. McLaughlin. (1982). "Strategic Choice in Federal Education Policy: The Compliance-Assistance Tradeoff." In *Policymaking in Education, 81st yearbook of the National Society for the Study of Education*, edited by A. Lieberman and M.W. McLaughlin (pp. 159–194). Chicago: University of Chicago Press.

Firestone, W.A., S.H. Fuhrman, and M.W. Kirst. (1989). *The Progress of Reform: An Appraisal of State Educational Initiatives*. New Brunswick, N.J.: Rutgers University, Center for Policy Research in Education.

Firestone, W.A., S. Rosenblum, B.D. Bader, and D. Massell. (1991). *Education Reform from 1983 to 1990: State Action and District Response* (CPRE Research Report Series RR-021). New Brunswick, N.J.: Rutgers University, Center for Policy Research in Education.

Florida Department of Education. (1984). *Student Performance Standards of Excellence for Florida Schools*. Tallahassee, Fla.: Author.

Gagnon, P., and the Bradley Commission on History in Schools, eds. (1989). *Historical Literacy: The Case for History in American Education*. New York: Macmillan.

Goertz, M.E. (1988). *State Educational Standards: A 50-State Survey*. Princeton, N.J.: Educational Testing Service.

Knapp, M.S., A.A. Zucker, N. Adelman, and M. St. John, M. (October 1990). *National Study of the Education for Economic Security Act (EESA) Title II Program (now the Eisenhower Mathematics and Science Education Program): A Summary of Findings*. SRI International, Menlo Park, Calif., and Policy Studies Associates, Washington, D.C. (Contract No. LC88029001). Washington, D.C.: U.S. Department of Education.

McDonnell, L.M., L. Burstein, T. Ormseth, J.M. Catterall, and D. Moody. (1990). *Discovering What Schools Really Teach: Designing Improved Coursework Indicators*. Santa Monica, Calif.: The RAND Corporation.

McDonnell, L.M., and R.F. Elmore. (1987). "Getting the Job Done: Alternative Policy Instruments." *Educational Evaluation and Policy Analysis* 9, 2: 133–52.

McNeil, L.M. (1988a). "Contradictions of Control, Part 1: Administrators and Teachers." *Phi Delta Kappan* 69: 333–39.

McNeil, L.M. (1988b). "Contradictions of Control, Part 2: Teachers, Students, and Curriculum." *Phi Delta Kappan* 69: 432–38.

McNeil, L.M. (1988c). "Contradictions of Control, Part 3: Contradictions of Reform." *Phi Delta Kappan* 69: 478–85.

Meyer, R. (1990). *Beyond Academic Reform: The Case for Integrated Applied and Academic Education*. Discussion paper prepared for the Institute for Research on Poverty, University of Wisconsin-Madison.

Missouri Department of Elementary and Secondary Education. (1986). *Core Competencies and Key Skills for Missouri Schools*. Jefferson City, Mo.: Author.

Murphy, J. (1990). "The Educational Reform Movement of the 1980s: A Comprehensive Analysis." In *The Educational Reform Movement of the 1980s*, edited by J. Murphy (pp. 3–55). Berkeley, Calif: McCutchan.

National Center for Education Statistics. (1988). *The Condition of Education: Elementary and Secondary Education*. Washington, D.C.: U.S. Department of Education.

National Commission on Excellence in Education. (1983). *A Nation at Risk: The Imperative for Educational Reform.* Washington, D.C.: U.S. Government Printing Office.

National Commission on Social Studies in the Schools. (1989). *Charting a Course: Social Studies for the 21st Century.* Washington, D.C.: Author.

National Council of Teachers of Mathematics. (1989). *Curriculum and Evaluation Standards for School Mathematics.* Reston, Va.: Author.

National Research Council. (1989). *Everybody Counts: A Report to the Nation on the Future of Mathematics Education.* Washington, D.C.: National Academy Press.

Pennsylvania Department of Education. (1987a). *Mathematics Content Lists.* Harrisburg, Pa: Author.

Pennsylvania Department of Education. (1987b). *A Recommended Science Competency Continuum for Pennsylvania Schools.* Harrisburg, Pa: Author.

Porter, A.C. (1989). "External Standards and Good Teaching: The Pros and Cons of Telling Teachers What to Do." *Educational Evaluation and Policy Analysis* 27, 4: 343–56.

Porter, A.C., D.A. Archbald, and A.K. Tyree, Jr. (1991). "Reforming the Curriculum: Will Empowerment Policies Replace Control?" In *The Politics of Curriculum and Testing: The 1990 Yearbook of the Politics of Education Associations* (pp. 11–36), edited by S. Fuhrman and B. Malen. London: Taylor and Francis Ltd.

Porter, A., R. Floden, D. Freeman, W. Schmidt, and J. Schwille. (1988). "Content Determinants in Elementary School Mathematics." In *Perspectives on Research on Effective Mathematics Teaching* (pp. 96–113), edited by D.A. Grouws and T.J. Cooney. Hillsdale, N.J.: Erlbaum.

Rosenholtz, S.J. (1987). "Education Reform Strategies: Will They Increase Teacher Commitment?" *American Journal of Education* 95: 557.

Rowan, B. (1990). "Commitment and Control: Alternative Strategies for the Organizational Design of Schools." In *Review of Research in Education* 16 (pp. 353–389), edited by C.B. Cazden. Washington, D.C.: American Educational Research Association.

Sabatier, P., and D. Mazmanian. (1980). "The Implementation of Public Policy: A Framework of Analysis." *Policy Studies Journal* 8, 4: 575–596.

Smith, M.S., and J. O'Day. (1991). "Systemic School Reform." In *The Politics of Curriculum and Testing, The 1990 Yearbook of the Politics of Education Association* (pp. 233–267), edited by S.H. Fuhrman and B. Malen. London: The Falmer Press.

South Carolina Department of Education. (1982). *Teaching and Testing Our Basic Skills Objectives.* Columbia, S.C.: Author.

Stecher, B.M. (1992). *Describing Secondary Curriculum in Mathematics and Science: Current Status and Future Indicators.* Santa Monica, Calif.: RAND.

U.S. Department of Education. (February 1988). *State Education Statistics.* Washington, D.C.: Author, Office of Planning, Budget and Evaluation.

Wise, A.E. (1988). "The Two Conflicting Trends in School Reform: Legislating Learning Revisited." *Phi Delta Kappan* 69: 328–332.

10

How Districts Mediate Between State Policy and Teachers' Practice

James P. Spillane

More and more government agencies are entering the business of curriculum and instructional policymaking. Over the past decade, state departments of education have begun to pay greater attention to instructional governance. These state-level efforts to govern curriculum and instruction, however, raise important questions about the role of local government agencies that have traditionally been responsible for curriculum and instruction. As state departments of education try to govern curriculum and instruction, we need to consider how those efforts might influence, and be influenced by, local curriculum and instructional government initiatives at the central office and school levels. Following a brief historical overview, I present a case study of such an effort and its effect at the district level.

Historical Perspective on State Governance of Curriculum

The U.S. educational governance system has changed dramatically since the 1950s. Both state and federal agencies have increased their share

Author's Note: I am grateful to Deborah Ball, David Cohen, S.G. Grant, Nancy Jennings, and Suzanne Wilson for their helpful comments and suggestions on drafts of this article. This research was partially supported by the Carnegie Corporation, Pew Charitable Trusts, and the Consortium for Policy Research in Education—a consortium of the Eagleton Institute of Politics at Rutgers University, the University of Wisconsin-Madison, Stanford University, and Michigan State University—funded by the Office of Educational Research and Improvement, U.S. Department of Education, under Grant No. OERI-R117G10007. The views expressed are those of the author and do not represent endorsement by the sponsoring institutions. An earlier version of this chapter was presented at the Association for Public Analysis and Management Annual Research Conference, Denver, Colorado, October 29–31, 1992.

of the funding of public schools. In 1979, state contributions surpassed local contributions (Doyle and Finn 1984). State departments have also grown, while the consolidation of schools and districts has increased (Meyer, Scott, Strang, and Creighton 1987).

The volume of federal and state-level educational policies has also increased. State and federal agencies have implemented policies that focus on educational equity, raising student achievement standards, and strengthening student graduation and teacher certification requirements. Most noticeable, perhaps, has been the increasing interest of state and federal policymakers in instruction and curriculum, issues that were traditionally left to the discretion of local educators. By 1990, many state governments that had previously confined their attention to school finance were expanding their scope of attention to include curriculum and instruction (Kaagan and Cooley 1989). By 1990, state-level curriculum and instructional policies were no longer a novelty.

Those developments have led many commentators to speculate that the autonomy and control of local educators over the school curriculum has decreased (Cantor 1980, Wise 1979). According to Cantor:

> The likelihood is that eventually a position will be reached whereby in some states the central authority is more or less in complete control of education throughout its territorial area. . . . The corollary of such a system is that school districts either disappear entirely or have their powers so attenuated as to become rudimentary (1980, p. 30).

From this perspective, when we centralize the policy-making and educational governance process at the state level, local educators merely follow the dictates of higher-level agencies.

Many education researchers, however, question that perspective. Centralized educational governance and policymaking at one level of the organization, they argue, does not result in a concomitant decrease in educational governance and policy-making activities at other levels (Cohen 1982, Berman and Pauly 1975, Berman and McLaughlin 1977, Fuhrman and Elmore 1990). "Power and organization have often grown in tandem, rather than growing in one place at the expense of another" (Cohen 1982, p. 476).

Yet another trend in educational policy raises further questions about local curriculum governance and decision making: In the late 1980s, states like California and federal education policies (such as *America 2000*) began to call for fundamental changes in how teachers taught and students learned (California State Department of Education 1985a, b; U.S. Department of Education 1991). Unlike earlier state-level policies, which focused mainly on the "ritual classifications of schooling"—teacher certification requirements, graduation credits, and testing—these "new" state policy initiatives focused on the "core technology of schooling"—teaching (Meyer and Rowan 1978). State instructional policies began to call for more ambitious visions of student learning that implied radical shifts in teachers' instructional roles and practices. This trend represented a new departure for state government because it involved detail about both the content of the school curriculum and its presentation to students. Most of these reform initiatives seem concentrated at the state level. And the role of school districts in the reform of curriculum and instruction has received little attention in these efforts.

Past research offers conflicting evidence on districts' roles in curriculum and instruction. One study of California school districts suggests that although the number of central office staff increased and job titles became more specialized between 1930 and 1970, curriculum and instruction received little attention (Rowan 1983). Other studies suggest that district central offices pay little attention to curriculum and instruction in their interactions with school principals and teachers (Hannaway and Sproull 1978–79; Floden et al. 1988). But some evidence suggests that districts can and do play an important role in curriculum and instructional reform. Central office personnel, for example, can play an important role in successfully introducing change at the school and classroom level (Berman and McLaughlin 1977, David 1990).

As state governments enter the realm of curriculum and instructional governance and policymaking, the question of the role of school districts in curriculum and instruction arises anew. What role, if any, do school districts play in curriculum and instructional reform in these new state-level instructional policy initiatives?

In this chapter, I explore this issue through the response of one school district to a new state reading policy in a large industrial state. Here, one school district's efforts to govern curriculum both influenced and were influenced by a state-level reading policy that was designed to reform not only the content of the reading curriculum but how teachers teach reading. I have drawn on data from an exploratory study of how two school districts responded to a state-level reading policy. The study involved interviews with state policymakers who developed and implemented the state reading policy, central office personnel in the two districts, and school principals and other school-level administrators in three schools in each district.

The chapter focuses on preliminary findings from one district, Parkwood (a pseudonym), and includes responses to interviews with four central office staff members, four school principals, three school-level curriculum specialists, and five teachers who were involved in district efforts to respond to the state policy. In addition, I have included analyses of state and district documents related to the policy and to reading instruction. These sources provide the basis for a discussion of the district's response to the new state policy. Two questions emerged from this study: How did the state's new reading policy shape the central office's reading curriculum in this district? How did the central office's response to the state's reading policy shape the policy itself?

The State Reading Policy

In 1985, after considerable preparatory work on the part of state Department of Education staff, the State Reading Association, and some university professors, the state Board of Education approved a revised state definition of reading. The revised state reading definition stated:

> Reading is the process of constructing meaning through dynamic interaction among reader, the text, and the context of the reading situation (*State Department Essential Goals and Objectives*).[1]

Compared to the previous state definition, which described reading as "a process of transforming the visual representation of language into meaning," the revised definition suggested a considerable shift in how state policymakers envisioned reading instruction in classrooms. The old definition focused on students' ability to recognize words. In contrast, the revised definition placed much greater emphasis on students' comprehension of text. The revised definition suggested that students should be able to construct meaning from whole texts, rather than merely figuring out words. Moreover, the new policy portrayed comprehension as an interactive process, shaped by readers' preexisting knowledge, the material being read, and the context in which the reading took place.

With a revised reading definition in place, state policymakers began to revise the state's "essential objectives for reading education" to reflect the new definition. Reading goals were written in terms of student outcomes under three headings:

- Constructing meaning,
- Students' knowledge about reading, and
- Students' attitudes to and self-perceptions of reading (*State Goals: Reading at a Glance* 1987).

One goal, for example, included the "ability to integrate textual information within sentences, within a whole text, with information outside the text, with information from the reader's knowledge" (*Reading at a Glance* 1987). The state department, with the assistance of the Reading Association and some local educators, conducted workshops across the state for teachers on the state reading policy. State workshops presented the definition from a cognitive psychology perspective, providing teachers and local administrators with information on research in cognitive psychology and reading strategies (e.g., KWL, DRTA).[2] Conference organizers developed scripted modules of the presentations with transparencies and handouts for participants to use to conduct their own staff development efforts in their districts and schools.

In addition, the policymakers revised the state's reading testing program, which was administered at grades 4, 7, and 11, to reflect the changes in reading that state policymakers were advancing. The revised reading test differed significantly from its predecessor. The previous test focused entirely on discrete reading skills and literal comprehension and included brief text selections that students had to read before answering questions that were written for the purpose of the test. In contrast, the revised test centered on students' ability to comprehend text, requiring students not only to respond to questions answered in the text but also to questions that drew on students' prior knowledge and experiences. Test selections were longer (500–2,000 words) and drawn from children's literature. And the test required students to respond to expository text, as well as narrative selections.

The state's reading policy was an ambitious effort. State policymakers had taken a bold new step in attempting to change how teachers taught reading. For the first time, they had gone beyond using state policy as a means of specifying the content of the reading curriculum and had tried to affect instruction. And the reading instruction that policymakers envisioned called for dramatic changes in how reading was taught in classrooms. Modal reading instruction focused on discrete reading skills, paying little attention to students' ability to comprehend text (see Durkin 1978–79, in the References). The policy, in contrast, called on teachers to move away from drilling students on isolated vocabulary, phonics, and decoding skills. Instead, teachers were encouraged to show students how to make sense of what they read by actively involving them in constructing meaning. Policymakers saw reading as a process of "constructing meaning" from text rather than as a process of extracting knowledge from printed matter.

How was the state's reading policy received at the local district level? Did central office personnel reform their existing reading curriculum? The case study that follows offers an opportunity for examining these questions.

A District Responds: The Case of Parkwood

Overview

Parkwood is a suburban school district with twelve elementary schools, serving more than 7,000 students. Fewer than 6 percent of the students are minorities; most of the students come from middle- and upper-middle-income families. The district has a modest-sized central office administration, including four professional staff members and an assistant superintendent employed to deal with curriculum and instructional issues.

The Parkwood community supports its school system. Education is highly valued, and residents have high expectations for the performance of the school district and their students. According to one senior central office administrator, the community "realizes that good schools contribute to good communities" (interview, May 7, 1992). Other indicators seem to support these suggestions. Over three-quarters of high school graduates, for example, planned to seek a place in higher education in 1990–91. Average district scores on both the verbal and math Scholastic Aptitude Test (SAT) are well above the national average. Average student performance on the state testing program in reading, math, and science are also above the state averages. According to both central office and school-level administrators, the community pays close attention to the district's performance in the state testing program.

The state's reading policy received considerable attention from central office personnel in Parkwood. They undertook numerous initiatives to disseminate ideas from the policy to Parkwood teachers, and they reformed the instructional guidance system (e.g., textbooks, curriculum guides, tests) in an effort to change reading instruction in Parkwood classrooms. Community interest in the district's performance on the state testing program no doubt provided considerable incentives for the Parkwood central office to attend to the state's reading policy. After all, the reading testing program was an integral component of state policymakers' efforts to reform reading instruction. But although those contextual factors mattered, they only partially explain the extent and nature of Parkwood's response to the state's reading policy. Central office administrators in Parkwood paid attention to the state policy for various reasons and responded to the policy in different ways. Individuals' beliefs about and knowledge of reading instruction and their existing reform agendas shaped their attention and response to the state policy. In other words, characteristics of individual central office administrators interacted with contextual features of the district to influence how Parkwood responded to the policy.

Jensen, the director of elementary education, and Roberts, a school learning specialist who chaired a central office committee to review the existing reading curriculum, played prominent roles in Parkwood's response to the state policy. (Jenson and Roberts are pseudonyms.) I consider their efforts, and the changes made in the central office instructional guidance system, next.

The Context of Change

Until the late 1970s, Parkwood did not have a district-mandated reading curriculum. In fact, the central office paid little attention to instruction, hiring no central office staff with responsibility for instruction until the late '70s. Each school within the district was, in effect, its "own little island" (Roberts interview, July 18, 1991), with individual principals and teachers taking responsibility for issues of curriculum and instruction. Different reading programs were used across the district, and for the most part reading instruction was "basal bound" (Principal 1 interview, February 19, 1991). There were few exceptions to this traditional approach to reading instruction.

In the late 1970s, however, the central office began to take a much stronger role in curriculum leadership, hiring three new staff members, including a new assistant superintendent, to deal with curriculum and instruction. First, the central office adopted a district reading textbook for all teachers. Teachers had to submit students' scores on the end-of-unit and end-of-book tests from the basal to the central office, and teachers administered a standardized reading test at each grade level. A new student report card was introduced, and all teachers had to participate in staff development in the Hunter Instruction Theory into Practice (ITIP) model. The central office's new reading curriculum focused on discrete reading skills (e.g., decoding) and, according to one principal, was a response to the national "back to basics movement" (Principal 2 interview, May 8, 1992).

A couple of schools supported more innovative approaches to reading instruction, using trade books to teach reading rather than basal programs. But those schools were the exception rather than the norm in Parkwood. It was into this environment that the new state reading policy was received in Parkwood in the mid-1980s.

Attending to the Policy

Despite the obvious differences between the state's new reading policy and the central office's existing reading curriculum in Parkwood, the state policy received considerable attention from central office personnel. Jensen, the director of elementary education, was eager to get the state's reading policy implemented in Parkwood. The state's ideas about reading instruction were not novel for Jensen; they fit with her beliefs about instruction (Jensen interview, September 23, 1992). Many practices that she had encouraged as a school administrator in the 1970s coincided with the ideas about instruction being pushed in the state's reading policy (e.g., focusing on reading comprehension, rather than drilling on isolated skills, and on using literature to teach reading). Taking a position at the central office in the early 1980s, she hoped to reform the elementary school curriculum districtwide by introducing many of the ideas about instruction that she had successfully implemented as a building principal (Jensen interview, September 23, 1992). The state's reading policy gave Jensen's instructional reform agenda considerable legitimacy. Jensen sent three district representatives to a curriculum review conference organized by the state Department of Education. According to Roberts, one of the three district representative who attended the curriculum review conference, the ideas presented seemed sensible, though not novel.

Roberts also saw the state's reading policy as a lever to shift some Parkwood central office administrators away from their emphasis on the Hunter instructional model and basic skills (Roberts, April 11, 1992). In Roberts's view, the state workshop provided an opportunity for changes in both curriculum and instruction in Parkwood:

> I saw [the state definition] as a real chance for our district to start moving away from some of the practices [drilling students in decoding skills] that I thought were holding kids back (Roberts interview, April 11, 1992).

When Roberts and her colleagues returned from the curriculum review workshop, they encouraged Jensen and other senior central office administrators to form a task force to review the district's reading curriculum in the light of the state's initiative in reading.

Reading Guidelines and Reading Philosophy

With the help of other central office staff and a committee of district teachers, Jensen undertook a major overhaul of the district's instructional guidance system. The central office published a revised district curriculum guide in 1988. Comparing those documents with earlier curriculum guides suggests that, in terms of reading instruction, Parkwood had undergone a revolution—at least on paper. According to the district's 1988 reading philosophy statement:

> Reading, one component of the language process, is dynamic. The meaning of the message which the reader constructs is dependent upon the interaction of the reader's background experiences, the author's purpose for writing the material, the type of material being read, and the reader's purpose for reading it (*Parkwood Reading Curriculum Guidelines*).

As a result, "Reading is taught as a process of thinking, not as a series of isolated skills" (*Parkwood Reading Curriculum Guidelines*). Mirroring the dramatic change in the state definition, the new reading philosophy represents a considerable departure from the old Parkwood reading philosophy statement, which portrayed reading as a process of decoding and recognizing words—a series of isolated skills.

The new ideas about reading instruction embedded in the district's instructional guidance system were many and suggested a radical departure from modal reading practice: Teachers would focus on reading comprehension instead of drilling students on isolated reading skills. They would use real literature to teach reading instead of selections with controlled vocabulary. They would teach reading through whole-group instruction instead of through ability groups.

The *Parkwood Reading Philosophy and Reading Curriculum Guidelines* reflected many ideas presented in the state's policy documents, including the state's staff development workshops and the revised testing program. The guidelines portrayed reading as an "interactive process." And they paid considerable attention to the reading strategies (e.g., KWL, QAR)[2] that state department staff were disseminating through workshops. The guidelines accorded a central role to reading strategies to emphasize comprehension over the learning of isolated decoding skills. In fact, the reading objectives, outlined in the Parkwood curriculum guide, were practically identical to the state's. Parkwood seems to have gone a step further than the state, matching specific strategies with particular learning objectives.

But despite the many similarities, there are also notable differences. Many instructional ideas in the Parkwood guidelines seem rather novel compared to the state policy documents. One whole section of the Parkwood guidelines is devoted to "Developmental Stages of Reading" that teachers should use to guide their reading instruction. The guidelines—which were not mentioned in the state policy—detail the stages of reading development:

- Emergent Reading
- Beginning Readers

- Reading for Consolidation
- Reading to Learn the New
- Reading for Independence
- Mature Readers

These guidelines highlight indicators for teachers to assess students' stage of reading development and delineate learning experiences helpful at each stage. The guidelines also encouraged teachers to integrate reading and writing instruction.

Some of these additional ideas came from Jensen, who saw the state's reading policy as an opportunity to push other instructional agendas, many of which she had embraced since the 1970s when she began to pay attention to the British Infant School philosophy. As an elementary school principal in the '70s, she had championed developmentally appropriate practices, encouraging teachers to develop instruction to meet the individual needs of students (Jensen interview, September 23, 1992). These beliefs seemed to have played a major role in the instructional agenda she began to advance in Parkwood in the mid-1980s. High on Jensen's agenda was "developmentally appropriate practices" (DAP). She described DAP as "recognizing that children . . . have very different rates of growth developmentally . . . and that school practices have to reflect that" (Jensen interview, September 23, 1992). According to another central office administrator, DAP was designed to promote classroom "instruction [that] is based around what the child already knows . . . and then taking a look at what the child is capable of doing and proceeding from there and allowing that child to grow and develop from the strengths that the child already has" (interview, August 19, 1991). In many ways, the state's reading policy gave Jensen a chance to revise the district's reading curriculum and to introduce the DAP curriculum and other ideas districtwide.

Jensen also believed that writing played a critical role in reading instruction (interview, September 23, 1992). Although the state policy made no reference to writing, Jensen's efforts to reform reading instruction in Parkwood in response to the policy encouraged teachers to integrate reading and writing instruction.

Textbooks and Materials

Jensen also aligned reading textbooks and other materials with the reading guidelines to better the chances of her ideas making their way into classrooms. New district textbooks were purchased; student report cards were redesigned; and new central office mandates on grouping students for reading, workbook use, and the role of learning specialists in reading instruction were put in place.

Three literature-based programs replaced the traditional skills-based reading program that the central office had mandated since the early 1980s. These texts seemed closely aligned with many ideas presented in the Parkwood reading guidelines. For example, one of the three district selections pays careful attention to using reading strategies to teach reading (Principal 1 interview, February 19, 1992). Schools were allocated funds to buy one of the three district textbooks. But they could opt to use this money to buy children's literature instead of the reading programs. Jensen seemed to be sending the message that real literature was the material to use to teach reading. Teachers could use their discretion to select textbooks that were literature-based or to select literature itself. But teachers didn't have complete freedom; the central office actively resisted the old drill-and-skill reading by cutting off resources that might support it. Jensen also told schools that they could no longer buy any of the workbooks or practice books that accompanied the reading programs, and the central office refused to process workbook orders. The message from the central office seemed clear: Drill in isolated skills is no longer acceptable reading instruction.

Jensen also used other strategies to implement these new ideas about reading instruction, including the student evaluation system. New district report cards moved away from letter grading in reading. The new report cards focused on students' attitudes toward reading and their comprehension of text. In addition, Jensen informed teachers that they were no longer to use ability grouping in reading instruction, and learning specialists were no longer to pull students out for remedial instruction in reading. Rather, the specialists were to work within the classroom as the classroom teacher saw fit.

These two directives made clear that Jensen did not want to see any more skill-and-drill instruction for poor readers. Learning specialists had traditionally operated with caseloads of readers who were reading below age level, as measured by standardized tests. They drilled those students on discrete word skills. Considering the focus on comprehension and on teaching skills in context rather than in isolation, Jensen's directives were designed to remove the occasions when skills-based instruction would occur. Jensen visited schools and classrooms to monitor the implementation of these directives. And principals and teachers seemed to take these visits seriously (interviews with school principals, May 8 and 13, 1992; February 19, 1991).

Staff Development

Roberts was selected as chair of the district's reading task force that was established to disseminate the state's new reading policy to Parkwood teachers. With the help of a state grant and other Parkwood staff members, Roberts began to design a district staff development program on the state's reading policy. As chair of the task force, she had considerable opportunity to shape Parkwood's response to the state policy.

Roberts interpreted the state reform efforts as support for her beliefs about reading instruction. As a remedial teacher in the 1970s and early '80s, she had many concerns about the drill in isolated skills that prevailed in many reading classrooms where reading and writing were defined too narrowly. Her experience as a Head Start and preschool teacher seems to have influenced her knowledge and beliefs about reading instruction:

> I taught preschool, so you know . . . when you work with young children and see what emergent reading is like, really observe that, it's very difficult to embrace this discrete skill thing when you see children come at these from so many different ways. So I thought [the state definition] was real refreshing, and I was real excited about it (Roberts interview, April 11, 1992).

For Roberts, the reading policy did not provide a one-best-answer to reading instruction; based on her knowledge of reading research, she believed that there was no one best approach to reading instruction (Roberts interview, July 30, 1990; April 11, 1992). Roberts believed that teachers should use different approaches, depending on their students and the context. She also believed that teachers needed to use the available research to construct their own practice. That belief had direct implications for the staff development she planned:

> My idea was not to present this uniform picture. . . . I said there really isn't any agreement out there [on reading instruction] . . . . With the new definition of reading, it looks like there is, but there really isn't, because I've kept up with reading [research] and stuff (Roberts interview, July 30, 1990).

Roberts organized an ambitious staff development effort at Parkwood. Teachers and other district employees attended a three-hour workshop each week over a ten-week period. The ten-week series of workshops was offered on three other occasions over an eighteen-month period. Nationally recognized reading researchers presented a number of the weekly sessions. Throughout the presentations, the reading researchers paid attention to the state definition and to much of the research behind the definition (e.g., metacognition). Several sessions focused on reading strategies (e.g., QAR, KWL), paralleling the state's staff development efforts. However, the presenters offered many other perspectives on reading. Some presentations, for example, focused on the connection between reading and writing instruction. Teachers had opportunities to learn about integrating reading and writing instruction in their classrooms.

Moreover, many presenters paid little attention to giving teachers practical techniques to use in their classrooms, focusing instead on getting teachers to develop their own philosophies of literacy that they could use to construct their own approaches to reading instruction. For example, one presenter focused on getting teachers to develop an understanding of literacy by getting them to define reading and writing. The session began with teachers' reading different text selections at different levels of difficulty to understand what reading means. Based on how they read and the difficulties they had with the texts, teachers developed definitions of the reading process and considered the implications of those definitions for how they taught reading.

Parkwood's staff development effort was distinctly different from the state's staff development efforts. For the most part, the state-sponsored workshops focused on giving teachers new approaches—especially reading strategies—to teach reading. In contrast, the Parkwood workshops focused on more than a strategy approach to reading instruction, offering teachers different perspectives on reading and writing instruction and challenging them to construct their own instructional approaches.

In 1987–88, the district's staff development efforts changed, focusing more on giving teachers reading strategies to use in their classrooms and moving away from giving teachers opportunities to internalize the definition and make it their own by considering different perspectives on reading. Roberts no longer chaired the district task force on reading, and the new chair concentrated more on giving teachers opportunities to learn how to use the reading strategies. Further, because the state was soon to implement the revised reading test, central administrators were anxious about students' test scores and wanted to ensure that all teachers knew the reading strategies.

Influence of Knowledge and Beliefs of Central Office Staff

Both Jensen's and Roberts's efforts to respond to the state's reading policy resulted in considerable refocusing of the Parkwood language arts curriculum. They both supported ambitious beliefs about reading instruction—such as integrating reading and writing instruction—and these beliefs shaped their efforts to reform the central office instructional guidance system. Jensen and Roberts interpreted the state policy to fit with their personal instructional reform agendas. As a result, state policymakers' calls for reform evolved in important ways as they were enacted in Parkwood's central office. The manner in which the state's reading policy influenced the central office reading curriculum in Parkwood, therefore, depended on the beliefs and knowledge about reading instruction that Roberts and Jensen brought to their efforts to understand the policy.

But there were important differences in their efforts to reform reading instruction, partly because of their different beliefs about how to change modal reading instruction. Jensen's beliefs about how best to change teachers' reading instruction influenced her efforts to reform reading instruction in Parkwood. Jensen's knowledge and beliefs about teacher change seemed to support an approach to reform that relied heavily on mandating the type of instruction she wanted to see in classrooms. Jensen believed that "if you don't mandate change, it doesn't happen" (interview, September 23, 1992). The district's instructional guidance mechanisms (e.g., textbook adoptions, curriculum guidelines) that Jensen had at her disposal also shaped the way she went about reforming Parkwood's reading curriculum. Although the district's instructional guidance system was an efficient, effective means of communicating new ideas about reading instruction to Parkwood teachers, it provided few opportunities for the central office to tailor those ideas to the individual needs of teachers and their learning styles.

Jensen's efforts to encourage change in reading instruction differed considerably from Roberts's. Roberts believed that teachers needed opportunities to construct their own reading practice, and she developed the staff development program to provide such opportunities for district teachers. In contrast, Jensen's efforts to promote change in reading instruction gave teachers few opportunities to construct their own practice. Instead, she mandated specific practices that she believed all teachers should follow in teaching reading—for example, abandoning workbooks and ability grouping. There were considerable differences between Jensen's mandates for change and Roberts's staff development workshops. Consequently, although both Jensen and Roberts supported ambitious change in the existing reading instruction in Parkwood, the two approaches suggested rather different routes to reforming modal instruction—one providing individual teachers with considerable flexibility, the other specifying rather definite pedagogical methods for teaching reading.

All in all, the Parkwood efforts to disseminate new ideas about reading to teachers were ambitious and extensive. And there was considerable consistency across the different initiatives: They all called for change in existing reading instruction. Although no uniform picture of what this change would look like emerged, all the ideas were different from the existing reading practice. The Parkwood case suggests that the central office in this district has taken a much stronger leadership role in curriculum and instructional governance and policymaking over the past decade. The central office used several instructional guidance mechanisms that led to stronger leadership in instruction and curriculum for teachers (e.g., textbooks, staff development). These mechanisms were changed to reflect many ideas from the state's reading policy, as well as other ideas that some central office staff were advocating. Although the state's reading policy affected the central office's reading curriculum, central office staff members also influenced the policy, using it as an opportunity to advance other ideas about reading instruction not mentioned in the state's policy documents.

Discussion

What does this case study suggest about the role of the school district in curriculum and instructional policymaking in the light of a new state reading policy that attempted not only to change *what* teachers taught but *how* they taught reading? Three observations are critical to answering this question.

The district central office plays an important role in the state policy implementation process.

The efforts of the central office ensured that many Parkwood teachers were exposed to the state's reading policy. Central office administrators refocused the district instructional guidance system and gave considerable incentives for teachers to pay attention to and learn about the state's reading policy. Central office curriculum guidelines, textbook adoptions, and student report cards, among other aspects of the system, changed to incorporate the ideas about reading instruction that the state policy promoted. In addition, the central office devoted considerable resources to organizing staff development workshops for Parkwood teachers. The response of central office administrators to the state's reading policy amplified the policy's message.

In a state where the Department of Education has limited resources to support widespread staff development, such district initiatives seem critical if reforms are to reach schools. Moreover, in a state where key instructional guidance mechanisms (e.g., textbooks) are controlled at the local level, the central office's response seems important if state-level initiatives to change instruction are to reach schools.

Central office administrators are more than implementors of state policy.

In the Parkwood example, the state policy changed at the central office level. The way central office administrators interpreted and responded to the state's reading policy reshaped it considerably. Although the central office took up and disseminated many key ideas of the state's reading policy (e.g., reading strategies, the need to focus on student comprehension), they also saw the policy as an opportunity to push many other ideas about reading instruction. The central office's efforts to reform reading instruction in Parkwood focused on many ideas about instruction that received no attention in the state's policy documents. For example, as mentioned previously, the Parkwood guidelines for reading paid considerable attention to developmental stages of reading, encouraging teachers to design reading instruction to fit each student's needs; and these guidelines and the staff development workshops encouraged teachers to integrate reading and writing instruction.

The central office's staff development workshops embellished the state policy in other ways. Though promoting many aspects of the policy, the staff development workshops also suggested some distinctly different ideas about reforming reading instruction. Many presenters, for example, focused on getting teachers to develop their own understanding of what reading means, encouraging them to reconsider their current reading instruction. Teachers heard different perspectives on reading research and were challenged to construct their own approaches to reading instruction—in stark contrast to the state's staff development efforts, where presenters concentrated on modeling highly structured approaches to reading instruction (e.g., reading strategies) for teachers and encouraged them to repeat the approaches in their classrooms.

A complex mix of organizational and individual factors shaped the central office's response to the state policy.

Several organizational factors explain how the central office responded to the state policy. The Parkwood central office had considerable financial resources for conducting an ambitious series of staff development workshops and for buying new literature-based textbooks that supported the state policy. Another important organizational factor that shaped their response was the district's instructional guidance system. For example, because the central office decided which reading textbook to adopt, central office administrators had an existing means for disseminating new ideas about reading instruction to Parkwood teachers. The literature-based reading textbooks they selected encouraged teachers to pay attention to the reading strategies and students' ability to comprehend what they read. Likewise, district curriculum guides and student report cards gave central administrators other mechanisms for disseminating the state policy to classroom teachers.

Organizational factors, however, only partly explain the central office's response to the state policy. The personal characteristics of key central office administrators—Roberts's and Jensen's beliefs and knowledge about reading instruction—also shaped the central office's response to the policy.

Roberts believed, from her experience with teaching young children, that drilling students on discrete reading skills hindered the development of good readers. She saw the policy as a chance to move reading instruction in Parkwood schools away from drilling students in isolated phonics, decoding, and vocabulary skills. She encouraged the central office to respond to the policy; but she also saw the policy as an opportunity for teachers to study the research on reading and construct their own approaches to reading instruction. Thus, she organized staff development workshops that exposed teachers to the reading research instead of modeling for them an alternative to modal reading instruction. In fact, Roberts was openly critical of the state's strategy-dominated staff development workshops.

Jensen's knowledge and beliefs about reading were no less important in shaping Parkwood's response to the state reading policy. Jensen, for example, encouraged teachers to integrate writing and reading instruction because students' knowledge of writing contributed to their reading ability—though the state policy paid no attention to writing. Similarly, her belief in the importance of designing classroom instruction to suit students' stages of development influenced how she interpreted and disseminated the state reading policy in Parkwood.

Jensen's beliefs about teacher change, however, seem rather different from those of Roberts. Jensen encouraged teachers to follow some well-defined instructional approaches (e.g., reading strategies) as dictated by central office mandates. In contrast, Roberts encouraged teachers to construct their own practices based on an understanding of reading research.

In sum, Roberts's and Jensen's beliefs and knowledge of reading instruction and teacher change were important in shaping the central office's response to the state policy. Still, organizational factors, like district funding resources, did play a role in the central office's response to the state policy. The knowledge and beliefs of central office administrators interacted with a host of organizational factors (e.g., financial resources and instructional guidance mechanisms) in influencing how the state policy evolved at the central office level. The importance of organizational factors depends on how central administrators perceive and use them. The district's financial resources, for example, enabled Roberts to organize extensive staff development. But Roberts was the important agent, taking the initiative to use the available resources to provide ambitious workshops for teachers on reading instruction. And her knowledge and beliefs shaped the nature of the staff development initiatives and the messages they conveyed to teachers about reading instruction.

In the past decade, the Parkwood central office has taken a much more active role in curriculum and instructional governance and policymaking. Since the early 1980s, curricular decisions that had traditionally been left to schools were brought under central office control. The central office has developed an elaborate instructional guidance system to influence classroom instruction in the district. This case study suggests that the state's reading policy, which represents a new kind of state-level policy designed to push more ambitious approaches to teaching, did not decrease local district governance and policymaking for curriculum and instruction. As the state government entered the instructional policy arena, central office activity in curriculum and instruction seems to have increased, not decreased. In fact, the central office expanded its policy-making arena to include reading pedagogy. Central office initiatives amplified the state's policy message and changed the state policy. The Parkwood case suggests that local districts contribute in important ways to state-level efforts to reform classroom instruction.

This case also suggests that in exploring the role of districts in the state-policy and classroom-practice relationship, we need to pay attention to both organizational and individual factors. Central office administrators' knowledge and beliefs about instruction and teacher change are critical to an understanding of how the central office responds to and enacts state policy.

Endnotes

[1] In the case study, citations from state, district, and local guidelines are fictitious; they do not appear in the References.

[2] KWL (Know/Want to Learn/Learned), DRTA (Directed-Reading-Thinking Activity), and QAR (Question and Answer Relationship) (mentioned later) are reading strategies that were developed from research in cognitive psychology and reading. According to the research, good readers use these and other approaches to reading.

References

Berman, P., M. McLaughlin. (1977). *Federal Programs Supporting Educational Change*. Santa Monica, Calif.: Rand Corporation.

Berman, P., and E. Pauly. (1975). *Federal Programs Supporting Educational Change, Vol. 2*. Santa Monica, Calif.: Rand Corporation.

California State Department of Education. (1985a). *Language Arts Curriculum Framework for California Public Schools*. Sacramento, Calif.: Author.

California State Department of Education. (1985b). *Mathematics Curriculum Framework for California Public Schools*. Sacramento, Calif.: Author.

Cantor, L. (1980). "The Growing Role of States in American Education." *Comparative Education* 16, 1: 24–31.

Cohen, D. (1982). "Policy and Organization: The Impact of State and Federal Educational Policy in School Governance." *Harvard Educational Review* 52, 474–499.

Cohen, D. (1988). "Teaching Practice: Plus ca change . . ." In *Contributing to Educational Change: Perspectives on Research and Practice* (pp. 27–84), edited by P. Jackson. Berkeley, Calif.: McCutchan.

Cohen, D., and D. Ball. (1990). "Relations Between Policy and Practice: A Commentary." *Educational Evaluation and Policy Analysis* 12, 3: 249–256.

David, J. (1990). "Restructuring in Progress: Lessons form Pioneering Districts." In *Restructuring Schools: The Next Generation of Educational Reforms* (pp. 209–250), edited by R. Elmore and associates. San Francisco: Jossey-Bass.

Doyle, D., and C. Finn. (1984). "American Schools and the Future of Local Control." *Public Interest* 77: 77–95.

Durkin, D. (1978–79). "What Classroom Observations Reveal About Reading Comprehension Instruction." *Reading Research Quarterly* 14, 4: 481–533.

Floden, R., A. Porter, L. Alford, D. Freeman, S. Irwin, W. Schmidt, and J. Schwille. (1988). "Instructional Leadership at the District Level: A Closer Look at Autonomy and Control." *Educational Administration Quarterly* 24: 96–124.

Fuhrman, S., and R. Elmore. (1990). "Understanding Local Control in the Wake of State Education Reform." *Educational Evaluation and Policy Analysis* 12, 1: 82–96.

Hannaway, J., and L. Sproull. (1978–79). "Who's Running the Show? Coordination and Control in Educational Organizations." *Administrator's Notebook* 27: 1–4.

Kaagan, S., and R. Cooley. (1989). *State Educational Indicators: Measured Strides, Missing Steps*. New Brunswick, N.J.: Center for Policy Research in Education, Rutgers University.

Meyer, J., and B. Rowan. (1978). "The Structure of Educational Organizations." In *Environments and Organizations*, edited by M. Meyer. San Francisco: Jossey-Bass.

Meyer, J., W. Scott, D. Strang, and A. Creighton. (1987). "Bureaucratization Without Centralization: Changes in the Organizational System of American Public Education 1940–1980." In *Institutional Patterns and Organizations: Culture and Environment*, edited by L. Zucker. Cambridge, Mass.: Bollinger.

Rowan, B. (1983). "Instructional Management in Historical Perspective." *Educational Administration Quarterly* 18: 43–59.

U.S. Department of Education. (1991). *America 2000: An Education Strategy*. Washington, DC: Author.

Wise, A. (1979). *Legislated Learning*. Berkeley: University of California Press.

11

Coordinating Top-Down and Bottom-Up Strategies for Educational Reform

Michael G. Fullan

Small- and large-scale studies of top-down strategies (whether employing voluntary or mandatory methods) have consistently demonstrated that local implementation fails in the vast majority of cases. The best known study of "voluntary" adoption is the Rand Change Agent study conducted by Berman and McLauglin and associates (1978). They investigated federally sponsored educational programs adopted in 293 sites and found that, even though adoption was voluntary, districts often took on change projects for opportunistic rather than for substantial reasons.

> Local school officials may view the adoption of a change agent project primarily as an opportunity to garner extra, short term resources. In this instance the availability of federal funds rather than the possibility of change in educational practice motivates project adoption. Or, school managers may see change agent projects as a "low cost" way to cope with bureaucratic or political pressures. Innovation *qua* innovation often serves the purely bureaucratic objective of making the district appear up-to-date and progressive in the eyes of the community. Or a change agent project may function to mollify political pressures from groups in the community to "do something" about their special interests. Whatever the particular motivation underlying opportunistic adoption there was an absence of serious educational concerns (Berman and McLaughlin 1978, p. 14).

As dissatisfaction with failed implementation grew in the 1970s, states and districts turned more and more to mandatory solutions. Corbett and Wilson's (1990) study of the impact of compulsory statewide testing in Maryland and Pennsylvania is a case in point. They found that new state testing requirements caused action at the local level, but in ways that narrowed the curriculum and created conditions adverse to reforms:

> Coping with the pressure to attain satisfactory results in high-stakes tests caused educators to develop almost a "crisis mentality" in their approach,

in that they jumped quickly into "solutions" to address a specific issue. They narrowed the range of instructional strategies from which they selected means to instruct their students; they narrowed the content of the material they chose to present to students; and they narrowed the range of course offerings available to students (Corbett and Wilson 1990, p. 207).

Corbett and Wilson also identified other unintended consequences, including the diversion of attention and energy from more basic reforms in the structure and practice of schools, and reduced teacher motivation, morale, and collegial interaction necessary to bring about reform. They concluded: "when the modal response to statewide testing by professional educators is typified by practices that even the educators acknowledge are counterproductive to improving learning over the long term, then the issue is a 'policymaking problem' " (p. 321).

On a more sweeping scale, Sarason (1990) argues that billions of dollars have been spent on top-down reform with little to show for it. Sarason observes that such reform efforts do have an implicit theory of change:

Change can come about by proclaiming new policies, or by legislation, or by new performance standards, or by creating a shape-up-or-ship-out ambience, or all of the preceding. It is a conception that in principle is similar to how you go about creating and improving an assembly line—that is, what it means to those who work on the assembly line is of secondary significance, if it has any significance at all. The workers (read: educational personnel) *will* change (Sarason 1990, p. 123).

Political impatience and expediency are understandable as motivators, but they are ineffectual as strategies for educational reform. Governments can't mandate what matters, because what matters most are local motivation, skills, know-how, and commitment. As Goodlad (1992) observes: "Top-down, politically driven education reform movements are addressed primarily to restructuring. They have little to say about educating" (p. 238).

In short, centralized reform mandates have a poor track record as instruments for educational improvement. This failure has led some to conclude that only decentralized, locally driven reform can succeed. Site-based management (SBM) is currently the most prominent manifestation of this emphasis. So far, however, the claim of superiority of grassroots initiatives is primarily theoretical. In reviewing evidence on site-based management in *The New Meaning of Educational Change*, I concluded that restructuring reforms that devolved decision making to schools may have altered governance procedures, but did not affect the teaching-learning core of schools (Fullan 1991, p. 201). The evidence continues to mount.

Taylor and Teddlie (1992) draw similar conclusions in their study of the extent of classroom change in "a district widely acclaimed as a model of restructuring" (p. 4). They examined classrooms in thirty-three schools (sixteen from pilot schools that had established SBM programs and seventeen from nonpilot schools in the same district). Taylor and Teddlie did find that teachers in the pilot schools reported higher levels of participation in decision making, but they found no differences in teaching strategies (teacher-directed instruction and low student involvement dominated in both sets of cases). Further, there was little evidence of teacher-teacher collaboration. Extensive collaboration was reported in only two of the thirty-three schools, and both were nonpilot schools. Taylor and Teddlie (1992) observe: "Teachers in this study did not alter their practice.... Increasing their participation in decision-making did not overcome norms of autonomy so that teachers would feel empowered to collaborate with their colleagues" (p. 10).

Other evidence from classroom observations failed to indicate changes in classroom environment and student learning activities. Despite considerable rhetoric and what Taylor and Teddlie saw as "a genuine desire to professionalize teaching.... The core mission of school seemed ancillary to the SBM project" (p. 19). Substantive changes in pedagogy (teaching strategies and assessment) and in the way teachers worked together on instructional matters proved to be elusive. These findings would not be noteworthy, claim the authors, except that "the study occurred in a district recognized nationally as a leader in implementing restructuring reforms" (p. 16). Similarly, Hallinger, Murphy, and Hausman (1991) found that teachers and principals in their sample were highly in favor of restructuring but did not make connections "between new governance structures and the teaching-learning process" (p. 11).

Virtually identical findings arise in Weiss's (1992) investigation of shared decision making (SDM) in twelve high schools in eleven states (half were selected because they had implemented SDM; the other half were run in a traditional principal-led manner). Weiss did find that teachers in SDM schools were more likely to mention changes in the decision-making process (e.g., composition of committees, procedures, and so on), but "schools with SDM did not pay more attention to issues of curriculum than traditionally managed schools, and pedagogical issues and student concerns were low on the list for both sets of schools" (p. 2).

Similar findings were obtained in the implementation of the Chicago Reform Act of 1989. In essence, this legislation shifted responsibility from the Central Board of Education to Local School Councils (LSCs) for each of the city's 540 public schools and mandated that each school develop School Improvement Plans (SIPs). The LSCs by law consist of eleven or twelve members (six parents, two teachers, two community representatives, the school principal—and, in the case of high schools, one student). Easton (1991) reports that the majority of elementary teachers said that "their instructional practices had not changed as a result of school reform and will not change as a result of SIP" (p. 41).

In sum, decentralized initiatives, as far as the evidence is concerned, are not faring any better than centralized reforms.

Given the absence of any clear superiority of top-down or bottom-up strategies, two patterns, both ineffective, persist. One pattern attempts to resolve the dilemma through the false clarity of ideological preference. Many of those in positions of authority opt for centralized reform—"almost always egregiously indifferent to the role of obstacles," says Goodlad (1992, p. 238). Advocates of decentralization, similarly (although from a different ideological perspective), push ahead with site-based management as an end in itself.

The other pattern, of course, rests on ambivalence about which way to go, usually resulting in flip-flops or swings from top-down to bottom-up emphasis. Both strategies are often pursued simultaneously, but in a completely disconnected manner. Rowley's (1992) case study of school district restructuring covering a twelve-year period is instructive and I expect represents a familiar story. Sequoia Valley School District in California engaged in a major restructuring effort in the early 1980s following the appointment of a new superintendent in 1979. By 1985, the district had created a mission statement and a comprehensive strategic plan. The superintendent and the board adopted a philosophy of school-based management. Over time, however, the board became dissatisfied with the uneven development and fragmentation of effort. The superintendent and board began to establish programs with external funds and consultants, small groups of teachers, and administrators in such areas as whole language, early childhood centers, cooperative learning, and so on. Observes Rowley (1992):

> Confusion and heated debate inevitably resulted from the lack of clear definition and from the overload of new programs. Was restructuring going to be a centralized, program-driven process in which schools would obligingly align with problems and solutions identified by Board members, the Superintendent, and district level committees? Or, was restructuring going to remain a school-based process with the district office playing a supporting role?
>
> The answer was both. The philosophy of school-based management and strong site councils continued to be heartily espoused by the superintendent and board. But they also had committed significant resources to new programs and had installed program specialists in key administrative roles throughout the district. Thus, it became apparent that Sequoia Valley's

leaders had inadvertently created oppositional dynamics for change and that during this middle stage the climate for restructuring had become more contentious than collaborative (p. 26).

The result, not uncommon, was the appointment in 1990 of a new superintendent known for advocacy of "tight school-based accountability and multiple methods of assessing student performance" (p. 28). Outcome-driven education became just the latest in the ebb and flow of district approaches. Because of its imposition and seeming incompatibility with preferred instructional approaches in many schools, conflict increased sharply. Within a year, the board expressed doubts about the new superintendent's leadership style and its adverse affect on the morale of teachers and administrators.

In conclusion, the whole matter of the relative roles and relationships of centralized and decentralized strategies for educational reform is a morass, badly in need of conceptual and strategic clarification.

Why Centralized and Decentralized Strategies Are Both Essential

I have provided evidence that neither top-down nor bottom-up strategies, by themselves, are effective, but it is necessary to probe deeper by asking *why* they do not work.

Top-down strategies are problematic because complex change processes cannot be controlled from the top. Senge (1990) calls it the illusion of being in control. "The perception that someone 'up there' is in control is based on an illusion—the illusion that anyone could master the dynamics and complexity of an organization from the top" (p. 290).

More fundamentally, the forces of educational change are so multifaceted that they are inherently unpredictable. As I have stated elsewhere, change is nonlinear and complex:

> How is change complex? Take any educational policy or problem and start listing all the forces that could figure in the solution and that would need to be influenced to make for productive change. Then, take the idea that unplanned factors are inevitable—government policy changes or gets constantly redefined, key leaders leave, important contact people are shifted to another role, new technology is invented, immigration increases, recession reduces available resources, a bitter conflict erupts, and so on. Finally, realize that every new variable that enters the equation—these unpredictable but inevitable noise factors—produces ten other ramifications, which in turn produce tens of other reactions and on and on (Fullan 1993a).

Controlling strategies do not work because there is too much to control. Even strong leadership and vision-driven change are seriously flawed because things are constantly changing. We need a new mindset to manage situations of constant flux (see Fullan 1993a; Beer, Eistenstat, and Spector 1990; Stacey 1992).

Given the difficulty of attempting to control change from afar, it is understandable that local participation and site-based management appear to many to be the solution. Yet this alternative is also fraught with fundamental deficiencies, four of which follow:

1. There is ample evidence that organizations in general are not likely to initiate change in the absence of external stimuli. Schools, in particular, are not known for their innovativeness.

2. As we saw in the previous section, when schools do have the opportunity to control the change process (through site-based management, for example), they do not necessarily take productive action. They are more likely to get bogged down or make superficial structural changes.

3. In decentralized systems, it is difficult to discern, let alone maintain, quality control (on the other hand, accountability fares no better in centralized systems).

4. One could speculate that it is possible for a given school to become highly innovative, despite the district it is in. I would venture to add, however, that it is not possible for such a school *to stay* innovative despite the district. District action or inaction—personnel transfers, hiring decisions, budget decisions, and the like—inevitably take their toll.

Stacey (1992) summarizes the problem of decentralized decision making and organizational learning:

> The whole point of flexible structures and dispersed power is to enable those below the top level in the management hierarchy to detect and take action to deal with a large number of changes affecting an organization that operates in a turbulent environment. This is supposed to enable the organization to learn about its environment and so adapt to that environment faster than its rivals do. However, studies have shown that widening participation and empowering people by no means guarantees that organizational learning will improve (p. 175).

When two alternative positions—opposite solutions, really—are both found to be basically flawed, it normally means that a paradox lies behind the problem. A shift in mindset is required—from either/or to both/and thinking. Beer and others (1990) summarize the situation:

> The top-down approach possesses some allure. It holds the promise of producing rapid change toward an elegantly conceived end state that is symmetrical and complete. Thus, managers can lead their employees in the desired direction. But the unilaterally directive approach also has traps into which renewal can fall. Employee commitment to the newly aligned

organization may be low, and employee knowledge of how things get done in the organization may not be considered in the solution.

> A bottom-up approach that allows, even demands, participation by employees seems to address many of the failings of unilateral top management direction. But it can suffer from a different set of problems. A participative approach to change may be too slow and ill defined to respond effectively to short-term business demands. It presents top managers with the problem of how to incorporate their perspective and knowledge into new solutions. It raises questions about the motivation and skill of employees to develop an ambitious solution that will "force" them, the employees to change their ways. Even worse, participative approaches to change can be derailed by resistant managers, unions, and workers.

> Our examination of revitalization efforts in 26 plants and business units across the six companies reveals that effective renewal occurs not when managers choose one alternative or the other. Instead, effective revitalization occurs when managers follow a critical path that obtains the benefits of top-down as well as bottom-up change efforts while minimizing their disadvantages (pp. 68–69).

Pascale (1990) draws a similar conclusion in examining the turnaround at the Ford Motor Company in the 1980s:

> Change flourishes in a 'sandwich.' When there is consensus above, and pressure below, things happen. While there was no operational consensus at the top as to precisely *what* should be done at Ford, the trips to Japan caused many senior managers to agree that the problems lay in the way the organization worked. This might not have led anywhere, however, were it not for pressures for change coming from the rank and file (pp. 126 and 128, emphasis in original).

Finally, research on effective and collaborative schools shows that such schools do not go it alone, but are actively part of a wider network in which external and internal influences are equally important. Collaborative schools, for example, are more likely to seek outside ideas, more likely to be linked to their districts, and more likely to engage state-level policies proactively (Louis and Miles 1990; Rosenholtz 1989; Nias, Southworth, and Campbell 1992). A study of forty-eight school districts in Illinois confirms that internal development and external involvement must go together (Baker, Curtis, and Benenson 1991). Thirteen of the forty-eight districts were classified as engaged in "systematic improvement" on a sustained basis. It is no accident that all thirteen successful districts used external support from regional educational service centers and several other sources. By contrast, there was no evidence of school improvement in the eight cases that had no external support. Time and again we find that seeking external support and training is a sign of vitality.

External linkages do not necessarily involve connections to a hierarchical center, but effective systems include two-way interactions with those in authority. Thus, the boundaries between external and internal systems, between top-down and bottom-up levels, become effectively permeable and mutually influential in successful organizations.

Coordinating Top-Down and Bottom-Up Strategies

Recognizing that both top-down and bottom-up strategies co-exist in effective systems means that the choice of reform strategies will never be entirely clear. Ambiguities and tensions always accompany complex change processes. In this final section, I intend to clarify this vexing problem by making two generic distinctions, and then by providing two case illustrations—one at the school (local)/district (center) level; the other at the district (local)/state (center) level.

The two generic distinctions pertain to *division of labor* (between the center and local), and the *sequence* of strategies. Division of labor concerns the relative roles of the center and local entities. In overall terms, the center's role in bilateral systems is to stimulate and respond to local action, help formulate "general direction"; gather and feed back performance data; focus on selection, promotion, and replacement; and provide resources and opportunities for continuous staff development. The role of the local unit is to take action, work on shared vision, develop collaborative cultures, monitor and solve problems vis-a-vis desired directions, respond and be proactive with external agencies and events, and basically develop the habits and skills of learning organizations. These relative roles will become clearer through the two case illustrations described here.

Even more problematic is the sequence of events and emphasis. In dynamic systems, there can be no step-by-step set of procedures. Recent research, however, shows that nonlinear change does work in approximate patterns that point clearly to the types of strategies that are more or less likely to be effective (Fullan 1993a). As heretical as it sounds, reliance on visions and a strong shared culture creates severe limitations for addressing complex change.

In studying "the critical path to corporate renewal" in twenty-six companies, Beer and others (1990) concluded the following:

> • Change efforts that begin by creating corporate programs to alter the culture of the management of people in the firm are inherently flawed even when supported by top management.

- Formal organizational structure and systems are the *last* things an organization should change when seeking renewal—not the first, as many managers assume.
- Effective changes in the way an organization manages people do *not* occur by changing the organization's human resource policies and systems.
- Starting corporate renewal at the very top is a high-risk revitalization strategy not employed by the most successful companies.
- Organizations should start corporate revitalization by targeting small, isolated, peripheral operations, not large, central, core operations.
- It is not essential that top management consistently practice what it preaches in the early stages of renewal, although such action is undoubtedly helpful (p. 6).

Beer and others (1990) found that isolated pockets of change reflecting new behaviors led to new thinking that eventually pushed structures and procedures to change. People learn new behaviors primarily through their interactions with others, not through front-end training designs. Training builds on and extends new momentum. We found this process very clearly in our work in Brock High School in the Learning Consortium (Durham Board of Education, Fullan 1993b). Change started in the behavior and culture of teaching and teacher relationships through small-scale inservice, which in turn spread and led to changes in structure.

This leads to the interesting hypothesis that reculturing leads to restructuring more effectively than the reverse. In most restructuring reforms, structural change is expected to result in cultural change, and mostly fails. There is no doubt a reciprocal relationship required between the two. But reform is much more powerful when teachers and administrators begin working in new ways, only to discover that school structures must be altered, than the reverse situation—when rapidly implemented new structures create confusion, ambiguity, and conflict, ultimately leading to retrenchment.

In any case, Beer and others (1990) found that organizations that underwent successful revitalization followed a particular sequence in which individual, small-group, and informal behavior began to change first (bottom-up, if you will), which in turn was reinforced and further propelled by changes in formal design and procedures (structures, personnel practices, compensation systems, etc.) in the organization (top-down). Both local and central levels can be active and influential at all phases, but *what* is attended to and *when* is critical.

School/District Relationships

Most school districts are not known for their focus on instruction (Elmore 1992). Given the absence of top-down initiatives from the district, schools in such jurisdictions are less likely to work on instructional improvement. Highly decentralized district curriculum development has a poor track record at the level of school and classroom implementation (Fullan 1991). What works is simultaneous school/district co-development, reflecting both top-down and bottom-up initiatives.

How can schools and districts interact, avoiding center dominance on the one hand, and individual school drift on the other?

Louis and Miles (1990) conducted case studies of five urban high schools that had undertaken major reform projects. Two of the five schools were successful. Most significant, relative to our interests, is that these two schools had different relationships with their districts than did the three schools that did not succeed. Louis (1989) analyzed these relationships. She found that two separate dimensions affected the quality of the relationship. One she called the degree of "engagement" (frequent interaction and communication, mutual coordination and influence, and some shared goals and objectives); the other she classified as the level of "bureaucratization" (the presence of extensive rules and regulations governing the relationship).

To oversimplify, in situations of low engagement and high bureaucracy, Louis observes that there is frequent reference to rules but limited enforcement because the schools and districts operate in isolation from each other. The principal, for example, often operates as a buffer to central rules. In the case of high engagement and high bureaucracy, Louis found conflict, interference, resistance, and ultimately failure. The third situation—low engagement and low bureaucracy—is one of loose federation, informality, and laissez-faire, in which people essentially did not try to engage in comprehensive change. The fourth scenario—high engagement and low bureaucracy—presented "the only clearly positive district contexts" (p. 161). Louis (1989) summarizes: "Essentially, the picture is one of co-management, with coordination and joint planning enhanced through the development of consensus between staff members at all levels about desired goals for education" (p. 161). Only the schools with this district profile experienced successful school improvement projects.

Similar findings, independently and more systematically arrived at, are contained in LaRocque and Coleman's (1989) analysis of "district ethos" and quality in school districts in British Columbia. The authors compiled performance data by aggregating school results on provincewide achievement tests. They rated the districts according to high, medium, and low performance and then selected ten districts for more detailed analysis, taking into account size and type of school community. LaRocque and Coleman (p. 169) hypothesized that positive district ethos would be characterized by a high degree of interest and concern relative to six sets of activity and attitude "focuses":

1. Taking care of business (a learning focus).
2. Monitoring performance (an accountability focus).
3. Changing policies/practices (a change focus).
4. Consideration and caring for stakeholders (a caring focus).
5. Creating shared values (a commitment focus).
6. Creating community support (a community focus).

Three of the ten districts were classified as having a strong district presence in the schools, described in the following terms:

> The district administrators provided the principals with a variety of school-specific performance data; they discussed these data with the principals and set expectations for their use; and they monitored through recognized procedures, how and with what success the schools used the performance data....
>
> The district administrators used their time in the schools purposefully to engage the principals in discussion on specific topics: school performance data, improvement plans, and the implementation of these plans....
>
> In spite of the emphasis on school test results, the nature of the discussions was collaborative rather than prescriptive. The district administrators acknowledged good performance. They helped the principals interpret the data and identify strengths and weaknesses, and they offered advice and support when necessary. Ultimately, however, plans for improvement were left up to the principal and staff of each school—this point was stressed by the principals—although their progress in developing and implementing the plans was monitored. The features of collaboration and relative school autonomy probably reinforced the perception of respect for the role of the principal and recognition of the importance of treating each school as a unique entity (LaRocque and Coleman 1989, p. 181).

All three of these districts had a high performance rating on the achievement tests.

At the other end of the continuum, three districts were characterized by an absence of pressure for accountability: Little or no data were provided to the schools, and no structures or processes were established to monitor or discuss progress. All three of these districts had a low performance rating on the achievement tests.

LaRocque and Coleman (1989, p. 190) concluded that effective districts have an active and evolving accountability ethos that combines interactive monitoring with a respect for school autonomy.

Rosenholtz (1989) studied seventy-eight "stuck" and "moving" schools from eight districts. She discovered that some school districts had higher proportions of stuck schools, and others had more moving schools. She concluded that districts can also be stuck or moving, and that this directly influences school effectiveness. In particular, she found that moving districts worked interactively and continuously with school personnel on (1) goal-setting and monitoring, (2) principal selection and professional development, and (3) teacher selection and professional development.

A last example comes from our Learning Consortium in the Toronto area, where we have been working for five years in a partnership with four large school districts and two higher education institutions. One of the focuses has been to link school and district development. The Halton (44,000 students) and Durham (55,000 students) districts provide illustrations of the complexity and components of school level and district level developments.

In Halton, for example, the strategies used to achieve correlated development include:

- The establishment of a broad-based mission statement and strategic directions statement that provide core foci while enabling flexibility;
- The development of a School Growth Planning process as a means of achieving continued growth geared to each community's context;
- The use of performance appraisal for teachers within the school and for vice principals and principals vis-a-vis the system that is integrated with the three strategic directions (instruction, school planning, and staff development);
- A selection and promotion process for new teachers, school administrators, and district personnel that stresses criteria such as collaborative skills, staff development participation and leadership, implementation planning, and knowledge of the change process;
- A systematic commitment to continuous development through allocating staff development funds to each school, conducting systemwide institutes, providing training and support in school growth planning, and establishing a range of in-depth leadership institutes for teachers, future administrators, and existing administrators (which allows, among other things, future vice-principals and principals to develop a track record of capability regarding promotion criteria);
- The development of an assessment and evaluation system for the district, which provides periodic feedback into the processes described above (see Fullan 1993b).

Similar patterns took place in Durham, including:

- A broad-based system mission plan;
- An emphasis on school growth team development and planning with many and varied examples of school-based initiatives;

- Massive staff development aimed at capacity-building (cooperative learning, conflict resolution, training school growth planning, training of trainers, and more);
- Changes in leadership training, performance appraisal, and selection and promotion criteria consistent with new directions;
- Central district reorganization that combined downsizing and devolution of authority to schools with refocussing the districts role on direction setting, information gathering and feedback, and regional support to families of schools (see Bennett and Green 1993).

To conclude, there is a broad pattern to the evolution of redesigning the relationship between schools and districts, similar to Beer and others' (1990) findings, cited earlier, about the critical path to revitalization. Initiatives occur at both district and school levels, at first in an uncoordinated fashion. Action and variation at the school level is allowed and encouraged. As people gain clarity and skills through experience, and as training and new approaches to selection and promotion begin to accumulate, greater consistency is achieved; and pressure mounts to alter the organization that is now experienced as ill-fitted to the new emerging patterns. As Beer found, formal procedures and formal reorganization are changed later in the process, not at the beginning.

It is also clear that independent action, as well as coordinated action (where possible), is needed from both school and district levels. In the mid to long run, there can be no district development without school development, or school development without district development. One inevitably takes its toll on the other, for better or for worse. In the very long run, it is possible to imagine very different systems that do not include local school districts at all (see Elmore 1992). Whatever the eventual pattern, some form of combined top-down/bottom-up relationship will be essential for effectiveness.

Finally, the pattern of evolution being described is complex and ambiguous. We are still at the very early stages of rethinking the relationship between schools and districts. Many, many questions remain unanswered, plaguing those working on school and district restructuring.

Local/State Relationships

The same problems apply, writ large, concerning local/state or local/national relationships. The same principles of top-down/bottom-up simultaneity also apply. Researchers have found that change occurs when top-down mandates and bottom-up initiatives "connect." As stated by Fuhrman, Clune, and Elmore (1988):

One of our most interesting and important discoveries is that many local districts are going far beyond compliance; they are responding very actively to state reforms. In over half of our local districts, administrators saw in the state reforms opportunities to accomplish their own objectives, particularly as the state reforms provided significant funding increases. Local districts are actively orchestrating various state policies around local priorities, strategically interacting with the state to achieve goals. For example, one major urban district coordinates almost all state teacher policies, including its mentor-teacher and alternate-route programs, to meet the prime objective of hiring a large number of new teachers (p. 247).

Similarly, in examining the impact of California's major reform legislation S.B. 813, Odden and Marsh's (1988) main findings were:

- Virtually all schools implemented key provisions of S.B. 813 in a manner consistent with state purposes.
- Education reform legislated at the state level can be an effective means of improving schools when it is woven into a cohesive strategy at the local level.
- Successful implementation of reforms at the local level reflects several key themes (district leadership, school collegiality, concern for all students, ongoing staff development, etc.).
- Attention to the substance of curriculum and instruction and to the process of school change correlates with high test scores and improved learning conditions for all students.
- Students with special learning needs—the poor, those with limited proficiency in English, and those at risk of dropping out—received increased services and attention. Unfortunately, the services were generally of a type that has produced insufficient levels of academic achievement in the past. Sample schools lacked appropriate strategies for mounting more effective interventions for at-risk students.
- Sample schools wanted to engage in even more complex school improvement, such as focusing the curriculum on problem solving and on higher order skills (pp. 595–596).

From a strategy perspective, the question is how to maximize the productive mix of top-down pressure, incentives, and responsiveness on the one hand, and bottom-up initiatives, development, and accountability on the other. In a commissioned paper to the Ontario government, we suggested four broad strategies to guide its current restructuring reform (Fullan and Kilcher 1992), as follows:

1. Articulate at the state level an overarching rationale and direction with reference to desired learning outcomes.
2. Local and regional capacity building should be a priority for schools, districts and regions.
3. Invest from the state level in value-added strategies to support and feed into local development (such as funding exemplary programs, research, evaluation and dissemination).

4. Work on defining roles and establishing partnerships and alliances across key constituencies (universities and schools, teacher unions, etc.) (p. 31).

Clune (1992) similarly opts for a "coordinated decentralized" approach to systemic reform rather than a "standardized centralized" approach. He argues that in complex and differentiated systems, centralized approaches do not achieve greater coherence, but rather add more layers of confusion. His recommended strategy is to find a "balance among central guidance, central provision of resources, a realistic network of change agents just above the school level, and provision for school improvement" (p. 19). In particular, he outlines a combination of tasks that include:

- Sponsor and facilitate a range of curriculum development efforts.
- Facilitate the creation of curriculum networks.
- Create incentives for schools to initiate and sustain approved processes of curriculum upgrading.
- Develop personnel policies that compensate skill and effort in the new curriculum.
- Develop a student assessment system that tracks progress and leads practice.
- Sponsor efforts to coordinate different parts of the delivery system.

The goal is to achieve greater coherence without centralization. Clune concludes that the strategy of direction setting and information monitoring, combined with increased decentralized capacity stimulated by change agent networks, "is both more feasible and more powerful as a tool for producing coherent, ambitious curriculum at the school level" (p. 14).

Although not addressed to the question of state/board relationships, Hampden-Turner's (1992) review of the Hanover Insurance Company is instructive. Investment in continuous skill development at all levels operates in a negotiated system of local and central give and take. The dilemma, successfully managed by Hanover, was

> how to make local branch staff stronger and more self-reliant, while also making the staff at the national office strong, capable, and responsive. There were two perils to be avoided: A strong central staff that suppressed local initiatives and made branches dependent, and a strong local staff that resented any interference from national HQ as an infringement of their autonomy (p. 25).

Hampden-Turner (1992) found that Hanover constantly works on the attainment of a larger vision that is tested by specific information and numbers gathered by the organization. It is recognized that local units are comparable in some respects, and different in others. Thus, the center and the locals negotiate goals, develop strategies for success, and seek data in relation to agreed-on directions.

Top-down strategies result in conflict, or superficial compliance, or both. Expecting local units to flourish through laissez-faire decentralization leads to drift, narrowness, or inertia. Combined strategies that capitalize on the center's strengths (to provide prospective direction, incentives, networking, and retrospective monitoring) and locals' capacities (to learn, create, respond to, and contribute) are more likely to achieve greater overall coherence. Such systems also have greater accountability, given that the need to obtain political support for ideas is built into the patterns of interaction.

Simultaneous top-down/bottom-up strategies are essential because dynamically complex societies are full of surprises (Senge 1990, Stacey 1992). Only the negotiated capacity and strengths of the center and the locals, in combination, are capable of pushing for improvement while retaining the capacity to learn from new patterns, whether anticipated or not. Finally, and paradoxically, one level cannot wait for the other level to change. Systems don't change by themselves. Individuals change systems, acting individually and together, regardless of how ineffective they perceive others around them to be. Breakthroughs occur when productive connections amass, creating growing pressure for systems to change (Fullan 1993a, b). The more that top-down and bottom-up forces are coordinated, the more likely that complex systems will move toward greater effectiveness.

References

Baker, P., D. Curtis, and W. Benenson. (1991). *Collaborative Opportunities to Build Better Schools*. Chicago: Illinois Association for Supervision and Curriculum Development.

Beer, M., A. Eisenstat, and B. Spector. (1990). *The Critical Path to Corporate Renewal*. Boston: Harvard Business School Press.

Bennett, B., and N. Green. (1993). "Beyond Mediocrity: Systemic Change in the Durham Board of Education." Unpublished paper, University of Toronto.

Berman, P., and M. McLaughlin. (1978). *Federal Programs Supporting Educational Change: Vol. VIII. Implementing and Sustaining Innovations*. Santa Monica, Calif.: Rand Corporation.

Clune, W. (1992). "The Best Path to Systemic Education Policy: Standard/Centralized or Differentiated/Decentralize?" Unpublished paper. Madison: Center for Educational Research, University of Wisconsin.

Corbett, H.D., and B. Wilson. (1990). *Testing Reform and Rebellion*. Norwood, N.Y.: Ablex.

Durham Board of Education, and Faculty of Education, University of Toronto. (1992). *Making Change at Brock High School*. [Video]. Oshawa, Ontario: Durham Board of Education.

Easton, J. (1991). *Decision Making and School Improvement: LSCs in the First Two Years of Reform*. Chicago: Chicago Panel on Public School Policy and Finance.

Elmore, R. (1992). "The Role of Local School Districts in Instructional Improvement." Paper presented at the Annual Meeting of The American Educational Research Association, San Francisco.

Fuhrman, S., W. Clune, and R. Elmore. (1988). "Research on Education Reform: Lessons on the Implementation of Policy." *Teachers College Record* 90, 2: 237–257.

Fullan, M. (1993a). *Change Forces: Probing the Depths of Educational Reform*. Bristol, Pa.: Falmer Press.

Fullan, M. (1993b). "Coordinating School and District Development in Restructuring." In *Restructuring Schools: Learning from Ongoing Effort* (pp. 143–164), edited by J. Murphy and P. Hallinger. Newbury Park, Calif.: Crowin Press.

Fullan, M., and A. Kilcher. (1992). *Implementation Strategies for the Restructuring of Education*. Commissioned Report, Toronto: Ontario Ministry of Education.

Fullan, M., with S. Stiegelbauer. (1991). *The New Meaning of Educational Change*. New York: Teachers College Press.

Goodlad, J. (1992). "On Taking School Reform Seriously." *Phi Delta Kappan* 74, 3: 232–238.

Hallinger, P., J. Murphy, and C. Hausman. (1991). "Conceptualizing School Restructuring: Principals' and Teachers' Perceptions." Paper presented at the Annual Meeting of the American Educational Research Association, Chicago.

Hampden-Turner, C. (January-February 1992). "Charting the Dilemmas of Hanover Insurance." *Planning Review*, 22–28.

LaRocque, L., and P. Coleman. (1989). "Quality Control: School Accountability and District Ethos." In *Educational Policy for Effective Schools* (pp. 168–191), edited by M. Holmes, K. Leithwood, and D. Musella. Toronto: OISE Press.

Louis, K. (1989). "The Role of the School District in School Improvement." In *Educational Policy for Effective Schools* (pp. 145–167), edited by M. Holmes, K. Leithwood, and D. Musella. Toronto: OISE Press.

Louis, K., and M.B. Miles. (1990). *Improving the Urban High School: What Works and Why*. New York: Teachers College Press.

Nias, J., G. Southworth, and P. Campbell. (1992). *Whole School Curriculum Development in the Primary School*. London: Falmer Press.

Odden, A., and D. Marsh. (1988). "How Comprehensive Reform Legislation Can Improve Secondary Schools." *Phi Delta Kappan* 69, 8: 593–598.

Pascale, P. (1990). *Managing on the Edge*. New York: Touchstone.

Rosenholtz, S. (1989). *Teachers' Workplace: The Social Organization of Schools*. New York: Longman.

Rowley, S. (1992). "School District Restructuring and the Search for Coherence." Paper presented at the annual meeting of the American Educational Research Association, San Francisco.

Sarason, S. (1990). *The Predictable Failure of Educational Reform*. San Francisco: Jossey-Bass.

Senge, P. (1990). *The Fifth Discipline*. New York: Doubleday.

Stacey, R. (1992). *Managing the Unknowable*. San Francisco: Jossey-Bass.

Taylor, D., and C. Teddlie. (1992). "Restructuring and the Classroom: A View from a Reform District." Paper presented at the Annual Meeting of the American Educational Research Association, San Francisco.

Weiss, C. (1992). "Shared Decision Making About What? A Comparison of Schools With and Without Teacher Participation." Paper presented at the Annual Meeting of the American Educational Research Association, San Francisco.

12

Commentary on the District and School Roles in Curriculum Reform: A Superintendent's Perspective

Thomas W. Payzant

In the 1983 report, *A Nation at Risk*, The National Commission on Excellence in Education called for many changes in U.S. public schools to stop the "rising tide of mediocrity" that the authors believed covered the educational landscape. Ten years later, we can describe the intervening periods as reflective of several different waves of reform. It is remarkable that educators, policymakers, and the public are still engaged in debate about the need for reform when experience suggests that our attention span for formulating and implementing change in the schools is short lived. Despite the continuing waves of reform, we have yet to see substantial change—we have yet to witness a turning of the tide.

What is different about the current debate on the need for change, the ways to effect it, the policies that support it, and the challenges of implementation? Certainly curriculum and instruction are central issues, but they are less likely to be addressed separately. Researchers and practitioners are increasingly concerned that these often fragmented efforts may not contribute to long-term institutional change in schools, or enhance teaching and learning in a lasting way for the increasingly diverse U.S. public school population. If reform is to be systemic, policies and practices must take into account the interconnectedness of all the elements—teaching, learning, governance, assessment, accountability, parent involvement, professional development, resource availability and allocation, and integrated services for children. A systemic approach to reform calls for a whole that is greater than the sum of its parts. Such reform requires new ways of thinking about change, as well as the leadership and policies required to initiate it.

The current organization and structure of most public schools in America assumes that the tasks of teaching and learning can be standardized. Teaching strategies and instructional materials are based on assumptions about learning and teaching that are out of step with current research. The expectations for what all children must know and be able to do go far beyond basic literacy. The policy implications for the development of new curriculum and its implementation are the focus of three chapters in this volume, the subject of my commentary.

Impact of Standards on Curriculum Initiatives

Porter, Smithson, and Osthoff, in "Standard Setting as a Strategy for Upgrading High School Mathematics and Science," conclude that policy must be clear, coherent, authoritative, and powerful to make a difference in teaching and learning. It is difficult for single curriculum initiatives in science or mathematics to achieve these goals without compatible policy initiatives in the areas of standard setting, assessment, professional development, and the preparation and adoption of textbooks and instructional materials. The dilemma is that, in formulating policies with clear goals and unambiguous specifications for attaining them, it is easy to ignore the complexity caused by the many variables that teachers and students encounter, even when those focused policies have the "authority and power" of the state behind them.

My own experiences in San Diego reflect many of the conclusions drawn from the research of Porter and others, but I am more sanguine than they are about the long-term impact of several policy initiatives in California. Increasing graduation requirements in science and mathematics may have been based on the faulty premise that doing more of the same for more of our students would improve achievement. There is evidence that graduation rates were not adversely affected by the tougher requirements and that more students have prepared themselves to meet post-secondary entrance requirements. In California, the policies of longer school days and years, tougher teacher certification standards, and stricter graduation requirements captured the public's attention in the early and mid-'80s; behind the scenes, however, work was progressing simultaneously on new curriculum, textbook adoption, and assessment policies that will have a more profound and lasting impact on subject content and how it is taught in California's schools. The policy direction is significantly different in that it is based on the assumption that there must be connections among curriculum, instruction, assessment, and teacher development. We are learning that it is easier to conceptualize the connections than it is to create new practices in schools that reflect them.

Porter and his colleagues might understand my more optimistic view. San Diego is the second largest district in California; and as they point out, in larger districts more staff members are available to help implement new policies. They conclude that educators seem to be more convinced of the need for change because so many of our students are not succeeding, and there may be a stronger commitment to "control" classroom practice. The timing perhaps was fortuitous, but we have been struggling locally with many of the same policy issues that have captured the attention of state policymakers. Rather than viewing the California curriculum frameworks as incompatible with our local efforts, we have embraced them as consistent with our own commitment to the establishment of high expectations in each of the major curriculum areas. We can see the connection with the state's more rigorous screening procedure to ensure that textbooks and instructional materials developed by publishers for the California market will meet those curriculum framework general content standards. Moreover, the evolution of the California Assessment Program during the '80s reflected the willingness of educators and policymakers to address the important issue of alignment. In the '90s, we are seeing the continuation of more systemic thinking as frameworks are revised, materials are developed, and the new state assessment program is created with more authentic assessments.

In the San Diego City Schools, we have implemented a common core curriculum based on the belief that all student are entitled to a strong academic program in all the basic subjects. This curriculum reflects the state curriculum frameworks. Our intent is to decrease norm-referenced achievement testing as the new California Assessment Program provides us with assessments that are aligned with the curriculum. Porter and others point out that standard setting has not resulted in the elimination of tracking. San Diego's common core curriculum has not eliminated tracking completely, but significant progress has been made by eliminating local courses in math and science that were offered only for low-achieving students. The challenge is to provide the support systems necessary to help students succeed with the more demanding curriculum that all students deserve to be taught. Like Porter and his colleagues, we have found bridging courses to be very helpful. They note that Math A in California is a good example of an effort to maintain high expectations in course content consistent with the state's mathematics framework, while committing to the development of creative and innovative instructional strategies that will engage students who have not been successful in traditional courses. We agree with the observation that the lack of materials at the time of expected implementation has been a problem, and that professional development has been insufficient. Although some believe that Math A is a watered-down course that will not enable students to meet the requirements of the common core, this is not the case.

Central Office Role in Curriculum Initiatives

James P. Spillane, in his chapter "How Districts Mediate Between State Policy and Teachers' Practice," uses a case study to show that "the district central office plays an important role in the state policy implementation process." The size and demographics of San Diego are quite different from the district he studied, but my own experience with the implementation of a new reading/language arts program is similar. In the 1990–91 school year, San Diego initiated an integrated, literature-based reading/language arts program based on the California framework and the reading and language art materials approved by the California State Board of Education for use in K–8 local school districts. The new framework and instructional materials reflected a fundamental change in philosophy about reading and writing and how to teach them.

Change efforts are always influenced by context, and San Diego's experience is a good example. In the early '80s, the district developed its own Achievement Goals Program (AGP) to respond to part of its integration court order, which required the district to meet specific achievement outcomes in reading, language arts, and mathematics for students in the court-identified racially isolated schools. AGP was a mastery learning program with a clear focus on basic skills acquisition, using a structured curriculum, direct instruction, frequent testing and reteaching, time on task, and administrative monitoring. The curriculum was prescribed and sequential. Teachers relied heavily on worksheets, pacing charts, and multiple-choice tests. Through the '80s, test scores for all racial groups improved significantly; and despite dissonance in the early years of the development and implementation of AGP, by the mid-'80s many principals and teachers had accepted the district policy initiatives that responded to the court order. When achievement results hit a plateau in 1988–89, the district was well into the discussion of setting higher expectations that would take all students beyond the skills required for basic literacy. Implementation of a common core curriculum would require a very different approach from that of AGP.

When the new California framework for reading and language arts appeared, educators at the central office and in schools in San Diego were eager to see it implemented. This combination of a new state policy direction and our own local analysis of the need for change combined to provide the impetus for a dramatic shift in philosophy and practice in teaching reading and language arts. As with the math and science initiatives, there was no real controversy about the state's policy direction; the dissatisfaction with the changes in reading and language arts focused on our local district's implementation plan.

We found, as Spillane did in his case study, that the beliefs of central office personnel were important in moving the change agenda forward. Several central office staff members strongly advocated a literature-based program, instructional practice based on the developmental stages of learning, teaching writing as a process, and new dynamic grouping practices. However, we underestimated the degree of readiness for change among some principals and teachers, and how difficult the implementation of the new effort would be without an extraordinary professional development effort. When the decision was made to implement the new program, we were unaware that we were facing several years of dramatic budget reductions that would further limit the professional development support we subsequently learned would be necessary to give principals and teachers the knowledge and skills necessary to meet the district's expectations. Moreover, we were switching to a new norm-referenced achievement test during the time that the new reading/language arts program was introduced. The policy decision to cut back districtwide testing to only two grades, 5 and 7, had been made with the expectation that the California Assessment Program results could be used at several other grade levels. However, a dispute between the state superintendent of public instruction and the governor resulted in the governor's withholding funding for the state assessment program in 1990–91. At a time when we were looking for assessments that would fulfill the promise of bringing curriculum, teaching, and assessment together, we were still relying on districtwide, norm-referenced achievement tests for all grades in Chapter 1 schools and grades 5 and 7 to determine the results of a reading/language arts program—with goals that exceed the acquisition of basic skills.

The 1993–94 school year is the fourth year of San Diego's literature-based reading/language arts program; and staff members have made it the top instructional priority. Because San Diego teachers and administrators are committed to systemic reform, they are trying to develop strategies that will bring into focus how decisions about professional development, resource allocation, assessment, accountability, parent involvement, and governance all affect changes in the teaching and learning of reading and language arts. In the best of circumstances, it is easy to underestimate the complexity of policy implementation. It is not easy to forge the links between instructional policy and teaching practice when the power of tradition is at best underestimated, or at worst, misunderstood. Spillane is correct in concluding that whether a central office is initiating policy or responding to state direction, there is a complex set of variables that will shape implementation outcomes. Unless there are strategies for convincing principals and teachers that change is desirable—that more of the same will not be good enough for students to meet the high expectations that we have for them—old knowledge and belief systems will prevail; and practitioners will fall short in fulfilling the promises that policymakers envisioned in their carefully crafted policies.

Blending the Central and the Local in Curriculum Initiatives

My own experience matches Fullan's conclusion in "Coordinating Top-Down and Bottom-Up Strategies for Educational Reform" that neither top-down nor bottom-up strategies—used alone—will work. In most instances, a blend of each is required. Certainly San Diego's experience with reading/language arts using the AGP approach of the '80s suggests the powerful impact that a top-down strategy can have with short-term gains, but there are complexities that cannot be controlled from the top. AGP may have been a program that worked to improve basic skills achievement in the court-identified racially isolated schools, but only a handful of other district schools chose to implement AGP. With the new reading/language arts program, it is clear that there are "multifaceted" and "unpredictable" forces that influence our implementation.

How then do we blend top-down and bottom-up approaches? San Diego educators (and others across the country) are still learning—and I believe that the central direction has to focus on the "what" questions:

- What are the standards our district expects all students to meet?
- What are the goals in teaching and learning that all schools should work to achieve?
- What is our vision for systemic reform whereby the whole does become greater than the sum of its parts?

- What is our common belief system that must be shared districtwide if we are to provide equal access to educational opportunity for all students and quality results?

Many opportunities for bottom-up approaches arise as we address the many "how" questions:

- How do we reach the district goals school by school?
- How will each school develop its own strategies, based on the needs of the students, to ensure that each child will be taught and will learn?
- How will each school allocate its resources to achieve the best results?
- How will each school demonstrate that it is willing and able to accept more responsibility for results as the quid pro quo for having more autonomy in decision making about teaching and learning?

In San Diego, teachers, principals, and central office staff still have more questions than answers; but most agree that the answers will come more easily if we learn from our own experience and the experiences of others who understand the complexity of creating a positive nexus between policy and practice. No longer can we indulge the continuation of past policy initiatives and practices that often fragment our efforts and detract from a focused systemic approach to reform that puts teaching and learning at the center of all that we do. The increase in compatibility between state and local school district policies and practices is encouraging.

Reference

National Commission on Excellence in Education. (1983). *A Nation at Risk: The Imperative for Educational Reform*. Washington, D.C.: U.S. Government Printing Office.

13

Education Professionals and Curriculum Governance

Richard F. Elmore and Susan H. Fuhrman

We began this yearbook with the argument that the United States is moving toward a more national, performance-based view of curriculum policy and that, in this movement, the country faces a number of important policy choices in which education professionals should play an important role. Four trends in curriculum policy and governance are now emerging:

1. Increasing focus on state-level governance of curriculum and teaching, in addition to the traditional state role in finance and organization, with an attendant growth in the importance of governors and state legislatures as policy actors.

2. Growth of certain nationalizing forces in the determination of curriculum policy, including professional subject-matter organizations in such areas as mathematics, science, and literacy; national organizations of state and local officials; and representative bodies formed around national goals.

3. A more direct connection between curriculum and student performance assessment in policy.

4. An increasing focus on the goal of providing ambitious academic instruction for a broad cross-section of American students.

These changes are being fueled by policymakers' perceptions that schools in the United States need to focus on the core task of providing high-quality academic instruction to virtually all students.

In this concluding chapter, we make a few observations about the implications of these changes and draw some conclusions about the role that education professionals might play in the future of curriculum policy and governance in the United States.

We focus first on the basic political realities of the emerging changes in curriculum governance and then on some practical ideas for how professionals might respond to these new realities.

Political Realities

Increasing State and National Influence

The first, most basic political reality is that curriculum decisions will be increasingly made in state and national arenas, rather than exclusively in local- and school-level arenas. We observe in Chapter 1 that the much-honored tradition of "local control" in the United States has never been quite as strong as its proponents argue.

Curriculum in the United States, in fact, has been subject to strong nationalizing forces for decades, especially through the textbook market and the influence of college and university entrance requirements on secondary schools. Likewise, many teachers and principals have grown accustomed to taking their cues about good educational practice not just from local sources but also from the national organizations to which they belong. So the new political reality is more an amplification of existing influences, rather than a fundamental change in the focus of decision making.

But we are witnessing the emergence of more assertive state policymaking around issues of curriculum and assessment and the development of national networks around debates on national standards. These unfolding processes will almost certainly mean that traditional conceptions of local control will become increasingly unworkable in the future.

The increasing importance of state and national arenas probably means that influencing curriculum decisions will become a more complex task. The more actors and interests who play a role in influencing what gets taught in classrooms, the more complex the decision-making processes and the more political sophistication it takes to makes one's influence felt.

Importance of Interdependence

The second basic political reality is that interdependence among levels of the education system will increase, and the parochial interests of levels will become increasingly difficult to defend. Michael Fullan argues that systemwide change requires both "top down" and "bottom up" views of policy implementation. Successful policies accommodate the need for broad strategic direction from the top and concrete problem solving at other levels. Likewise, the chapters in this yearbook that deal with state and local attempts to formulate and implement ambitious curriculum goals all point to the importance of strengthening connections among all levels of the system. As the higher-level policymakers become more interested and involved in the details of teaching and learning, it becomes increasingly important to have people in the system who are able to work across institutional boundaries.

As these interdependencies among levels—national, state, local, and school—increase, institutional autonomy for its own sake will become increasingly difficult to defend. As we develop increasing consensus on national purposes and as these purposes become adjusted to local realities and appear in state and local policies, it will be increasingly difficult to argue that schools or districts should be allowed to operate as if they were not part of a broader system.

Autonomy will probably be increasingly defined as the capacity to push against state and national standards, to participate in the political and professional networks that influence those standards, and to develop innovative solutions to the basic problems posed by the standards, such as how to bring more challenging academic content to traditionally underserved students. In other words, autonomy will be defined less in terms of exercising power and authority for one's own ends and more in terms of using one's power and authority to challenge and influence broader state and national purposes.

Opportunities for Problem-Solving and Influence

The third basic political reality, to take a hint from Murphy's Law, is that new policies create problems. A corollary of this principle is that the more complex the policy, the more unanticipated problems it produces, and the more opportunities it offers for people to exercise influence by engaging in problem- solving. Increasing national and state influence over curriculum in the United States, if accompanied by well-designed and well-implemented policies, probably will increase student access to high-quality academic instruction. This influence will also generate many new problems. This yearbook gives a hint of what kind of problems these might be (to name a few):

• Designing new forms of organization at the state and district level that center more on providing assistance to schools and less on ensuring bureaucratic oversight;

• Providing more effective professional development to teachers and principals; and

• Designing more effective ways of communicating curriculum guidance from the state and local levels.

The issue is not whether policy creates problems—policies always do—but whether policy surfaces problems that lead to improvement and whether it provides the wherewithal to solve those problems.

From a political perspective, we must recognize that problems present opportunities, not just inconveniences. Problems like the design of new forms of organization, new types of training, and new approaches to giving policy guidance are invitations to exercise influence. Ambitious reforms, of the type we are experiencing now, are usually predicated on relatively weak knowledge. The success of reforms is determined less by whether they are "realistic," in the sense of being based on well-understood principles, and more by whether they mobilize the problem-solving skill and commitment necessary to make them work. People have to believe that the problems presented by new policies are worth solving, and they have to have the skill and commitment to craft the solutions that will make the policy work. Mobilizing this skill and commitment is as much a political talent as it is a technical or administrative talent. New policies surface opportunities for people to develop and use such talents.

Practical Advice

These three basic political realities—a state and national focus, increasing interdependence among levels, and new problems and opportunities for influence—lead us to five pieces of practical advice for education professionals. We must learn more, focus our efforts, network with each other, emphasize "best practice," and push against the limits of policy.

1. Develop Expertise. We, as education professionals, must develop the greatest political asset we have in policy debates—expertise. As governors, state legislators, and school board members are drawn into national debates on the improvement of instructional quality, they increasingly confront issues for which they are relatively unprepared by their own backgrounds and experiences.

Most policymakers recognize their limitations and look to people with expertise for advice. But expertise is often a fragile and perishable commodity in policy debates. Policymakers are most interested in hearing from professionals who are willing to confront the problems they, policymakers, think are important, not just the problems that professionals think are important. Hence, as the policy agenda shifts, for example, to the question of how to make ambitious, high-quality academic instruction available to a broad cross-section of students, policymakers will value the kind of expertise that deals with the practical problems and possibilities of that agenda, not just the general professional interests of educators. General expertise is not enough; policymakers want effective expertise that focuses on the relevant problems—our second piece of advice.

2. Focus on Important Policy Arenas. We should focus attention on the policy arenas where important decisions will be made. Important daily decisions will continue to be made at the school and district level, but the context for these decisions will increasingly be shaped by strong forces from the state and national level. Hence, we must be knowledgeable about the nature of policy debates at the national and state levels and within our national professional associations. Being knowledgeable about the issues is the first step toward being influential. An effective way to influence decisions is through networking.

3. Cultivate Professional Networks. Education professionals should cultivate and use professional networks to increase expertise and to exercise influence. If, as this yearbook suggests, policies will depend increasingly on institutional interdependencies and on people with boundary-spanning skills, professional networks should become increasingly influential in determining both the content of policy and its implementation. One can see evidence of this phenomenon already in the role that professional organizations, such as the National Council of Teachers of Mathematics, have played in giving form and substance to the abstract policy idea of national standards. In the presence of a well-organized professional network, standards become, in effect, what professionals say they are. In other areas, where professional interests are less well organized and less focused in the application of their expertise, policy will probably be influenced more by diffuse political interests.

State and local policymakers have thus far shown a willingness to rely heavily on professionals to develop and implement policies where it is clear that professionals are mobilized and willing to participate, as in the formulation of state curriculum frameworks, for example. In most instances, policymakers are sufficiently aware of their own limitations in areas like curriculum policy that they will readily seek professional advice when it is well formed and articulated. Policymakers will seldom refrain from making policy, however, in the absence of sound professional advice, when they are responding to strong pressures to act. Hence, sound policy advice depends heavily on the willingness of professionals to develop and use networks to cultivate expertise and influence.

4. Promote "Best Practice," Not Professional Self-Interest. In providing advice to policymakers, we must recognize the difference between policy advice based on expertise and that based solely on professional self-interest. Education professionals have political interests like any other organized constituency. Teachers and principals would like to increase their visibility in political decisions and would like, incidentally, to improve their own material well-being in the process.

These interests are like many others in the political process. Educators, however, have another, distinguishable interest to bring to policy debates: an interest in promoting good educational practice through policy, or at least in preventing bad practice from becoming entrenched through policy. Both types of interests—those based on the personal well-being of professionals and those based on professionals' assessment of the best available practice—will play a role in policy debates; and often the two types of interests reinforce each other.

Teachers' primary motivation—enhancing student learning—should attract them to policies that support improvements in teaching and learning and that lead to a greater focus on student performance. But if educators are to play a strong role in bringing expertise to bear on policy, they need to recognize that expertise will sometimes be at odds with professional interests that are narrowly defined. Sometimes good practice, defined as practice based on solid research and strong connections to classrooms and schools, will be at odds with what many or most teachers or principals want to do. In such cases, it is important for some segment of the professional community to argue for "best practice" solutions, not just for the solutions that satisfy most practitioners. Sometimes this is an uphill struggle.

5. Push Against the Limits of Policy. A final piece of advice is to push against the limits of existing and new policies. The greatest strength of current changes in curriculum policy and governance is that they provide an opportunity to bring a higher quality of academic content and teaching to a broader segment of children. Their greatest weakness is that they increase the complexity of decisions about what gets taught to whom, and with what effect.

To capitalize on the strengths and minimize the weaknesses requires that education professionals be willing to call policy failures to the attention of policymakers and to use their expertise to invent solutions to those problems. The difference between policies that bog down in their own complexities and those that succeed is that the latter mobilize the problem-solving capacities of people.

Pushing against the limits of existing policies—using expertise to define problems worth solving and to produce solutions to them—can increase the effectiveness of the current generation of policies and, incidentally, increase the influence of those who craft the solutions.

About the Authors

Richard F. Elmore, the co-editor of the 1994 ASCD Yearbook, is Professor of Education at the Graduate School of Education at Harvard University, 409 Gutman Library, Appian Way, Cambridge, MA 02138.

Susan H. Fuhrman, the co-editor of the 1994 ASCD Yearbook, is Director of the Consortium for Policy Research in Education (CPRE), Eagleton Institute of Politics, at Rutgers University, 86 Clifton Avenue, New Brunswick, NJ 08901.

Michael G. Fullan is Dean of the Faculty of Education at the University of Toronto, 371 Bloor Street West, Toronto, Ontario, Canada M5S-2R7.

Susan Follett Lusi is a Predoctoral Fellow at the Malcolm Wiener Center for Social Policy, John F. Kennedy School of Government, Harvard University, 79 JFK Street, Cambridge, MA 02138.

Diane Massell, a Research Associate at the Consortium for Policy Research in Education, is a doctoral candidate in the School of Education at Stanford University, Stanford, CA 94305.

Richard P. Mills is Commissioner of Education in the Vermont Department of Education, 120 State Street, Montpelier, VT 05602.

Ken Nelson is an Education Consultant and is Senior Fellow in the College of Education at the University of Minnesota, 4201 Garfield Avenue, South, Minneapolis, MN 55409.

Jennifer O'Day is Assistant Director of the Pew Forum on Education Reform at the School of Education at Stanford University, Stanford, CA 94305.

Eric Osthoff is Project Assistant at the Wisconsin Center for Educational Research, University of Wisconsin-Madison, 1025 West Johnson Street, Madison, WI 53706.

Thomas W. Payzant, former Superintendent of the San Diego, California, City Schools, is Assistant Secretary for Elementary and Secondary Education at the U.S. Department of Education, 400 Maryland Avenue, S.W., Washington, DC 20202.

Andrew C. Porter is Director of the Wisconsin Center for Education Research, and Professor of Educational Psychology at the University of Wisconsin-Madison, 1025 West Johnson Street, Madison, WI 53706.

Marshall S. Smith, the former Dean of the School of Education at Stanford University, Stanford, California, is Undersecretary of the U.S. Department of Education, 400 Maryland Avenue, S.W., Washington, DC 20202.

John Smithson is Project Assistant at the Wisconsin Center for Education Research, University of Wisconsin-Madison, 1025 West Johnson Street, Madison, WI.

James P. Spillane is a Research Associate in the College of Education at Michigan State University, Erickson Hall, East Lansing, MI 48824-1034.

ASCD 1993–94 Board of Directors

Elected Members as of November 1, 1993

Executive Council

President: Barbara Talbert Jackson, Executive Director, Grants Development Branch, District of Columbia Public Schools, Washington, D.C.
President-Elect: Arthur W. Steller, Boston Public Schools, Boston, Massachusetts
Immediate Past President: Stephanie Pace Marshall, Executive Director, Illinois Math and Science Academy, Aurora, Illinois
Thomas Budnik, Coordinator for Planning, Research, and Evaluation, Heartland Area Education Agency #11, Johnston, Iowa
Robert Clark, Associate Superintendent, Marietta City Schools, Marietta, Georgia
Robert Garmston, Co-director, Institute for Intelligent Behavior, El Dorado Hills, California
Ruud Gorter, Director, Association of Educational Advisory Centers, The Hague, The Netherlands
Edward Hall, Assistant Superintendent, Talladega County Board of Education, Talladega, Alabama
Frances Jones, Executive Director, Piedmont Triad Horizons, Greensboro, North Carolina
Margret Montgomery, Grapevine-Colleyville Independent School District, Grapevine, Texas
Irving Ouellette, Director of Elementary Education, Portland Public Schools, Portland, Maine
Sheila Wilson, Director of Staff Support, Schaumburg, Illinois
Isa Kaftal Zimmerman, Acton-Boxborough Public Schools, Acton, Massachusetts

Review Council Members

Chair, Phil Robinson, Detroit, Michigan
Carolyn H. Chapman, Associate Professor, College of Education, University of Nevada-Reno
Art Costa, Kalaheo, Kauai, Hawaii
Maryann Johnson, Assistant Superintendent for Curriculum and Instruction, South Kitsap School District, Port Orchard, Washington
Marcia Knoll, Assistant Superintendent, Valley Stream Central High School District, Valley Stream, New York

Elected Members-at-Large

Bonnie Benesh, Director of Curriculum and Instruction, Newton Community School District, Newton, Iowa
Marguerite Bloch, Superintendent of Schools, Butler District 53, Oak Brook, Illinois
Sharon Bevel, Drew Elementary School, Washington, D.C.
Sandra Braithwait, Clinton School District, Clinton, Missouri

Marguerite Cox, Director of Instruction, Glenbard Township High School, Glen Ellyn, Illinois
Mary Francis, Superintendent, Petersburg City School District, Petersburg, Arkansas
Esther Fusco, Principal, Babylon School District, Stony Brook, New York
Sandra Gray, Director, K–12 Laboratory School, Southwest Missouri State University, Springfield
David Jones, Jr., Metropolitan Public Schools, Nashville, Tennessee
Joanna Kalbus, Superintendent, San CLASS Regional School District, San Bernardino, California
Sharon Lease, Western Heights School District, Oklahoma City, Oklahoma
Ina Logue, Director of Curriculum and Instruction, Allegheny Intermediate Unit, Pittsburgh, Pennsylvania
Lynn Murray, Principal, Williston Central School, Williston, Vermont
Annemarie Romagnoli, Principal, Little Tor Elementary School, New City, New York
Judy Stevens, Director of Elementary Instruction, Springbranch I.S.D., Houston, Texas
Joseph Taylor, Jr., New Orleans Public Schools, New Orleans, Louisiana
Nancy Vance, Colonial Heights, Virginia

Affiliate Presidents

Alabama: Max Stripling, Coordinator of Federal Programs, Pickens County Board of Education, Carrollton
Alaska: David Hagstrom, Professor, University of Alaska, Fairbanks
Alberta, Canada: Jim Tayler, Teacher, H.D. Cartwright Jr. High School, Calgary
Arizona: Virginia McElyea, Phoenix Union H.S. District, Phoenix
Arkansas: Paula Cummins, Coordinator, Gifted Programs, UA-LR, Little Rock
British Columbia, Canada: Norm Bradley, Springvalley Secondary School, Kelowna
California: Joanna Kalbus, Assistant Superintendent, San Bernardino County Schools, San Bernardino
Colorado: Ken Humphrey, University of North Colorado, Greeley
Connecticut: LeRoy Hay, Superintendent of Schools, Windsor Locks Public Schools, Windsor Locks
Delaware: David Campbell, Superintendent, Colonial School District, New Castle
District of Columbia: Amy Jones, P.R. Harris Education Center, Washington, D.C.
Florida: Lee Dixon, Assistant Superintendent, Okeechobee County Schools, Okeechobee
Georgia: Tom O'Rourke, Dekalb County Schools, Decatur
Germany: Gerry Schiele, Principal, DoDDS-Buechel Elementary School
Hawaii: Mamo Carreira, Lincoln School, Honolulu
Idaho: Gary Delka, School of Education, University of Idaho, Lewiston
Illinois: Janet Dews, Principal, J.B. Nelson School, Batavia
Indiana: Evelyn Sayers, Indiana Department of Education, Indianapolis
Iowa: Brad Colton, Grantwood AEA #10, Cedar Rapids
Japan: Maria Rubio, Office of District Superintendent, DoDDS-Pacific, Tokyo
Kansas: Pat Anderson, Director of Secondary Education, USD #475, Junction City
Kentucky: Mona Goodman, Glasgow Independent Schools, Glasgow
Louisiana: Lisa Mowen, Principal, West Jefferson High School, Harvey
Maine: Rodney Hatch, Superintendent, Maine School Administrative District #74, North Anson
Maryland: Lorraine Costella, State Department of Education, Frederick

Massachusetts: Caroline Tripp, Assistant Superintendent of Schools, Shrewsbury Public Schools, Shrewsbury
Michigan: Elba Berlin, Jackson Public Schools, Jackson
Minnesota: Kenneth Kelsey, Department of Teacher Development, St. Cloud State University, St. Cloud
Mississippi: Doris Smith, Superintendent, Winona Public Schools, Winona
Missouri: Sandra Gray, Southwest Missouri State University, Springfield
Montana: Bryan Dunn, Assistant Superintendent, Bozeman Public Schools, Bozeman
Nebraska: Michaelene Meyer, Principal, Hillrise Elementary, Elkhorn
The Netherlands: Martijn Dingemans, Bergen Op Zoom
Nevada: Teddy Brewer, Principal, Wooley Elementary School, Las Vegas
New Hampshire: Susan Newton, Peterborough Elementary School, Peterborough
New Jersey: James Wasser, Freehold Regional H.S. District, Englishtown
New Mexico: Delbert Dyche, Principal, Aspen Elementary School, Los Alamos
New York: John Cooper, Assistant Superintendent, Canandaigua City Schools, Canandaigua
North Carolina: John Schroeder, Principal, Northeast Middle School, High Point
North Dakota: Ann Clapper, FIPSE Project Director/Lecturer, Valley City State University, Valley City
Northwest Territories: Denrick Richardson, Deninoo School, Fort Resolution
Ohio: Margaret Edwards, Middletown City Schools, Middletown
Oklahoma: Sandy Wisley, Director of Middle Schools, Putnam City Public Schools, Oklahoma City
Ontario: Doug Gruber, Assistant Superintendent, Waterloo Region RCSSB, Kitchener
Oregon: Kenneth Settlemier, Director of Education, Lincoln County Schools, Newport
Pennsylvania: John Linden, Assistant Superintendent, Fairview School District, Fairview
Puerto Rico: Haydée Piris-Maldonado, Catholic University of Puerto Rico, Ponce
Rhode Island: John Harrington, Assistant Superintendent, South Kingstown Public Schools, Wakefield
St. Maarten: Celia Stewart, St. Peter's Hillside School, St. Peter's
Singapore: Kan Sou Tin, Curriculum Planning Division, Ministry of Education
South Carolina: Steve Hefner, Associate Superintendent for Instruction, Richland County School District #2, Columbia
South Dakota: Bryan Monteith, Director of Curriculum, Watertown School District 14-4, Watertown
Tennessee: Betty Sue Sparks, Supervisor, Knox County Schools, Knoxville
Texas: Janice Rosson, Principal, Big Spring ISD, Big Spring
Trinidad & Tobago: Annette Wiltshire, Diego Martin
United Kingdom: Martha Parsons, DoDDS-Lakenheath Elementary School
Utah: Martha Kupferschmidt, Principal, Horizon Elementary School, Murray
Vermont: Doug Harris, Superintendent, Franklin Northwest S.U., Swanton
Virginia: Sarah Armstrong, Director of Instruction/Personnel, Nelson County Public Schools, Lovington
Virgin Islands: Dolores Clendinen, Coordinator, Alternative Education, Department of Education, St. Thomas
Washington: Sherrelle Walker, Assistant Superintendent, Federal Way School District, Federal Way

West Virginia: Judy Szymialis, Department Chairperson, Wheeling Park High School, Wheeling
Wisconsin: Chuck Larson, Assistant Dean of Educational Outreach, UW-Eau Claire, Eau Claire
Wyoming: Robert Krisko, Curriculum Director, Carbon County School District #1, Rawlins

THE GOVERNANCE OF CURRICULUM

ASCD Headquarters Staff

Gene Carter, *Executive Director*
Diane Berreth, *Deputy Executive Director*
Frank Betts, *Director, Education and Technology Resources Center*
John Bralove, *Director, Administrative Services*
Ronald S. Brandt, *Executive Editor*
Helené Hodges, *Director, Collaborative Ventures*
Susan Nicklas, *Director, Field Services*
Michelle Terry, *Director, Professional Development*

Diana Allen
Meleanie Bell
Vickie Bell
Jennifer Beun
Steve Blackwood
Gary Bloom
Maritza Bourque
Lorraine Bradshaw
Joan Brandt
Dorothy Brown
Kathy Browne
Robert Bryan
George Bryant
Colette Burgess
Edward Butler
Elizabeth Byrne
Angela Caesar
Kathryn Carswell
Sally Chapman
John Checkley
RC Chernault
Eddie Chinn
Sandra Claxton
Lisa Manion Cline
Adrienne Corley
Christine Craun
Agnes Crawford
Sandi Cumberland
Elaine Cunningham
Brian Curry
Marcia D'Arcangelo
Keith Demmons
Becky DeRigge
Gloria Dugan
Shiela Ellison
Kathie Felix
Gillian Fitzpatrick
Frederick Fleming
Chris Fuscellaro

Troy Gooden
Regina Gussie
Nora Gyuk
Dorothy Haines
Vicki Hancock
Nancy Harrell
Dwayne Hayes
Davene Holland
Julie Houtz
Angela Howard
Debbie Howerton
Harold Hutch
Peter Inchauteguiz
Jo Ann Jones
Mary Jones
Teola Jones
Stephanie Kenworthy
Leslie Kiernan
Crystal Knight
Shelly Kosloski
Diane MacDonald
John Mackie
Indu Madan
Larry Mann
Jan McCool
"Biz" McMahon
Clara Meredith
Ron Miletta
Ginger Miller
Frances Mindel
Nancy Modrak
Cerylle Moffett
Kenny Moir
Karen Monaco
Bill Monroe
Margaret Murphy
Dina Murray
Kimber Nation
Peter Neal

Mary Beth Nielsen
Jonathan Nobles
John O'Neil
Jayne Osgood
Millie Outten
Kelvin Parnell
Margini Patel
Carolyn Pool
Jackie Porter
Ruby Powell
Pam Price
Lorraine Primeau
Gena Randall
Hope Redwine
Melody Ridgeway
Judy Rixey
Rita Roberts
Gayle Rockwell
Cordelia Roseboro
Carly Rothman
Jeff Rupp
Marge Scherer
Beth Schweinefuss
Judy Seltz
Bob Shannon
Valerie Sprague
Lisa Street
Judi Wagstaff
Mary Dern Walker
Judy Walter
Dave Warren
Milton Washington
Vivian West
Kay Whittington
Linda Wilkey
Pam Williams
Scott Willis
Carol Wojcik
Sue Young

ASCD Networks and Facilitators, 1993–94

ASCD sponsors numerous networks that help members exchange ideas, share common interests, and establish collegial relationships. Contact the **ASCD Networks Program Liaison** for additional information about these and other networks, or write or call one of the facilitators listed here.

Alliance for the Teaching of Science
Thomas Jones
700 Diamond St.
Berlin, PA 15530
TEL (814) 267-5618

Curriculum Teachers
India L. Broyles
220 Bailey Hall
University of South Maine
Gorham, ME 04038
TEL (207) 780-5375
FAX (207) 780-5315

Designing District Evaluation Instruments for Math & Science Process Skills
Shelley Lipowich
Math/Science Consultant
6321 North Canon del Pajaro
Tucson, AZ 85715
TEL (602) 299-9583

Educational Futurists
Barbara Vogl
Consultant
Change Management Systems
5300 Glen Haven Rd.
Soquel, CA 95073
TEL (408) 476-2905

High Schools Networking for Change
Gil James
Principal
Sprague High School
2373 Kuebler Boulevard, South
Salem, OR 97302
TEL (503) 399-3261
FAX (503) 391-4046

Instructional Supervision
J. McClain Smith
Coordinator, University Programs
Hilliard City Schools
5323 Cemetery Rd.
Hilliard, OH 43026
TEL (614) 771-4273
FAX (614) 777-2424

Network for Restructured Schools
Richard Ackerman and
Chuck Christensen
Center for Field Services and Studies
University of Massachusetts-Lowell
1 University Ave.
Lowell, MA 01854
TEL (508) 934-4633
FAX (508) 934-3002

Quality Schools/OBE
Rick Scott
Chetwynd Secondary School
School District #59
P.O. Box 447
Chetwynd, BC
CANADA V0C 1J0
TEL (604) 788-2267
FAX (604) 788-9729

Science, Mathematics, and Technology Education
Dennis W. Cheek
Supervisor of Math, Science, and Technology
Rhode Island Department of Education
22 Hayes Street, Rm. B-4
Providence, RI 02908
TEL (401) 277-2821
FAX (401) 351-7874

Teacher Leadership
Ronnie Konner
West Essex Regional School District
West Greenbrook Rd.
N. Caldwell, NJ 07006
TEL (201) 228-1200
FAX (201) 575-7847

Teaching Thinking
Esther Fusco
Principal and Director of Curriculum
Port Jefferson School District
24 Hopewell Dr.
Stony Brook, NY 11790
TEL (516) 473-8710
FAX (516) 928-0293

Workforce 2000: Work and Workers for the 21st Century
Linell Burrell, Jr.
Grants/Training Specialist
UAW-Chrysler National Training Center
2211 East Jefferson Ave.
Detroit, MI 48207
TEL (313) 567-3300
FAX (313) 567-8080

ASCD Networks Program Liaison
Susan Nicklas
Director of Field Services
ASCD
1250 N. Pitt St.
Alexandria, VA 22314-1453
TEL (703) 549-9110 X506
FAX (703) 549-3891